PRAISE FOR *SECRET KEEPING*

"A timely book! John Howard Prin takes the reader on a wonderfully exciting journey of self-exploration and the development of personal insight. He provides practical methods to free ourselves of our 'hidden secrets' so that ultimately we can be at peace with who we are even when no one else is around."

— Patrick DeChello, PhD,
author of *Understanding Self-Injury*

"John Howard Prin's *Secret Keeping* is the first book I've read that explores the origins and essence of secrets — how they help us and when they hurt us. Using examples from his own life and the lives of others — from public figures to the guy next door — Prin skillfully weaves a new quilt of understanding of the Jekyll and Hyde in each of us. He also provides new and necessary hope with a series of practical exercises we can use to transform ourselves and our world."

— Terrence Daryl Shulman, JD, MSW, CAC,
author of *Something for Nothing*

"Recovery means escaping from the labyrinth of one's own lies. John Prin's book on keeping secrets lays bare the essential connection between image management and a 'secret life.' A useful, well-written book by someone who has been there."

— Patrick J. Carnes, PhD, author of *Out of the Shadows*

SECRET
KEEPING

SECRET KEEPING

Overcoming Hidden Habits and Addictions

JOHN HOWARD PRIN

NEW WORLD LIBRARY
NOVATO, CALIFORNIA

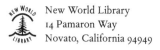 New World Library
14 Pamaron Way
Novato, California 94949

The material in this book is intended for education. It is not meant to take the place of diagnosis and treatment by a qualified medical practitioner or therapist. No express or implied guarantee about the effects of using the recommendations can be given, nor liability taken.

Case histories of individuals may be composites of two or more actual people, and names have been changed to respect the privacy of those persons.

Secret Keepers® and Secret Keeping® are registered trademarks of John Howard Prin. The Four Squares of Life™ is a trademark of John Howard Prin.

Brain diagram on page 12 by Robert Rath (www.robertrath.net) courtesy of Deidre Combs.

Text design and typography by Tona Pearce Myers

Library of Congress Cataloging-in-Publication Data
Prin, John Howard.
Secret keeping : overcoming hidden habits and addictions / by John Howard Prin.
    p.   cm.
Includes bibliographical references and index.
ISBN-13: 978-1-57731-534-6 (pbk. : alk. paper)
1. Secrecy—Psychological aspects. 2. Self-defeating behavior. 3. Compulsive behavior.
I. Title.
RC455.4.S43P75 2006
616.85'84—dc2   2006012255

First printing, September 2006
ISBN-10: 1-57731-534-0
ISBN-13: 978-1-57731-534-6
Printed in Canada on acid-free, partially recycled paper
Distributed by Publishers Group West

10   9   8   7   6   5   4   3   2   1

To Susie, whose loving patience and support have never been a secret

CONTENTS

INTRODUCTION

*E*VERYONE KEEPS SECRETS.
Some people who keep secrets do not feel guilty, while others do.

It's the second kind of people who keep secrets, those who feel guilt or shame, that *Secret Keeping: Overcoming Hidden Habits and Addictions* is meant for. In my career as a therapist and counselor, I've come to call these kinds of people Secret Keepers®. A Secret Keeper can be anyone from a housewife hiding vodka bottles from her family to a compulsive gambler, a food addict, a cybersex fanatic, or anyone who is secretly leading a double life.

Sometimes people just daydream about a taboo world, not acting on their fantasies. This is secret keeping® in its mildest form. If this describes you, relax. This form is passive, benign — hardly a problem. Although this book will help you, you're not in major trouble. Think of yourself as a human being like everybody else. We all dream of the forbidden, so be easy on yourself.

Other Secret Keepers go beyond musing about their fantasies to living them out. They willingly take risks and consciously push boundaries that move them toward something that is, or will become, a problem for them and for others. This is secret keeping in its active form. It's dynamic, volatile — and highly problematic. Individuals who engage in this behavior stretch ethical, moral, and relational boundaries in search of something that is missing in their lives, often to escape some pain or hurt. If you think you fit this category, this book will help you to climb out of the dark hole you've dug yourself into. It will urge you to rethink your reasons for secret keeping and prompt you to examine your options, including seeking outside help. It will open the door to hope — the hope of living freely without deception, lies, alibis, guilt, or shame.

Still other kinds of people act outside accepted ethical, moral, and relational limits; they break the law. They take great risks and commit crimes that endanger or damage themselves, others, and society. This is secret keeping in its criminal or psychotic form. It's malignant, destructive — and highly injurious. Two types of individuals fit in this category: the decent, regular sort of person whose secrecy makes them cross the line into crime or psychosis, and the hardened, antisocial career criminal such as a serial rapist or murderer. This book will deal only marginally with the latter type.

What's essential to realize is that secret keeping, in all of its forms, involves some degree of criminal thinking. And almost any functioning member of society can think like a criminal at times. How about the millions of everyday citizens who drive over the speed limit and who — despite their awareness that they're breaking the law — hope they never get caught? The likelihood for any Secret Keeper of slipping down the slippery slope from *passive* to *dynamic* to *malignant* always exists.

As you read this book, you will find that it describes people with good hearts and curious minds who are seeking, many times inappropriately, wholeness and fulfillment. It tells stories of everyday working adults with families, homes, jobs, and responsibilities who are trapped in the dynamic stages of "stealing hours" from their public lives. The risks, thrills, and taboo nature of their habits prove too strong to resist. By participating secretly in hidden activities that are shameful or stigmatizing, they risk their reputations. If anybody knew about their secret lives, their good standing in the community would be destroyed — and they are fully aware of that.

This book's aim is to prevent such disasters. Because chronic Secret Keepers' dual identities are in conflict, they are stressed-out people. Their parallel worlds never come together. Their forays into unhealthy habits develop into lifestyles that erode physical, mental, emotional, and spiritual well-being. A key purpose of this book is to help readers understand the problem and to see the merit of finding the solutions. It offers ways to stop living a *secretive, closed, risk-filled* life and to start leading an *honest, open, transparent* one instead.

In part 1, you will discover the Continuum of Secrets, which details the degrees of keeping secrets from benign to malignant and shows where secret keeping fits on that continuum. You will also explore the Eight Splintered Mind-sets of Secret Keepers. In part 2, you will have the chance to benefit from some time-tested ways to reverse those mind-sets and the distorted thinking and emotions that keep you, or someone dear to you, trapped. Help is offered through the Blueprint for Gaining Freedom, an easy-to-follow set of actions, along with some 12-step principles I've seen clients use to their benefit. Also available to assist you is the

Four Squares of Life diagram, showing various ways dysfunction and addiction can twist someone's youthful development physically, mentally, emotionally, and spiritually. Most important, the diagram also opens the door to healing. It shows the many possible ways that recovery can empower, restore, rejuvenate, and reconnect us to our core self, to the wholeness and serenity that secret keeping destroys.

CONFESSIONS OF A LIBERATED SECRET KEEPER

I speak from the perspective I've gained by having both personal and professional encounters with secret keeping. Between the ages of eleven and fifty-one, I lived parallel lives. Outwardly I looked normal, made a good impression, and was a high-functioning teenager and adult. The drama of my hidden addictions, however, and the ways my secrets gained control over me, are another story altogether. In time I learned the simple truth: *We are as sick as our secrets.*

This inner story that I alone experienced — and how I kept everybody else fooled — is only a small part of the picture. The bigger part is that my life mirrors the experience of thousands, no doubt millions, of other people, a few of whom you will meet in these pages. In my case, the forty years that I lived in two worlds, ricocheting between public respectability and private temptations, was a time I would never choose to repeat. Yet ultimately, these "stolen" years taught me invaluable lessons that led to the rewards of whole-mindedness. You will hear more about my story in the opening chapters and occasionally throughout the book.

In my current professional role as a counselor, I've heard numerous stories of secret keeping from clients who have told me about their double lives: hospitalizations for eating disorders, financial ruin from credit card debt, jail time for shoplifting, arrests for sexual crimes, and career crashes from compulsive gambling and extramarital affairs.

I've discovered numerous ways in which people keep secrets and become sick from their destructive habits. The clients I counsel often feel sabotaged by their self-defeating habits and end up hating their split reality — and these people walk among us every day. My counseling work has centered on developing effective therapies to help people struggling with the tension created by keeping a secret life.

Today I devote my waking efforts to assisting troubled individuals to free themselves from the detours, deceptions, and dead ends of secret keeping so they can have the highest-quality lives possible. With *Secret Keeping* I hope to make this motivating knowledge available to many more people than I could ever help personally.

The simple truth? We are as sick as our secrets...but there's hope!

PART 1

THE SELF DIVIDED

Problems and Consequences

Chapter 1

WHO ARE
THE SECRET KEEPERS?

Man is not truly one, but truly two.

—— ROBERT LOUIS STEVENSON,
THE STRANGE CASE OF DR. JEKYLL AND MR. HYDE

SECRET KEEPERS ARE TROUBLED PEOPLE. They steal hours away from their public lives to act out destructive behaviors or passions in private. They are "not truly one, but truly two," as Robert Louis Stevenson observed in his classic tale of split personality. By picking up *Secret Keeping*, you are showing curiosity about your own habits or the habits of those living close to you. If you are reading this book to help yourself, perhaps you want to regain control of the inner chaos and stress that weigh on you so heavily. If you are reading this because you suspect someone close to you is indulging in a secret life, you may want answers and guidance on how to deal with that person and how to regain equilibrium in your own life.

That's exactly what this book is intended to help you do.

Let's start by identifying who qualifies as a card-carrying Secret Keeper. Think of everyday citizens, hardworking professionals, and family men and women who are high functioning on one level but in bondage to a deeply held secret on another. Occasionally we read about individuals like these in the news:

- A university professor of religious studies concealed on his work computer 1,200 Internet photos of children having sex. His secret became so burdensome that when he was arrested, he stated, "What a relief to be caught."

- A college coed induced vomiting several times a week and continued doing so for years to "purge the fat cow inside" her. No one discovered her secret until she collapsed and had to be taken to the emergency room.

- A county commissioner filed for bankruptcy incurred by gambling debts when the public learned that he was visiting casinos several times a week during business hours. He had concealed his identity by wearing wigs and other clever disguises.

- A suburban mother of three children hid bottles of vodka for years in the laundry room and binged while the kids were at school...until they arrived home one day and found her passed out on the floor.

- A school board chairperson arrived habitually late to meetings because she couldn't leave the house until checking dozens of times to make sure the stove was turned off and the water taps were turned extra tight.

- A churchgoing father of four secluded himself in hotel rooms to dress up in women's clothes, then stepped out in public whenever he felt the need to express his "inborn nature."

- A priest molested a child in a secluded cabin, then threatened her life by saying she would die if anyone ever discovered their little secret.

- A homeowner allowed four hundred cats to overrun her house until the stench from years of accumulated urine and feces prompted neighbors to report her residence to public health authorities.

Around the globe, everyday people like these comprise the one out of every fifteen people who actively live double lives.[1] They are your next-door neighbor, the shopper ahead of you in the supermarket line, the driver behind you on the freeway — and they may be *you*. They are among the more than twenty million Americans who become trapped in hidden double lives yet still function in their jobs, homes, and families.[2]

Secret Keepers steal hours away from their "normal" lives to act out private behaviors, rituals, and fantasies whenever their secrets overpower them. They cleverly elude getting caught, seldom appearing in tomorrow's headlines or ending up in police custody. The people closest to them may suspect their excuses at times, thinking to themselves "how odd or eccentric Joe is" or "Jane seems lost in a private world of her own." But hard evidence almost never surfaces. Telltale clues, if any, go unnoticed.

Secret Keepers, even when they seem to be high functioning, carry with them concealed knowledge about themselves that nobody knows — not the boss, not friends, not siblings, not parents, not spouses. Ben Franklin once quipped, "Three can keep a secret if two are dead." That leaves just one person who knows, the key point of this disorder. Secret keeping means that *no one else knows*. Sadly, keeping secrets takes a toll on the physical, emotional, and spiritual health of the *one who knows*.

Secret Keepers may skirt the law, but they hardly ever get arrested. They may push ethical and moral boundaries, but they seldom overstep legal boundaries (with rare exceptions). Whether they secretly drink or do drugs alone, whether they are pathological gamblers, pornography lovers, compulsive shoplifters, obsessive shoppers, or video game freaks, nothing they do is obvious to the casual observer. Projecting a wholesome self for all to see and approve of, they carefully conceal two opposing selves struggling to coexist in one being. Over time, the competing selves within them wage war and wear them down until a crisis threatens either their sanity or their health, or both. As their emotions battle their reason, the pressure to disclose intimate knowledge to somebody builds up inside them, wreaking daily suffering on themselves and, inevitably, on everyone around them.

Here's an inside look at the experiences of two people, each of whom could be living down the street or working in the cubicle next to you at your job. They are both pleasant human beings whom you could easily grow to like, respect, and trust.

Caroline: Dying Inside but Hiding It Well

Growing up on the prairies of Kansas, Caroline loved animals. She spent afternoons and weekends petting rabbits, lambs, dogs, and cats on her parents' ranch. In junior high school, she became "rather lonely," she says. "I'd spend what seemed like hours checking and rechecking details about the animals' feeding and care before leaving home to go to school." Being late for the bus meant that her dad had to give her rides to school, where her classmates would tease her. "I'd shrug and act like so-what," Caroline says. After a while she felt that "something wasn't right" with her. But she managed to keep her behavior under control until she graduated from high school.

Her first major move at eighteen involved attending a large university in a city two hundred miles away, where she also worked part-time. Caroline worked hard and studied long hours, graduating four years later with honors. She dated in her senior year and moved in with a boyfriend, who kept two pet cats and a dog. Her love of animals reawakened. She landed a prestigious starting position as an accountant. Yet, as the months passed, she "fell into despair over spending up to two hours every morning trying to leave the apartment!"

Caroline performed the ritual of going through the apartment time and time again to make sure everything was turned off and the place was safe. She even turned the water taps supertight so "the pets wouldn't go crazy listening to the drip-drip sound." Caroline chided herself for never getting to her high-profile new job on time, no matter how early she set her alarm. "I couldn't tell my boss why I was late. I just couldn't. I was dying inside — a prisoner in my home until the clock said, 'You *really* are late, now get out!' "

Caroline knew her secret wouldn't keep indefinitely, and she agonized, fearful of the day when somebody would find out. The dread of being discovered, of facing the uncertain consequences, ate at her every day, causing dark moods. No one ever guessed why she fretted so much.

BRAD: BETTING ON MARBLES

As a child of seven, Brad watched his parents having a rollicking time playing their bridge games and betting on poker with friends. He learned that playing cards and betting meant having fun. It seemed only natural, then, that he picked up these pastimes too. Growing up during the 1960s, Brad watched TV shows like *Mr. Lucky* and *Maverick*, whose heroes, says Brad, "were charming gamblers with romantic mystiques — guys I admired and wanted to be like."

Cards were banned at school, so Brad brought his bag of marbles to class and secretly made bets with schoolmates during recess. He enjoyed the daring action and face-to-face haggling.

Whether he was winning or losing, it hardly mattered. By the sixth grade he habitually skipped classes in order to run a playground betting operation. In time Brad stole money from his mom's purse to pay back losses. Whenever a teacher tried to stop his betting, he would make witty quips to defuse the tension, but eventually his hours in detention threatened his academic standing.

At home, he joined his parents' card games and became so skilled at bluffing and cheating that he frequently won large pots. Brad would then put back the money taken from his mom's purse and bet the remainder on the playground. As a sophomore, he woke up one day and realized that his whole focus was on gambling instead of grades or girls or sports. He was hooked, and he dropped out of high school. From that day on, he put extra energy into turning his habit into a livelihood — and keeping it a closely held secret. His parents tried to talk him into going back to classes, but he would hear nothing of it and moved out to his own tiny apartment.

In his twenties, Brad earned his GED and successfully completed three years of college, but military service rekindled his love affair with gambling. When he returned to civilian life and a well-paying sales job, he kept his gambling clandestine for the next nineteen years until a mental breakdown loomed, prompted by financial losses and thoughts of suicide. Those close to him, especially his wife, tried to get him to admit his secrets but grew tired and alienated.

MASKED FEELINGS: HOW WE HIDE THEM

What is going on beneath the surface in these brief biographies? Both Caroline and Brad learned at a young age to mask their true feelings and to act in ways that did not reflect their inner worlds. While Caroline felt genuine affection for animals and Brad felt thrilled about betting, they both learned to express the opposite of these feelings, shrugging passively or making witty quips to deflect scrutiny.

As Caroline put it, "I cared so deeply for animals and their safety that it made me anxious, eventually so paranoid that I chewed my fingernails. I was also afraid of imaginary things like monsters. My parents frowned at me, and my brothers and sisters teased me, so I hid my feelings and acted numb. I learned to smile on cue whenever I ached inside or was afraid of monsters under my bed."

Brad described how he also hid his true feelings: "I loved the thrills of betting and winning until it became obvious that classmates and teachers thought I was weird. Later I hid any hint from employers and my family, sneaking to casinos at midnight or whenever I had an alibi. I plastered on a 'bright-and-happy' face, even though my urges got stronger. Letting my feelings show was the worst thing I could do. I just acted 'normal' like others expected me to."

This trait of substituting what's false for what's real, called *incongruence*, showed up early in my own childhood as well. When I was five, I prided myself on being a good boy, never wanting to be a problem. My greatest offense back then was stealing cookies, especially Mom's home-baked peanut butter or chocolate chip specialties. I'd climb up on a chair next to the kitchen counter, crawl quietly to the cookie jar, lift the lid ever so slowly, and swipe a handful — always listening carefully for her footsteps from the next room. Part of the thrill was knowing that she could walk in on me any second and catch me in a forbidden act.

In this way I learned early that the key factors leading to secret keeping were:

- the *excitement* of breaking rules,
- the *pleasure* of indulging in what's forbidden (eating stolen treats), and
- the *delight* of not getting caught.

This triple whammy became the first of several secret-keeping dynamics that gripped me. In later years I came to call it the Triad of Secret-Keeping Emotions. Various forms of this combination of temptation, craving, indulgence, and guilt held me captive for decades, as I've learned it does for other Secret Keepers. For many kids, stealing cookies is an everyday part of growing up and leads to nothing more serious. But for me stealing cookies started a behavior pattern that I later perfected as secret keeping, although I never thought of the word *secret* until midlife. While for most kids pilfering treats may be as far as this kind of behavior goes, for me it started a "guilt pocket," a reservoir of dualistic thinking. This kind of double-mindedness kept sneaking up on me and eventually took hold. Much like it did Caroline and Brad, masking what was true inside me became an ingrained habit. Like them, I too began slipping into the secret-keeping trap early in my teen years, what I've come to call the first of the eight splintered mind-sets of a Secret Keeper: *acting one way while feeling another*. We'll be exploring this mind-set further in this chapter.

Whether or not to surrender and to admit being out of control from balancing two separate worlds is the predicament many Secret Keepers eventually find themselves in, and it is at this precarious point when their investment in clandestine activities breaks down. At this juncture they must choose between two options that feel very difficult: disclosure can lead to health and sanity but also to shock and dismay for those who learn the painful truth. Meanwhile, denial and delays can lead to dire, even violent, consequences, even though the sufferer remains safe for the time being, albeit enslaved.

The Roots of Duality in Us All

These three examples indicate the innocent ways in which secret keeping can start. The notion of two selves existing within one being is as ancient as that of saint and sinner inhabiting the same person. Throughout Western literature, authors from Saint Paul to Saint Augustine to Goethe to modern writers such as Sigmund Freud, Robert Louis Stevenson, Carl Jung, and Joseph Campbell have all plumbed the depths of humankind's dual personality in an effort to unwrap its mysteries. The stark opposites of kindly Dr. Jekyll and menacing Mr. Hyde in Stevenson's classic tale of one person's dual, and dueling, personalities represent this dichotomy in fiction.

Author and researcher Daniel Goleman, in his ground-breaking book *Emotional Intelligence*, describes the inherent duality human beings experience. Basing his research on recent scientific studies, he has this to say about the splitting of one's psyche: "In a very real sense we have two minds, one that thinks and one that feels. These two fundamentally different ways of knowing interact to construct our mental life. One, the rational mind, is the mode of comprehension we are typically conscious of. But alongside that there is another system of knowing: impulsive and powerful, if sometimes illogical — the emotional mind."3

How often have you observed the tension, whether in works of fiction or in your own life, between "heart" and "head"? The conflict between the emotional and the rational seems universal, yet the two often combine harmoniously in the countless daily decisions we make. When the emotional and rational minds are in balance, they inform and enhance each other. If we didn't have both ways of perceiving, our world would seem flat and dull.

Goleman goes on to explain how the brain's distinct components (see the diagram that follows) comprise the architecture that manifests the "perennial tension between reason and emotion. The fact that the thinking brain grew from the emotional brain reveals much about the relationship of thought to feeling; there was an emotional brain long before there was a rational one. . . . [So] when passions surge, the balance tips: *it is the emotional mind that captures the upper hand, swamping the rational mind.*"4

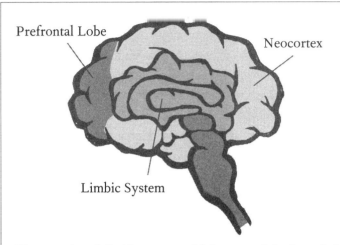

Prefrontal Lobe

Neocortex

Limbic System

The emotional *limbic system*, with its *amygdala, hypothalamus, nucleus accumbens,* and *hippocampus,* reacts to our environment (feelings and memory), while the rational *neocortex*, with its *prefrontal lobes,* evaluates and tempers our reactions (thinking and decision making).

Two circuits, or pathways, in the brain are especially relevant to secret keeping: the *"alarm" circuit* and the *"pleasure" circuit.* The alarm circuit plays a key role in how we remember things, especially traumatic events, and the pleasure circuit (often called the "reward" pathway) plays a key role in survival activities we wish to repeat like eating, drinking, and lovemaking that make us "feel good."

Important note: Both the *alarm* and *pleasure* circuits originate in, and are functions of, the emotional limbic system. The rational neocortex may influence these functions after the fact — once an event, favorable or traumatic, occurs — but only then.

I believe that these passions are at the core of a Secret Keeper's psyche. Secret keeping is an attempt to satisfy one's emotional demands, despite societal constraints. Sooner or later, something has to give. This conflict, as experienced by Caroline and Brad, led to their habit of stifling their genuine feelings and then masking those feelings to fit their environment. Perhaps Secret Keepers instinctively realize that an honest display of emotions will clash with others' expectations and elicit disapproval.

This phenomenon, described by Goleman as *display rules*, is learned very early by human beings. "An education in display rules is imparted when we instruct a child not to seem disappointed, but to smile and say thank you instead, when Grandpa has given a dreadful but well-intentioned birthday present.... The rule being learned by the child is something like, 'Mask your real feelings when they will hurt someone you love; substitute a phony, but less hurtful feeling instead.' "⁵

It is this kind of lesson that Secret Keepers master over time. (We will examine this concept in greater detail in chapter 5, when we explore Jung's theory of the Shadow.) Young Secret Keepers skillfully learn to display socially acceptable emotions while hiding their true — and unacceptable — feelings. The false trumps the true and sets them up for future clandestine behavior. To some degree this happens to everybody. For Secret Keepers, though, putting this into practice becomes a habit and develops into *acting one way while feeling another* — the first splintered mind-set.

Essentially, when we display socially acceptable emotions we win approval from elders and authority figures; when we display socially unacceptable emotions, we get into trouble. These socially unacceptable emotions can lead to the *excitement/pleasure/delight* cycle with its risk-taking and thrills that the tame, conventional world never knows or enjoys. This lesson is a common one for young Secret Keepers, as I myself was to learn.

My Story: Falling into the Secret-Keeping Trap

One evening when I was eleven my world flipped upside down. Seldom do children appreciate their childhood bliss until it ends, and that's precisely what happened to my twin brother, Dave, and me that night in October 1955. We had just crawled under the covers and turned out the lights. We shared a bedroom on the second floor of a white colonial house in Minneapolis, a home we loved, the place where we had built a tree fort high up in the crab apple tree in the backyard and where we'd played games with neighborhood kids like kick-the-can and hide-and-seek on the lawn until dark. But our carefree joys ended when Mom came into our room that night and sat on the edge of the bed. Something about the way she cleared her throat made us flinch. Then she blindsided us with an announcement that knocked me for a loop.

"Boys, I have exciting news! We're moving to a big new house! Daddy and I have been dreaming about it for a long time. Now, with a new variety show of his own on television, we can finally afford it."

"But we like it here!" I cried.

She kept talking as if she hadn't even heard me. Dad's musical talent at the piano entertained innumerable fans and had won him a place in people's hearts through the new apparatus with wire rabbit ears called television. A musical showman with a bald head and a big smile, known for his girth (he weighed three hundred fifty pounds), Toby Prin basked in the love of thousands of Twin Cities residents who watched him on their black-and-white TVs and asked for his autograph when they bumped into him on the street. We rarely saw him at home, though, other than when he napped on the couch, because of his long work hours.

It was Ellen Prin's fate that she couldn't plan simple meals or social occasions like other housewives whose husbands arrived home at 5:00 or 6:00 P.M. I watched Mom become more and more frustrated, and her volatile moods cast a shadow over we three boys. My brother Tommy, who was three years older, sometimes ran to his room when she hollered. Years earlier, when Dave and I were in kindergarten, she'd suffered from a nervous breakdown and, after six weeks in the hospital, returned home dazed and shuffling like a robot. Clearly things would be very different. I noticed that Mom took pink pills to calm her nerves and yellow ones to help her sleep, then in the morning she took blue ones to "snap herself out of it" and white ones in the afternoon to pep her up. Her pill bottles filled a shelf in the medicine cabinet.

Trying to soothe our fears as she tucked us in, she declared, "Now, now boys, you'll love the new house. You'll see. You can build another tree fort and play games all day long in the woods."

"Woods? But what about our friends?" Dave demanded.

"Do we have to?" I pleaded, inching away from her.

Dave looked at me, and we both knew the answer. She made it sound like making new friends and going to a new school would be some kind of special adventure.

"But why can't we stay here?" I asked.

Mom sat there talking on and on about her dream house, about how it would be nestled on a lovely lake miles away from the city, a kind of country manor for all the world to see and admire. She whispered in a dreamy sort of way, "The house will overlook the lake, and you boys will have lots of room to run around in, with wide-open spaces to shoot your BB-guns...."

I looked at Dave. I sensed that everything would be different and very strange.

Days later, on a Saturday, we all piled into Dad's Chevy and visited the natural wild beauty of the lake property she'd talked about, the subdivision called Chippewa Hills. The maple and oak and elm trees, with their thousands of orange and yellow and brown leaves, filled my view in every direction. Suddenly, without warning, Mom ordered us boys to move a grove of young birch trees two hundred yards to the lakeshore, where she could enjoy viewing them someday through the then-imaginary picture window. We looked at Dad, who shrugged meekly, and our visit turned into a work project. The sunny day became hot, and we sweated in our T-shirts as we hauled the heavy, sloshing pails of lake water, uprooted dozens of trees, loaded them into a rickety wheelbarrow, dug deep holes, and replanted them — all because "Mom said so." We lifted, we carried, we labored until dark.

Mom acted hurt when she observed how angry we were becoming and finally called it quits. She displayed no consideration for us — I'd never seen her act this way. When we boys dropped into our beds at last in our "real" home, we gazed with sunken eyes at one another and shook our heads. Our fears about the move had materialized: we were miserable. Was this a foretaste of how life would be?

Weeks later we moved from our beloved home in Minneapolis. I gazed out the rear window of Dad's Buick, a fancy new model he'd just purchased that was more in keeping with our showier new residence. I watched our old house disappear from view, tears dripping down my cheeks.

From that day on, I felt less secure, and my secret keeping became a pattern — outwardly I showed respect for Mom, while inwardly I seethed with anger toward her. I held this secret buried inside me, choking on the disturbing duality of wanting to love and appreciate her but covering up my fury with a smile. I began doing what came to be a habit. Without my knowing it, very subtly, I'd fallen into the trap of *acting one way while feeling another.*

That day I became a fledgling Secret Keeper. Of course, I

didn't put it into those words back then. Months passed, and my anger spiraled from dislike of Mom to hostility. Seeing the ways Dad caved in to Mom's mounting demands for our expensive lifestyle made me resentful. Things took a turn for the worse at the new house, and my new pattern of keeping secrets imbedded itself deeper and deeper. I began living two lives, one an outward happier life and one an inward hapless life.

OUR COMMINGLED NATURES

Let's return to the question, What is a Secret Keeper? We could say that he or she is a "charming deceiver." Charming deceivers escape suspicion, thanks to their charming personalities. They are seldom the first people anyone thinks of acting suspicious. Consider these clues:

- *They present well.* Male or female, regardless of ethnic origin, they appear to function well in productive jobs and careers. They pay taxes and attend their kids' soccer games and musical concerts.

- *They are heavily invested in a positive image.* Secret Keepers generally dress well, have good hygiene, and take active roles in their communities. Their homes or apartments look nice, and they get along with neighbors.

- *They have much at stake (a lot to lose).* Their greatest fear is being found out, having their double lives exposed. At stake are their hard-earned reputations, career potential, borrowing credentials, and overall standing in the eyes of people who matter — family, friends, co-workers.

- *They seldom have criminal histories.* To safeguard their positive images, Secret Keepers isolate on the sly. They wait to indulge until they can withdraw inconspicuously from being observed by anybody, thereby avoiding any reason for arrest. Maintaining a clean record is one of their cleverest cover-ups.

Yet behind their public masks, they are fearful of being caught. While they ingeniously flaunt conventional norms, they consciously calculate ways to cover their tracks in order to elude public exposure. Blowing their cover is their greatest worry. So they bluff very skillfully and rely on camouflage, priding themselves on blending in and never arousing concern. In short, Secret Keepers live primarily through their feelings, exhibiting a keen sense of emotional intelligence. They have a strong sense of adventure and risk-taking, and an equally strong dread of disapproval and criticism.

Perhaps Robert Louis Stevenson captured this dichotomy best when he penned these words for his main character, Dr. Henry Jekyll, the kindly physician in Victorian England who succumbed to the diabolical part of his psyche named Mr. Hyde:

> All human beings, as we meet them, are commingled out of good and evil. I saw that, of the two natures that contended in the field of my consciousness, I was radically both. All things therefore seemed to point to this; that I was slowly losing hold of my original and better self, and becoming slowly incorporated with my second and worse self.[6]

Chapter 2

WHAT ARE
UNHEALTHY SECRETS?

We call him a good man who reveals himself to others.

—— MEISTER ECKHART

*I*N MY PRACTICE AS A COUNSELOR, a question I often hear from clients and family members is, "What makes secrets good or bad?" My answer always is, "Good question."

As voters casting our ballots, we rely on secrecy to protect our vote from the knowledge of others. As planners of surprise birthday parties, we create a benign conspiracy that conceals our plans from the person being honored. As scientists, we study the secrets of nature to learn more about ourselves and our world. As lovers, we protect our privacy by closing the curtains, shutting the bedroom door, or taking a vacation to a secluded setting.

All these qualify as harmless secrets that are neither shameful nor morally wrong. We engage in intentionally hiding or concealing information from others to protect what is vulnerable without giving it a second thought. But negative views of secrecy are common. "The link between secrecy and deceit is so strong in the minds of some that they mistakenly take all secrecy to be deceptive," writes Sissela Bok in her scholarly book entitled *Secrets*. "To confuse secrecy and deception is easy, since all deception does involve keeping something secret."[1]

The deceptive nature of keeping secrets is what concerns us here. Once a person with a stigmatizing habit decides that deception is necessary, he typically withdraws or isolates from other people (to prevent them from getting nosy). If questioned, he replies vaguely or with minimal information (to avoid being found out). He plays an avoidance game. If you are wondering how your private habits stack up, the essential question to ask is, *How often do secrets play a role in my behavior?* If the answer is "often," then, assuming you wish to make vital changes in your life, the next question to ask is, *How do I move from living a secretive, closed, risk-filled life to living an honest, open, transparent one?*

Helpful suggestions await you, provided you're committed to living authentically. Authentic living, as you will see, is the heartbeat at the source of healing, what some practitioners have called having "rigorous honesty" and being "willing to go to any lengths."[2] *Integrity* is another word for it. Knowing your truth and living it with integrity takes work. And guts.

The above examples of voting, planning a surprise party, and so on are all actions without guile. They depend on the protective aspect of secrecy. That's the good news about secrets: *they protect*. In understanding the destructive power of secrecy, it helps to distinguish between *secrecy* and *privacy*. These concepts are closely linked. Often they overlap, so let's carefully discern between them and see how they differ.

Privacy can be defined as limiting unwanted access by others. It means keeping something from the view of strangers. People rightly seek to protect innocent, harmless, legitimate

activities they do in private. We keep a folder of tax returns in a
filing cabinet, our underwear in a drawer, and our prescriptions
in a medicine cabinet. We take for granted the legitimacy of hiding jewels or computer files from burglars and busybodies.

Bok adds, "But secrecy hides far more than what is private.
A private garden may not be a secret garden; a private life is
rarely a secret life.... One's purpose [in using secrecy] is to
become less vulnerable, more in control."3

We want to be less vulnerable and more in control. In addi-
tion to protecting us, secrecy's main aim is control. Protecting
our privacy means protecting our identity, personhood, plans,
and/or property. We do this by defining boundaries that others
should observe and respect. A sign on a neighbor's fence says
"Private Property: No Trespassing." A door in an airport is
marked "Authorized Personnel Only." These act to separate the
public from the private. However, should anybody jump that fence
or open that door, then the owner may opt for a system that provides more secrecy because *secrecy offers additional protection.*

It works like this. For decades I've kept a journal; I now have
more than one hundred spiral-bound notebooks. These notebooks contain numerous private, often secret, thoughts and
ideas. Because the people in my life respect my privacy, I make
no attempt to hide them. Should I ever feel vulnerable, however,
I would certainly seek to write entries in code, or lock the notebooks up, or hide them in some ingenious place. The added level
of secrecy offers additional protection.

Another way of ensuring additional protection is holding
back information about yourself. To maintain control over how
we direct the flow of information to others increases our personal power. In short, influencing how you are seen by others
gives you *power* and *control.* The critical issue here is the nature

of what is being kept secret. If it is something innocent, like your use of antidepressant meds, then your secrets aren't "bad."

But some people's secret habits conceal behaviors that are shameful, taboo, perverse, or harmful. Their secrets have power over them and motivate them to misbehave, become sick, or violate others. Burdened by intense impulses to act out secretly, they steal hours away from their public lives to indulge in unhealthy behaviors or passions — sometimes for decades without being detected. I once learned about some family members who had made the sickening discovery of a husband and father's secret life when they uncovered evidence in a storage locker he'd kept hidden for years. It contained sadomasochistic artifacts, photos, sex toys, and letters to unknown lovers, all of which violated their perceptions of him. This was not the man they thought they knew!

Then there is the story of a man whose wife died after the couple had celebrated sixty years of happy marriage. A few weeks after her funeral, he was cleaning out her closet and found a loose floorboard. Lifting it, he discovered a shoe box jammed with love letters. As he read through them, it became clear they were responses to letters his wife had sent to a man he'd never met — perhaps, he deduced, the former teenage flame of hers with whom she'd danced at their fiftieth high school reunion. You can just imagine his pain. His grief was compounded by keen disillusionment, making him ponder the hidden identity of his wife, whom he had loved so faithfully.

THE CONTINUUM OF SECRETS

To help illustrate the basic distinctions between the kinds of secrets that functioning adults tend to keep, I have provided the chart on the following page. This continuum gradually came into being as I counseled clients. Use it to help answer some of the questions you may be asking about secret keeping. Keep in mind that the first and second categories, simple secrets and silent secrets, are typical of human beings in general and are *not* the concern of this book.

CONTINUUM OF SECRETS			
NO HARM TO LESS HARM		MORE HARM TO MUCH HARM	
1	2	3	4
SIMPLE SECRETS	SILENT SECRETS	SECRET KEEPING	CRIMINAL-PSYCHOTIC BEHAVIOR
(everybody has)	*(dark and taboo but passive)*	*(acting out ethical and moral wrongs but nothing illegal)*	*(arrestable offenses or hospitalizations)*
BENIGN	PASSIVE	DYNAMIC	MALIGNANT

1. *Simple Secrets* emerge from isolated, rare events, the kind of harmless mistakes or lapses in judgment that seldom require self-disclosure or therapy — often memories of childhood or adolescent activities. A young student peeks at her classmate's test answers, or an underage driver takes his dad's car out for a joyride, and nobody finds out. Indirectly, secrets like these open the individual to dualistic thinking, which in some cases can develop and then take hold.

2. *Silent Secrets* become ingrained thoughts or attitudes and can pose a risk to one's mental health. Fantasies that are not acted out fit here. So do acts of deceptive omission, as in the story of three college fraternity brothers who got drunk and went boating together.

One fell overboard, and the other two jumped in to save him. Those two drowned, but the first guy survived. He felt intense guilt and made no mention of their drinking at the young men's funerals. Years later he feels exhausted, dirty inside, and burdened by having caused his pals' deaths and by having deceived their families. One act (getting drunk) led to another (falling overboard while boating), which turned into a tragedy (two drownings), which resulted in a cover-up (concealing truth from the victims' parents), which led to years of torment from silently keeping the truth secret.

3. *Secret Keeping* goes one step further and includes *acting out*, more specifically, indulging in habits or rituals that can lead to risking one's safety, health, or sanity and that of others. These are the kind of harmful patterns that make one sick, and the person caught up in them can benefit from disclosure and therapy. Secrets in this category include behavior patterns and rituals that lead to sneaking away to do things that make one feel better. These hidden acts stretch, and eventually transgress, *ethical/moral standards* and *relational boundaries* but do not cross the line into breaking the law or psychosis. The head pastor of a leading-edge metro church engaged in a furtive, on-going extramarital affair of eight years, which broke ethical, moral, and biblical rules. His secret keeping led to divorce, career exile, months of counseling for family members, and news headlines describing harmful consequences to thousands of parishioners. Nevertheless, he did not break the law, never wore handcuffs, or sat in a jail cell.

4. *Criminal-Psychotic Behavior*: Secrets in this category may include a mixture of secrets from the previous categories, but the acting out of them violates *legal boundaries/standards*, thereby making them crimes punishable by law, such as shoplifting. Certain acts may not constitute crime, but they sink to the level of *serious psychological pathology*. Sara Jane Olson's actions fit the criminal definition. After evading arrest for attempted murder in California as a fiery member of the rebellious Symbionese Liberation Army in 1975, she lived for twenty-four years inconspicuously as a suburban mother and housewife in St. Paul, Minnesota, until being discovered and sent to prison. A psychotic person is one who loses touch with reality and becomes captive to paranoia, delusions, and hallucinations, leading to hospitalization or institutionalization. Like the delirious Mr. Hyde, the individual's split personality divides too far, making the healthy psyche lose its governing power over the unhealthy psyche. Movie characters like Billy in *One Flew Over the Cuckoo's Nest*, Cy Parrish in *One-Hour Photo*, or the kidnapper in *Silence of the Lambs* fit this description.

Remember that the categories of simple secrets and silent secrets are typical of human beings in general and will not be examined in this book. While we may keep these kinds of secrets at some point in our lives, this level of secrecy *does not* cross the line into the third and fourth categories, secret keeping and criminal-psychotic behavior, which *are* the focus of this book.

To avoid any potential confusion, let's make clear what secret keeping is *not*: It is *not* the behavior of adults who hold family of origin secrets — memories of abusive home lives or their parents' stigmatizing secrets. Such secrets may surely influence current adult beliefs and behavior, and those keeping them may require therapy, but they fit into the silent secrets category, because these secrets were *somebody else's* and *in the past.*

Nor is secret keeping the behavior of citizens oppressed by tyrannical governments such as those of Hitler or Stalin or Idi Amin. These victims' secrets were kept to avoid capture, prison, torture, and death. Included in this category of secrets are those of paid professional spies such as CIA or FBI agents. These concern political or governmental conflicts, not the interpersonal relationships or inner universe of Secret Keepers.

Further, we are not engaging in secret keeping when we keep things from ourselves. In psychological lingo, these kinds of secrets are the result of *repression.* Unlike conscious concealment, or the "predisposition to actively conceal from others personal information one perceives as distressing or negative," the term *repression* means "keeping painful thoughts and impulses out of conscious awareness," writes Professor Anita Kelly of Notre Dame University.[4]

Below is the definition I've settled on that spells out these enigmatic forces in one sentence: *Secret Keepers live in a parallel universe based on the intentional concealment of what is shameful or discreditable beyond the limits of privacy.* That's quite a mouthful, so let's look at this sentence one phrase at a time.

Parallel universe refers to an entire world separated from the day-to-day realities of one's public or family life, a world that requires dual awareness and the ongoing "mental burden of remembering the secret so it won't be told but at the same time not thinking about it because it might be leaked."[5]

Intentional concealment describes the motive to conceal consciously, as distinguished from people who keep secrets from themselves without knowing they are doing so (called *repression* or *self-delusion*).

Shameful or discreditable suggests the negative or damaging content of what is concealed and the emotional toll that the acted-out secret habits or compulsions can take. If these secrets were exposed, various kinds of harm would come to the Secret Keeper as well as to people dear to him or her.

Beyond the limits of privacy speaks to the *control* and *power* and *additional protection* that Secret Keepers gain from hiding stigmatizing knowledge from every other human being on the planet.

Does this description fit you or someone you love?

Research psychologists Julie Lane and Daniel Wegner state, "Secrecy is an act of deceptive omission. People keep secrets from others for fear of the real or imagined repercussions the hidden information would bring with exposure, not realizing that the intrapsychic consequences of this silence can be devastating."[6] It is these internal stressors to a person's psyche and health that bring Secret Keepers to the breaking point (which could be either a breakdown or a breakthrough).

Besides the fact that they create inner stress and escalating turmoil for habitual Secret Keepers, the troubling thing about secrets is that they exclude others, and exclusion breeds conflict. An outsider/insider tension develops that says, "You don't belong." This means the social fabric between the Secret Keeper and everyone else frays because the people who don't know the secret remain outsiders to what is concealed. Sometimes this lends a sense of superiority to the Secret Keeper because she knows something that no one else in the world knows — and everybody is fooled. The conflict is felt by others because they may sense that something is vaguely "off," that excuses or explanations by the Secret Keeper don't quite make sense or jibe with reality.

Consider that human beings all live on a spectrum, with *secrecy* at one end and *transparency* at the other. Think of an arrow that looks like this:

SECRECY   HEALTHY   TRANSPARENCY
                     BALANCE POINT

What determines how openly or secretively we act and behave? In the case of privacy, we legitimately guard personal information we believe is ours, as well as our need to control the flow of this information.

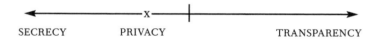

SECRECY   PRIVACY   TRANSPARENCY

In the case of secret keeping, the stakes are much higher. Because of the shame and guilt attached to the information we are hiding or covering up, we *block* the flow of information and *shut down* avenues of communication or discovery as a way to protect our vulnerability.

SECRET KEEPING   HEALTHY   TRANSPARENCY
                    BALANCE POINT

Maintaining privacy is an act of choosing healthy boundaries and staying comfortably within them. Secret keeping is an act of avoiding the embarrassment of crossing unhealthy boundaries by behaving in ways that violate one's values/ethics/morals/spiritual beliefs.

Eventually, stigmatizing behavior covered up by secrecy affects one's character and judgment and can lower one's resistance to the irrational or pathological. The inner, unshared world of the Secret Keeper stifles sanity and free choice, although former Secret Keepers will tell you that while they were active they believed with all sincerity that their secret compulsions enhanced both their sanity and their free choice. But Secret Keepers are divided people. Major parts of their inner world get walled off, compartmentalized, and acted out in dark, lonely places (more on this dynamic in later chapters when we discuss the concept of the Shadow). They often carry on an act, a performance scripted daily for others to buy into. All the tricks and ploys, the constant guile and deception required to deal with their pangs of conscience and conflicting emotions, breed illness.

"Studies show that people who tend to conceal personal information have more physical problems, such as headaches, nausea, and back pains, and are more anxious, shy, and depressed than people who don't," writes Anita Kelly.[7] "The more serious the secret," adds one of Kelly's colleagues, "the lower the self-esteem and worse the physical condition. Serious secret-holders had significantly lower satisfaction with life, and were emotionally worse off."[8]

As noted, the challenge for Secret Keepers remains whether to live a *secretive, closed, risk-filled* life or an *honest, open, transparent* life. Let's be clear about what *honest, open,* and *transparent* mean. They don't mean you are made like a glass window that people can see through; they do mean that *you let people see through to the real you.* Think of it as being H.O.T. (Honest-Open-Transparent). Being H.O.T. requires a careful and thorough self-examination of the reasons you refuse to let people see through to the real person you are. It's a goal worth aiming for, and the chapters in part 2 offer exercises and tips to guide you in this process.

The seeds of secret keeping are often planted early on, and a history of woundedness gets lived out unconsciously in adult lives — what I've come to call *developmental deficits* (explained more fully in chapter 6). To illustrate, I will continue with the story of my own boyhood.

MY STORY: INNOCENCE LOST

The new lakeshore house our family moved into was a landmark to my mother's ego. A sprawling edifice built in an affluent exurb on a wooded multiacre lot, it commanded more than twice the space of our old home. Its grand scale became the epitome of "appearances before reality." Mom's work projects for us boys multiplied — tiling floors, painting bedrooms, building shelves, planting flowerbeds — always accompanied by more of her unreasonable orders. She treated us more like hired hands than like sons. As her intensity increased, she no longer showed us affection or treated us like part of the family.

To top it off, no sooner had we moved in than Dad's health deteriorated because of his long hours of work at the TV station, which typically lasted from 5:30 A.M. to late evening six days a week...and his unceasing efforts to make Mom happy. He suffered blackouts from low blood sugar and spent days hospitalized because of what had become severe diabetes. He loved smoking cigars, ate lots of red meat, and rarely exercised. A parade of doctors' offices, more hospitalizations, and erratic employment followed — even the amputation of his right leg owing to poor self-care.

Mom's relentless decorating and landscaping projects increased, as did her treatment of us as hired hands. Dad could never protect us (while hospitalized) or rescue us (postamputation) from her tyrannical decrees; lying in bed became his existence. Because of my artistic skills, her work assignments often started with me. A typical decorating project entailed working long hours, like the time we tiled the entire sixteen hundred square feet of the basement. Tommy had fled to his room and slammed the door, so we twins stared at the concrete floor and the boxes of vinyl floor tiles and five-gallon bucket of black, sticky glue. As an eighth-grader, I had no experience, but I knew the end result had to meet professional standards. Dad was in bed. That day Mom rattled off directions, departed, and left us to fend for ourselves.

After many hours, Dave and I wiped the sweat from our faces and stood back. Pleased, we saw how professional the tiled portion of the floor looked. Except for finishing the edges, which needed tiles cut to size, we'd done the impossible.

All in all, the tiling took about two weeks, without the benefit of knee pads, the proper tools, Tommy's help, or Mom's gratitude. Dad got up from bed once a day to inspect our labor: "You boys are doing a fine job," he'd say, then he'd point out some area needing improvement and stumble back upstairs on his crutches.

Dave and I kept the secrets of our home life to ourselves, of course. We never dreamed of telling a teacher or anyone outside the family.

Those years of upside-down priorities overwhelmed my ability to cope and led to escapist — think secret keeping — behavior. I was a pubescent male, almost fourteen, dejected and hurt. Whenever Dave and I arrived home from school in the afternoon, we played a new game called Getting Lost. Evading Mom before she could trap us, we ran from the house and stayed out in the woods as long as possible, sometimes until dark.

I also slipped into a fantasy world. Getting Lost turned into another way to steal hours. Whenever possible I thumbed through *National Geographic*, looking at naked tribal women, and at the *Playboy*s hidden in my older cousin Roger's bedroom closet. One hot summer day when I was alone in the neighboring woods escaping reality by playing Getting Lost, a flood of sensual thoughts aroused me, and I removed my shorts and T-shirt and underwear. Exhilarated, I ran barefoot along the wooded path fully naked — feeling high and totally removed from the ugly reality at home. This first experience was so powerful that I "floated" through the next few days until I could plan my next escape and repeat the familiar excitement/pleasure/delight cycle. The "pleasure circuit" in my brain was getting stroked and stoked. At home or at school, I put on the appearance of a normal teenager, cleverly hiding the secret of behaving shamelessly in the woods. The Secret Keeper in me was growing.

Then something cruel and traumatic happened that set off my brain's alarm system. An incident that generated intense negative memories erupted on a hot bright sunny day in August 1958, when Dave and I awoke to our fourteenth birthday. We'd invited five of our friends over to our party. By noon the heat soared above ninety-five and was still rising. Dad promised to drive us and our friends downtown to a movie, but he appeared unexpectedly with a grim look on his face before anybody arrived.

"Boys, I have tough news. Your mother just heard on the radio that the highway department is ripping apart Lyndale Avenue. New freeway construction. She says the paving stones are being thrown away, and today is the only day they can be claimed."

"What about it?" I asked.

He looked away. "She thinks the stones are perfect for a backyard patio and rock garden. And they're free."

"Dad!" Dave exclaimed. "You can't be serious!"

But serious he was. We left a note on the door telling our

guests we'd return as soon as possible and to please stick around for the party. At the hot and dusty construction site, Dave and I lifted the discarded concrete paving stones into the trailer. These two-foot slabs weighed about sixty pounds each, and we worked without gloves. The heat baked our faces, and our bodies dripped with sweat.

When we arrived home four hours later, only two friends were waiting. We thanked them for their patience and begged them to excuse our tardiness.

But Dad announced, "Sorry, boys. But the trailer has to be returned before 6:00 P.M. And the stones have to be unloaded first." We groaned, then pleaded with our pals to go home so they wouldn't get sucked into helping us haul the stones. For the next hour we furiously finished the task, and Dad drove off to return the trailer. Dave and I stormed into the house, ripped off our clothes, and took long, cool showers. At dinner, Mom made a big show of saying "happy birthday" and cutting the cake — but we wouldn't touch it; we turned our backs and left her staring at us. We "got lost," and I wept for an hour while watching the sunset and swatting mosquitoes.

I harbored this new fury in my secret world — and how I struggled to reconcile it with my genuine feelings of love for her! But murderous thoughts sprang into my mind one afternoon after school when I stepped off the bus and started walking home, resentful about encountering Mom and having to play Getting Lost again. I fantasized taking a butcher knife from the kitchen and . . . stabbing her. That night, with Mom one wall away, I lay in bed petrified of my homicidal thoughts and fearful of acting on them. I needed some escape, some outlet for my hostility.

I came to depend on the thrill I experienced whenever I ran naked in the woods. Each time I snuck out and romped along the deer trail in bright daylight beside the lake, my heart jumped to my throat. My mind calculated the risks, but I kept telling myself I'd never been caught before, so why would anyone catch me this time? With my shirt and shorts tossed on a nearby shrub, I savored the soft breeze on my bare thighs as I jogged carefree in the gallery of nature. Au natural, I glided gleefully along the deer path.

These escapades made up for everything. My pleasure soared, my misery plunged. Each time I secretly went running, spending hours in sensual solitude, the ritual became bolder and more daring. Escaping the intense, unbearable tensions I harbored in my private world was the answer to my raging anger. But lurking in my gut and my ever-darkening moods remained the deepest and darkest secret of all: my fantasies of killing Mom.

Chapter 3

HOW SECRET LIVES
SEDUCE US

There are some secrets we think we're keeping,
but those secrets are actually keeping us.

— FRANK WARREN, FOUNDER OF POSTSECRET.COM

O NE WAY WE LEARN about secret lives is through the Internet. Websites like postsecret.com invite anonymous postcards from people describing their fears, betrayals, erotic desires, confessions, or childhood humiliations — "as long as it is true and you have never shared it with anyone before."[1] While fascinating and thought provoking — as well as affirming of this book's premise — these kinds of secrets pale in comparison to the Internet's capability to provide anonymity to stalkers and sexual predators. Talk about secret keeping! No other venue allows such wide-open access to unwitting victims like our children. Just go online to dateline.msnbc.com or perverted-justice.com to learn about how many scam artists use chat rooms to endanger kids and seduce the gullible by concocting phony aliases.

Another way we learn about secret lives is through newspaper and television coverage. Stories about the duality of famous celebrities abound. Former president Bill Clinton kept countless secrets and covered up his sexual escapades. Who can forget Monica Lewinsky and the years of tumultuous scandal and headlines? Clinton even admitted in his autobiography, *My Life*, "Life required me to be a secret keeper...if you have a whole part of your life you can't talk about, then you wind up living parallel lives."[2]

Another celebrity, the Reverend Jesse Jackson, fathered a baby in 1999 as the result of an affair with a government office worker while he was advising President Clinton about Monica.[3] CBS journalist Charles Kuralt's twenty-nine-year secret affair became public when his mistress arrived at his funeral and Kuralt's wife discovered the "other woman," who wanted her share of his estate. A judge later awarded her ninety acres of prime mountain property valued at $600,000.[4] Charles Lindbergh, the world-famous aviator, fathered two families, one in full view with his American wife, and the other hidden for decades with his German mistress, who gave birth to three children.[5]

Secret lives can also be found in literature. The tale of Robin Hood is a classic example. He and his merry men performed all kinds of exciting deeds in secret, and the Sheriff of Nottingham never did learn Robin's "daytime" identity. Superman also fits into this mold. As reporter Clark Kent he could hardly summon the nerve to say hi to Lois Lane, but after racing into a phone booth and ripping off his suit, he would emerge in a red cape and blue tights as the strong and indomitable force for good. Wonder Woman, Batman, and Spiderman are also incarnations of these fight-for-justice heroes, whose double lives dazzle and seduce viewers. Movies and television flash images of these dashing double identities, subtly conditioning young people by role-modeling secret lives. How? By portraying the adventurous secret lives of these alter egos as more exciting and glamorous than the routine daily lives of these heroes — or than our own.

From stories like these, whether real ones like President Clinton's or folktales like Robin Hood's, we learn that almost any human being — however privileged or disadvantaged — is capable of two-faced living. Culturally, the seduction begins early in our youth. And deception goes hand in hand with duplicity. In the late 1950s Tony Curtis starred in *The Great Imposter*, a movie about a clever con man who successfully impersonates a doctor, a naval officer, and several other identities in a wildly adventurous game of deception. The weekly TV show *I Led Three Lives* was about a corporate executive/father/spy. The lead character juggled three entirely separate identities, working in an office, parenting at home, and outsmarting Soviet secret agents on the sly.

Let's not leave out the business or sports worlds. Consider the CEOs of megacorporations Enron, Worldcom, Adelphia, and Tyco, who were all charged with defrauding their investors and employees by using secret accounting schemes and who made away with personal millions. Or how about former baseball heroes Pete Rose and Kirby Puckett, who hid from the public their secret gambling obsession and eighteen-year extramarital affair, respectively, behind their dazzling on-the-field, superstar images?

The focus of this book is on everyday people, however. Their secret keeping is just as prevalent, and probably more so, given their vast numbers. Their two-faced habits may start in childhood long before any addictions have developed. Brad's betting on marbles as a boy on a school playground fits this phenomenon: his secret keeping became a full-blown gambling compulsion when he reached adulthood. Caroline's excessive affection for animals also led to cover-up behaviors, as did my own efforts to clamp down on my fury by running in the woods or "getting lost."

IMPRESSION MANAGEMENT

In chapter 1 we explored the first splintered mind-set of a Secret Keeper: *acting one way while feeling another*. In this chapter we will explore the second: *placing appearances first and reality second*. This mind-set results from consciously preventing others from observing or learning about the secret activities dictated by our secret self — the voice in us that whispers radical and subversive ideas to ponder and act on. Psychologically, this dynamic is called *impression management*: making deliberate choices about facial expressions, body language, tone of voice, hygiene, and apparel to prompt a desired impression in others.

A concept introduced by sociologist Dr. Erving Goffman in 1959, at its simplest impression management means manipulating others' impressions to our benefit. It is based on his premise that theatrical performance pervades most human beings' everyday lives, what he called "the presentation of self."[6] After years of study, Goffman maintained that generally people behave like performers in a play and portray character traits they want their audience (other people) to believe. As Shakespeare so aptly put it, "All the world's a stage, / and all the men and women merely players."[7]

"In everyday life," Goffman wrote, "it is usually possible for the performer to create intentionally almost any kind of false impression without putting himself in the indefensible position of having told a clear-cut lie." Goffman goes on to show how using calculated techniques such as innuendo, ambiguity, half-truths, and what he called "crucial omissions" "allow[s] the misinformer to profit from lies without, technically, telling any. Some performances are carried off successfully with complete dishonesty."[8]

It's the objective (outer) cues that count, observed Goffman, more than the subjective (inner) state of a person. Mastery of these "presentation" techniques is a Secret Keeper's specialty, and they are often incongruent with the individual's actual feelings — exemplified by *acting one way while feeling another*. To illustrate, I will introduce two people whose stellar impression management skills demonstrate the dynamics of *placing appearances first and reality second*.

TRACY: PURGING THE "FAT COW"

The youngest of three sisters, Tracy realized early on that her sisters "were very thin." One of them got modeling jobs and received compliments on how great she looked, especially from their grandmother. Tracy remembers, however, "always hearing about how chubby [she] looked" whenever she visited their grandmother. Tracy would then scurry into an adjacent room and find a place to cry. "No one ever knew this," she reflects. "I kept my humiliation hidden."

In short order, Tracy came to value appearances over reality.

For years she felt depressed, like a "fat cow," and felt guilty every time she ate a full meal. In high school, despite being five-foot-five and weighing 120 pounds, Tracy lived with the terrible fear of "blowing up." As a sophomore, she and a friend joined the gymnastics squad, inspired by the USA women's Olympic team. "Their bodies were so sleek, so perfect. Who wouldn't want to be just like them?" Besides the strict exercise regimen and workouts, some girls restricted foods, while others went further and purged. During practices, Tracy discovered that her teammates quietly vomited up their meals to stay trim. "The coaches must have known, but no one talked about it. It was all very secretive."

Soon Tracy and her friends were routinely bending over the

toilet and sticking their fingers down their throats. "Nobody talked about it, but everybody did it." In time Tracy lost control of her purging episodes. "When I felt sick, which was every time I ate, I would just bend over, and it became automatic." Eventually Tracy dropped to one hundred pounds. She felt proud of herself. She finally felt in control, and she liked herself. Everyone told her how good she looked, and she thrived on the attention.

But the lack of nutrition and spending thirty-five hours a week at the gym took a toll on her health and energy. Tracy fibbed about feeling sick from the "stomach flu" and about not joining family members during meals "because of too much homework." Along with purging and simply refusing to eat, she began taking laxatives and enemas. Tracy's continuing weight loss finally forced her to drop out of gymnastics. "The sneaking, hiding, lying, and isolating had taken over. I'd run water in the sink whenever I purged or think up new excuses to leave the table quickly almost every day. It got overbearing."

Tracy became a cheerleader for a while, but that didn't boost her self-esteem either because deep down she knew she was destroying herself and believed that nobody could help her with her secret. "My mom had no idea that I was purging almost every day," she admits. In her quieter moments, the darker side of her secret keeping bothered her: "I knew I had to stop. I hated how it made me feel. The dishonesty felt worse than the vomiting. But how to stop?"

KEVIN: MIXED-UP GENDER ROLES

At the tender age of four, Kevin remembers walking through malls and department stores with his mother and watching "all the beautiful women." "Inside I longed for some kind of connection with those beautiful strangers." At home he avoided his blue-collar dad, whose abusive teasing and face-slapping made him feel like "damaged goods." While playing with his older sister one day, he tried on her dresses and shiny shoes. She exclaimed how cute he looked. Suddenly, he felt a connection to the beautiful women he adored who made him feel so complete.

At age ten, Kevin was captivated by his first centerfold photo. "Nothing had prepared me for the wave of good feelings that washed over me." Kevin wanted to *be* inside the picture and to feel the attention and love of the stunning, desirable woman. Instead, he did the next best thing. "I fantasized about being with her and got dressed in my sister's clothes to look like the centerfold in the shots where she was dressed. I adored who I saw in the mirror, a glamorous 'me' entirely unlike the 'damaged goods' I felt I was."

In junior high school, Kevin lived a double life of academic success, athletic achievements, and church attendance mixed with private sexual fantasies and searches for pornography. He tried entering "adult" bookstores but was too young. Nothing like the Internet existed in the mid-1970s, so he fantasized for long stretches of time, creating his own X-rated world in which he won the admiration of every woman he lusted after. He fed his fantasies with images from lingerie sections of newspapers and copies of *Playboy* or *Penthouse*. Kevin encouraged his sister to buy lacy slips and dresses, then snuck into her closet to try on the new apparel. His secret cross-dressing ritual continued unabated — and undiscovered.

In college, Kevin's dating patterns reflected the double life he was leading. Being sensitive and caring, he genuinely believed that he loved each girl he dated. "But at the same time," he admits, "I hid from the realization that I was only using her as an object of my sexual fantasies." Inevitably, when the relationships did not resolve his gender confusion, he reluctantly moved on to someone else. The last thing he dared do was to tell anybody about his secret obsession, including his fiancée, whom he married soon after they graduated from college.

SHINY ON THE OUTSIDE, SLIMY ON THE INSIDE

To some degree, at some time in our lives, all of us encounter duality in ourselves. Our experience of the external world includes the polarities of hot/cold, day/night, sunny/cloudy, and calm/stormy. So does our experience of the world within us (and internal/external itself is a polarity). As a student, haven't you felt torn at times between completing homework that's due the next day and partying with your friends instead? As a professional, haven't you ever debated ironing your work shirt so that you'd look presentable to your client the next day and then watched late-night sports till you stumbled, exhausted, into bed at 1:00 A.M. — and appeared unkempt the next day?

Take your pick. You govern your life.

Renowned therapist and author M. Scott Peck has written about this dualistic dynamic in his book *People of the Lie*.[9] Here are some of Dr. Peck's thoughts on the extremes of this phenomenon:

> Utterly dedicated to preserving their self-image of perfection, [people of the lie] are unceasingly engaged in the effort to maintain the appearance of moral purity. They are acutely sensitive to social norms and what others might think of them. They dress well, go to work on time, pay their taxes, and outwardly seem to live lives that are above reproach.... While they seem to lack any motivation to *be* good, they intensely desire to appear good. Their "goodness" is on a

level of pretense. It is, in effect, a lie. This is why they are the "people of the lie."[10]

Here Peck lists several characteristics that describe Secret Keepers, although he does not use that term. His description highlights the "self-image of perfection" as well as the "appear good/be good" characteristics of the *appearances first and reality second* mind-set. He also discerns the effort and the "unceasingly engaged" exertion required to maintain the Secret Keeper's carefully constructed facade that hides the real self. Each of these traits also fits Goffman's definition of "impression management," as well as my own pet phrase, the "shiny outside/slimy inside" aspects of secret keeping.

Peck continues: "What possesses them, drives them? Basically, it is fear. They are petrified that the pretense will break down and they will be exposed to the world and to themselves. . . . There is no need to hide unless we first feel that something needs to be hidden."[11]

As we saw in chapter 2, keeping secrets gives a person power, control, protection, and in many cases *pride* — the pride that comes from the awareness that *only* he or she knows certain information, while everybody else remains clueless. Fear of losing this high opinion of self strikes at the hearts of Secret Keepers. Secret keeping is fear-based behavior. The choice facing weary Secret Keepers who suffer from years of rigidly compartmentalized duality becomes: Do I continue living a *secretive, closed, risky* life based on *fear*, or do I begin living an *honest, open, transparent* life based on *courage?*

Peck's statement "There is no need to hide unless we first feel that something needs to be hidden" nails the inner-outer dichotomy of the Secret Keeper's terrain: the inner need to hide what is shameful or discreditable about the false self behind a mask of "moral purity" and the outer need to manipulate the impressions of others favorably to bolster the "presented self." This view of secret keeping supports my "charming deceiver" interpretation in chapter 1.

One more element of the seductive pull of secret keeping remains to be examined — that of danger. As we also observed in chapter 1, socially unacceptable emotions can lead to the *excitement/pleasure/delight* cycle that promotes the risk-taking and thrills. Think again about the Internet. Can you think of anything else that has promoted a safer place for secrecy to flourish for double-minded deceivers? Abductions, rapes, and murders fill the headlines, scaring us all. But it's not only the perpetrators. Unfortunately, many teens and preteens enjoy going online and flirting dangerously as fictional characters of their own creation, often unknown to parents. Exhilarated, they blog and chat like it's a big game but may give out too much personal information about themselves, making themselves easy prey. Sadly, the fun of their online secret lives sets them up for dire consequences. About two-thirds of teens surveyed in 2006 (62 percent) said they believe "most teens do things online they would rather their parents not see," according to a Pew Internet survey.[12] Danger not only lurks in the hearts of perpetrators, but it also lures the hearts of secret-keeping "innocents."

My Story: Teenage Turmoil

An essential component of leading a double life — *placing appearances first and reality second* — got burned into my brain while I was living in Mom's dream house bordering the lake. Fortunately, in April 1960, after five years of living hell, good news came at last: Mom and Dad had to sell the huge house because they could no longer afford it. Between Dad's worsening health and Mom's extravagances, we were stretched to the limit. Our choices were to cash in on our only asset, or go broke. A new lease on sanity began. We moved to a smaller, less expensive house in the same suburb closer to the center of town. I felt more connected socially, both in the new neighborhood and at school. We boys acted more like regular brothers again than worn-out workers and even invented silly games. Laughter returned to our lives.

For Mom, however, nothing was funny. The move from Chippewa Hills meant the painful demise of her dream. No sooner had we moved into our new house on Parkside Circle than she insisted on renovating the rooms and grounds. Determined to resurrect the glory of her Chippewa Hills projects, her expectations and bossiness reached new heights. Sick of her tyranny, we "mutinied." I pretended not to hear her shrill demands. She blew up at me, but I just ignored her.

Dad had just come home from the hospital after being fitted for an improved artificial leg, and Mom managed to get him to paint the exterior siding of the house. Dave and I couldn't stand to see him wobble and struggle, so we picked up paintbrushes and began slapping on paint, begging him to sit down and rest. Tommy relied on his former strategy and isolated himself in his room. I seethed inside: "She'll pay someday, just watch."

I was in my sophomore year at high school. In biology class, I lucked out and got to sit next to the prettiest cheerleader in school, Bonnie Witten. My spirits soared. When certain young women enter a room, all heads turn. That was Bonnie. She noticed me one day and smiled at me, sending me into orbit. I took this as a favorable sign and made jokes that she actually found funny. We soon bonded and were exchanging quips daily. At times it felt to me like we were dating. She'd pass notes or whisper silly one-liners, and my confidence grew. I could now hold the attention of the prettiest and most popular girl in my world.

In that soul-stirring manner I sailed through sophomore year, enjoying classes and girls and playing B-squad ice hockey as a goalie. Alfred Hitchcock's *Rear Window* captivated my imagination at the movies. I marveled at Jimmy Stewart's powers of observation as he spied on residents in his New York City apartment complex with his telephoto lens. His prying served a noble purpose, that of helping to solve a murder. But something else about his voyeurism hooked me, and my burgeoning dual nature and growing inclination toward escapism from home hit a new low in my junior year. Using Stewart as my role model, I acted out a new secret behavior: window-peeping.

During a pep rally for our football team, I sat in the bleachers of the gym watching six gorgeous cheerleaders. Next to Bonnie, who was a senior, stood a sophomore girl new to the squad, Cindy Foster. After Bonnie, Cindy was the prettiest and the peppiest of the bunch. She smiled like Debbie Reynolds and exuded the energy of Lucille Ball on *I Love Lucy*. Her every jump and "Go team!" excited me. Secretly, I was already thinking about seeing her again later that night — through her window. She lived only two blocks away.

That night, after washing the dinner dishes and studying for my history test, I obeyed the irresistible urge to satisfy my curiosity. I slipped out after dark and crept up to the windows of Cindy's house, staying in the shadows. I peered inside. From one window to the next I tiptoed. Through a crack in the bathroom curtains, I saw the silhouette of a young woman undressing. Her blurry figure appeared out of focus through the foggy glass — like an impressionist's painting of a nude. My heart pounded madly.

So risky, so reckless!

As had running naked in the woods, this new thrill, with its profound rush, led me into another variation of my double life, a new habit that stroked my brain's pleasure pathway and proved hard to resist. The neural rewards of window-peeping numbed my persistent conflicted feelings. I felt powerful and mighty. The emotions of secret keeping — the *excitement* of breaking rules, the *pleasure* of spying on Cindy, the *delight* of getting away with it — now became even more deeply ingrained.

At school, I behaved "normally," practicing my own version of impression management and *appearances first, reality second.* But I did make bona fide efforts to study and do well on my homework. I tried out for the class play, *The Mousetrap*, and worked hard to play varsity hockey, even though as a second-string goalie I saw very little game time.

Once, during a lopsided game when our team was ahead by six goals, I sat on the end of the bench holding my goalie stick. Late in the game I turned my head to look for Dad in the stands of the indoor rink. His faithful attendance at many of our varsity games humbled me. As always, he would hobble to a seat in the bleachers on his artificial leg, ever the loyal father supporting his earnest son. Sure enough, there he was that night sitting near the top row, his face looking sunken from his weight loss of hundreds of pounds.

"Prin!" my coach hollered. "Prin, get in goal!"

My heart leapt to my throat. I came out of my reverie. Our first-string goalie skated toward the bench, and the coach gestured for me to take his place on the ice. I heard cheers from Bonnie and Cindy. I made my way on wobbly legs past the players to the ice. Skating to the empty goal, I warmed up, taking a dozen practice shots from our players. Then the referee's whistle blew, and the game resumed.

A whirl of jerseys and sticks. I moved with the action but felt stiff. The opposing players attacked us with fury, outmaneuvering my teammates. A pass came to an open opponent, and he fired a high shot that I reached for, but the puck sailed past my open glove.

I heard the noise every goalie detests, the buzzer signaling a goal.

The opposing crowd roared, my teammates kicked their sticks, and our cheerleaders stood mute. I tried to locate Dad in the stands and imagined the hangdog look on his face. With just a few minutes of game time to go, I'd failed to compete. I was a worthless joke of an athlete.

My failure at sports (think failure at impression management, at *appearances first*) mirrored my sense of my parents' failure at home. My attempts to succeed at something visible to others became my way of trying to counterbalance the grim reality of home that was invisible to others. Like any boy in his midteens hoping to make his mark in the eyes of his peers, I felt I had to excel in at least one of the ways available to me: academically, artistically, or athletically.

But while my developing dual nature was causing identity confusion and emotional struggles, I knew deep in my core that I was an okay person with a strong work ethic and worthwhile life goals. Regardless of poor results at sports, beyond the craziness of secret keeping, I could affirm to myself my good intentions and point to character traits of lasting significance like hard work and fortitude to build my life on.

By springtime, which provided pleasant weather for making nocturnal visits to Cindy's, I ventured out more frequently. I dropped my guard eventually, and after one close call, a bright floodlight over Cindy's back door flicked on one night. Her dad flung open the door and shouted at me, "Who the hell are you? What the hell are you doing here?"

Stunned, I couldn't reply. Luckily I was closer to the back fence than the house, about thirty feet from the door, and somehow

I had the presence of mind to wave hello instead of running. "I was just cutting through your yard! That's all!" I kept walking nonchalantly, looking for a way to duck into the dark shadows, but Cindy appeared at the back door and identified me. The look on her face was ghastly.

"Oh, my God! John! It's John Prin!"

My heart flip-flopped, then sank. I could hear her tell her dad and mom about me.

I waved again, acting as if everything was normal, and kept walking. I couldn't decide from their expressions whether or not they believed my story. I cringed when I arrived home, waiting for the dreaded phone call — the exposure that would cause my secret world to cave in. I'd be labeled a pervert. But nothing was ever said, and I felt very, very grateful. For some reason I was spared. In an odd way I even felt blessed by something supernatural.

My shame and the aftermath of getting caught motivated me to stop peeping. In time I learned that if my external motivation was strong enough, then my internal impulses could be curbed. Balance and sanity returned to my life. Did I have the courage to keep it that way? School remained my haven, home my hell. But I knew deep down that secret keeping, both a curse and a blessing, still held me in its grip.

A Concluding Analysis

Some people seem able to solve the duality in their lives, the issue of opposing desires and motives, rather easily and completely. Some never do and feel torn and bullied by internal opposing forces all their lives. Others, perhaps the majority of us, find compromises and partial solutions that lead to a peacekeeping truce — at least much of the time. If you are in this latter group, welcome to the club.

One way to look at this duality is how the father of modern psychiatry, Sigmund Freud, did. He postulated that the human personality consists of three components: the id, the ego, and the superego. All three interact with one another continuously.

- The id is the seat of instincts. Ruled by the *pleasure principle*, it is impulsive, immature, demanding, and insistent.

- The ego mediates between the instincts and the surrounding environment. Ruled by the *reality principle*, it is intelligent and rational and governs the personality.

- The superego is the seat of the conscience. It internalizes the standards of parents and society, determines a person's moral code, and represents *the ideal rather than the real*.

Later on, psychologists like Eric Berne labeled these three the Child (id), the Adult (ego), and the Parent (superego). Another psychologist, Dr. Carl Jung, labeled these the Shadow (id), the Self (ego), and the Persona (superego). The diagram below, while a bit simplified and from an earlier day, shows a popular version of these theories — that of an angel on one shoulder and a devil on the other, each whispering into the person's ears. It

Superego   *Ego*   *Id*

illustrates the tensions and temptations brought to the ego by the conflicting drives of the id and superego.

Because temptations can come in so many forms (taking drugs, gambling, overeating, turning to sex, shopping, surfing Internet porn) these tensions can be triggered continually. The "average" person's dual-mindedness results from listening to both opposing forces and acting according to one, then the other, then the first one again, then the second again... on and on in an endless tug-of-war. Take eating, for example. The overweight person who needs to lose fifty pounds is caught between saying no to a piece of chocolate cake (the superego's goal = angel whispering "don't") and saying yes to it (the id's goal = devil whispering "go ahead"), never quite resolving which to obey.

In the case of the Secret Keeper, a decision is made to weigh the "devil/id" side very carefully, partly to end the tug-of-war and partly because it "feels good and it feels good *now*." But the Secret Keeper also still wants to avoid the disapproval, blame, and rejection of parents, society, laws, religion, conscience — this is supremely important. By using highly developed strategies of secret keeping such as clever cover-ups, alibis, excuses, and hiding places, the Secret Keeper perpetuates the risky ways to satisfy the id *and* the superego simultaneously — until the inevitable moment when the clashing forces halt the charade in a crash (public exposure) or a collapse (private breakdown). Or the Secret Keeper never gets caught.

Simply put, one answer to the question, How do secret lives seduce us? is, If we allow ourselves to get seduced, it's because our duality has set us up to be seduced. Duality is in our genes. It takes on many forms and varieties of behavior and can lead to painful consequences and emotions:

- shame, guilt, fear, embarrassment: harm to self
- surprises, shock, dismay, anger: harm to others
- loss of reputation, social standing, job, or career

Everyone struggles with duality. How about you? Does it drive you crazy? Or do you manage it? Is it your master, or are you its master?

Chapter 4

WHERE OUR SECRETS
STAY HIDDEN

What happens in Las Vegas stays in Las Vegas.

— LAS VEGAS, NEVADA, ADVERTISING MOTTO

*I*N THE PREVIOUS CHAPTERS we looked at what distinguishes privacy from secrecy. We've named four categories of secrets. We've started a list of the "splintered mind-sets" of Secret Keepers. And we've touched on how the media influences, even glamorizes, those who lead double lives. We've also glimpsed a few of the mysteries of duality. Now let's explore the places where we hide our secretive actions and thoughts.

THE JOHARI WINDOW: THE DYNAMICS OF HIDING

The dynamics of secret keeping and the places where we hide secrets can be observed in the diagram on the next page, called the Johari Window.[1] Named after its two creators, sociologists Joe Luft and Harry Ingham, who introduced it in 1955, this simple but ingenious illustration offers many helpful insights.

JOHARI WINDOW

    Known to Self Unknown to Self

	A	B
Known to Others	OPEN	BLIND
	C	D
Unknown to Others	HIDDEN	UNKNOWN

  The four areas of information shown in the figure — Open, Blind, Hidden, and Unknown — pertain to two-party relationships. (If you have already guessed that the Hidden area is where secret keeping fits, you are correct.) Let's take a closer look at these areas:

A. The Open area contains information *known both to you and to others*. Everything you know about somebody, such as her name, gender, race, hair color, and speech patterns is Open information. The same information about you is known by others. Every conversation, fact, or opinion that you and she share fits in this area.

B. The Blind area contains information *unknown to you but known to others*. Let's say you are unaware that your fly is unzipped or that your hair is sticking up in back. Another person sees that you aren't aware of these embarrassing details and whispers this information to you. "Feedback," which involves another choosing to inform you, is the way Blind information gets conveyed.

C. The Hidden area contains information *known to you but unknown to others.* Here is where we hide all our secrets. Here is where we store wounded feelings, as well as forbidden fantasies, hearsay, fibs, and knowledge of mistakes we've made. Hidden information gets conveyed via voluntary "self-disclosure," which requires your choosing to inform others.

D. The Unknown area contains information *unknown both to you and to others.* Certain vague impulses or motives reside here. The terms *subconscious, unconscious, Shadow,* and *implicit memory* apply here. In later chapters we will explore this area in greater depth.

The interplay of these areas in real life works something like this: when two people trust each other and are communicating with one another, the Open area (A) grows larger, and the other areas shrink proportionately. The more information that is shared in the Open area, the healthier the relationship. If one party starts holding back information, the communication between them diminishes, and the Open area remains static or grows less quickly. If this pattern persists, the Open area will expand only because the willing partner wants it to. Should this partner tire of the one-sidedness of the communication, he or she will generally feel frustrated, resentful, and hurt.

The person desiring to increase communication may start pressuring the reluctant member, who may sooner or later communicate grudgingly, feeling threatened or annoyed by the pressure. As the tension builds, conflict develops and struggles erupt. The relationship becomes jeopardized and may reach an impasse. Several rules govern these dynamics:

1. The more information that's shared in the Open area, the healthier the relationship.

2. The person who says the least controls the level of openness.

3. If the Open area stops growing, the relationship can falter and may dissolve or erupt in conflict, arguments, violence, or divorce.

In real life, the Blind area (B) gets smaller when both people trust each other, are communicating with one another, and are willing to give the other feedback. In this scenario, trust builds, and the Open area grows larger. But should one of the partners start withholding feedback, the Blind area shrinks because communication becomes one-way, and trust and intimacy decrease. One example of this dynamic is the wife who complains, "My husband hasn't said a word since our wedding about how I look or dress or wear my hair. I don't know what he likes or doesn't like anymore."

4. The Blind area grows smaller when both parties are willing to give the other feedback, and the Open area automatically grows larger.

5. When one partner withholds feedback, the Blind area shrinks slowly because communication becomes one-way and trust and intimacy decrease.

In real life, the Hidden area (C) grows smaller when both people trust each other and are communicating with one another, since both are willing to disclose to the other. This requires vulnerability, a key building block of trust and intimacy. Again, the Open area grows larger as more information (usually sensitive data) is shared, and therefore the relationship becomes healthier. But should one of the partners start resisting disclosure, the

JOHARI WINDOW

Self

	A OPEN	B BLIND
Others	C HIDDEN	D UNKNOWN

Hidden area will *increase* in size because more information gets added to it. If disclosure is one-way, trust and intimacy stagnate. This can occur in the most "normal" of relationships, when neither party is a Secret Keeper, meaning that each is in the non-pathological zone of simple or silent secrets on the Continuum of Secrets. This pattern is as common as the air we breathe!

It is here in the Hidden area where clever Secret Keepers learn to hide out for years.

In real terms, nobody can compel anyone's disclosure or confession about something that he or she has no awareness of. Thus Secret Keepers retain power and control and remain protected because their secret-keeping skills prevent anybody from learning their secrets, or that the secrets even exist. What becomes complicated for Secret Keepers is that all this trickery and subterfuge takes energy and cunning, not to mention an Oscar-worthy acting performance, thus mentally draining the individual.

6. The less information that is shared from the Hidden area, the more stagnant or diminished the relationship will be.

7. The Hidden area increases in size whenever sensitive information or secrets are withheld (that is, when disclosure is one-way), leading to a drop in trust and intimacy.

8. The Hidden area is where Secret Keepers learn to hide out, sometimes for years, concealing their secret lives and developing double-minded behaviors and addictions while wearing a mask of normality.

9. Nobody can compel disclosure or confession from someone about something he or she has no awareness of.

10. Trickery and subterfuge take extra energy and cunning, draining the Secret Keeper while requiring an acting performance to cover up the concealed truth.

In real life, the Unknown area (D), even when both people trust each other and are communicating, may remain basically the same or in a nebulous state. What's unknown generally stays unknown and beyond either's control. Neither person has any leverage or advantage. As we will see in later chapters, information or motives from this area may eventually influence the relationship, surfacing as behavior generated by the Secret Keeper's Shadow — the long-buried, distasteful, despised, disdained, and disowned attributes of an individual's personality.

11. The Unknown area exerts indirect influence on the two parties' interactions. Certain behaviors, of either person, may be understood only after insights are gained from therapy, study, or introspection.

From the Everyday to the Extreme: Illustrative Vignettes

To get a better grasp of these dynamics, let's take a look at the lives of three fictional people.

First Vignette

Ahmed is driving to an important job interview. The interview is his second and perhaps final opportunity to impress the future employer. Ahmed wants to put an end to months of unemployment and lost income. He arrives early, making a snappy, gung-ho impression. He parks his car in a metered space on the downtown street outside the office building. Ahmed sees that forty-five minutes remain on the meter and declines to add more coins, deciding to chance getting a ticket. He enters the building and goes to the reception lobby, where he waits for Ms. Marston, the hiring manager.

Ahmed mentally runs through the key points he wants to make. Time ticks by, and after twenty minutes, he thinks about running outside to put more coins in the meter but fears being absent should Ms. Marston appear. Ahmed recalls that the city has recently doubled the fines for parking violations. He walks to an area where he can look out a window and see his car. He sees that a uniformed patrol officer is in the vicinity. Just then Ms. Marston walks up and greets him, "Welcome!" Ahmed shakes her hand, offers a forced smile, and follows Ms. Marston to her office.

For the first few minutes they review the first interview. According to the Johari Window, their interaction operates in the Open area (A). Ahmed manages to put his fears of a parking ticket out of his mind, but his agitation leaks through. Ms. Marston notices it, but Ahmed remains unaware that it shows — this is Blind (B) information. As they settle into a conversation focused on the new job duties, Ahmed masks his upset feelings about an inevitable parking ticket so as not to sabotage this all-important interview — this is Hidden (C) information. For the remainder of their dialogue, he wrestles inwardly about the parking ticket while putting his best professional self forward to impress Ms. Marston.

This kind of incident takes place in the lives of thousands of people every day. For Ahmed, keeping his upset feelings about the parking ticket from interfering with the job interview makes sense. His aggravation, if known, would sidetrack the purpose of the interview. For Ahmed, keeping irrelevant or damaging information locked away in the Hidden area is a smart strategy.

Second Vignette

An hour later, someone else, let's call her Jasmine, is driving to an important job interview. She wants to put an end to months of unemployment and lost income. Jasmine drives over the speed limit in order to arrive on time, having left her apartment late. She weaves through traffic and tailgates, then speeds up to change lanes. Jasmine hears a shrill siren. Flashing red lights appear in her rearview mirror.

A police officer writes Jasmine a speeding ticket. She fumes. She is angry at herself because this will be her third speeding ticket in twelve months, including one DUI. Jasmine frets because the fine will be sky-high, as will her next round of auto insurance premiums — *if* she can stay insured. Worse, she will now be late for her interview with Ms. Marston. Jasmine believes she made an excellent impression on her the first time they met.

Fifteen minutes late and trying not to appear flustered, Jasmine shakes hands with Ms. Marston. Their interaction, according to the Johari Window, operates in the Open area (A) for the first few minutes: small talk and a review of the first interview.

Once the interview begins, Jasmine is sure that she's blown it, that this crucial interview has started off on the wrong foot. She tries to put the speeding ticket out of her mind, but her agitation still shows, and Ms. Marston notices it. But Jasmine remains unaware that it shows — this is Blind (B) information.

As the conversation continues, Jasmine talks about one topic while her mind dwells on another, the aftermath of the speeding ticket incident, including how her life in general is out of control. She prevents any information about the speeding ticket mess from passing her lips, yet her raw feelings and low opinion of herself sabotage her — this is Hidden (C) information. For the rest of their dialogue, while putting her best professional persona forward to impress Ms. Marston, Jasmine wrestles inwardly about the speeding ticket and everything that's wrong in her world.

Jasmine's attempt to keep her upset feelings about the speeding ticket to herself didn't work. Although she could hide the reason for her being late (by holding the damaging information in the Hidden area), the goal of giving a solid interview got sidetracked. Her feelings put her on the defensive, and at some level she sabotaged her chances, as she feared she would.

Jasmine is keeping an out-of-control life covered up in the Hidden area, but she is blindsiding herself. She projects the Blind information to perceptive people like Ms. Marston, and it gets noticed. Days later, when Jasmine hears that she did not get the job, she blames the police officer and the slow-moving driver in front of her — in other words, anybody but herself. Although technically not a Secret Keeper (she fits in the second category, of one keeping silent secrets), Jasmine is on track to becoming one.

Third Vignette

Two hours later that same afternoon, Troy is also driving to an important job interview — the second and perhaps final opportunity to impress a future employer. Troy is eager to put an end to months of unemployment and lost income. He drives over the speed limit in order to arrive on time, having left his favorite strip club late. He clears each nostril, sniffs cocaine, and wipes his nose, making sure that no white residue shows. Troy steps on the gas and speeds around a slow-moving car, daydreaming about an exotic nude dancer at the "gentlemen's" club whom he couldn't stop staring at. He flips open his cell phone and calls Ms. Marston's secretary. He explains that he will be ten minutes late and, hanging up, feels better that he called ahead. He weaves through traffic on busy downtown streets, driving even faster and honking and cursing. Troy hears a shrill siren. Flashing red lights appear in his rearview mirror.

Moments later, a police officer requires Troy to perform a walk-the-line roadside test and to take a Breathalyzer test. Troy walks steadily enough and, although the Breathalyzer meter indicates a blood alcohol content of half the legal limit, neither test is enough for a DUI. Troy is relieved when the officer writes only a ticket for speeding, thankful the officer has not detected his cocaine use or searched his car. Also, now he doesn't have to worry about another DUI being added to his record of three priors. Troy feels another rush of gratitude, realizing his wife won't find out anything serious this time. But he feels angry at himself for having to arrive thirty minutes later than he said for the job interview, and he curses under his breath because the cop took his sweet time writing the ticket.

Looking sharp and well groomed in his designer suit and tie, Troy shakes hands with Ms. Marston. Before they walk to her office, she asks him why he arrived thirty minutes late. He smooth talks her, but Ms. Marston doesn't buy it. Their interaction, according to the Johari Window, has operated in the Open area (A) for a brief moment, but Blind (B) information sealed his fate — she smells the alcohol on his breath and says so. Company policy prohibits her from conducting an interview, she tells him. Troy realizes that he can't be honest with her because it will kill his chances of getting the job. According to the Johari Window, the information in the Hidden area (C) that he won't disclose (the strip club, snorting cocaine, getting a speeding ticket) would doom him. Instead, he decides to bow out graciously. Shaking hands cordially with Ms. Marston, he suggests that his busy schedule includes other job interviews and leaves.

The interview ends before it has begun.

For Troy, the concealed Hidden information is extensive — strip clubs, cocaine and alcohol use, today's speeding ticket, prior DUIs — qualifying him as a Secret Keeper (the third category on the Continuum of Secrets). For him, protecting his clandestine habits comes first. Far behind is being a responsible employee, husband, father, or citizen. Troy's into immediate and frequent self-gratification, as his acting out the risky habits of his secret life attests. He is caught in the third splintered mind-set: *stealing hours doing what is required to feel better.*[2]

Because Troy's habits are expensive and he's jobless, his debts are mounting. For the past several months his family has depended solely on his wife's income from her part-time job. He's furious at himself for blowing the interview with Ms. Marston. He feels trapped because he can't come clean about the nasty things he's hiding; he'd be too vulnerable to criticism *and* he doesn't want to give up any habit. With his job prospects no rosier elsewhere, he's considering ways to steal from his elderly, widowed aunt. By becoming her legal guardian, Troy could make himself look like a family hero and at the same time skim funds from her estate.

Notice Troy's thinking. It revolves around his secret life and ways to protect and perpetuate it. He depends on stylish clothes and grooming to present a good image, and he depends on *plac-ing appearances first and reality second* in order to make a favorable impression. Notice his self-centeredness and double-mindedness. He is on the brink of embezzling money, something he must *feel one way about while acting another.* Notice how his thinking is basically criminal. Should he act on that thinking with his aunt, he will have committed a crime and crossed the line into criminal behavior, the fourth category on the Continuum (besides his already illegal regular use of cocaine).

Crossing lines from one category to another on the Continuum is easy when one's priority is leading a double life. Consider also the actual and eventual damage to his wife and family because of what he is keeping in the Hidden area.

Now let's turn to the continuing saga of my own youthful secrets.

My Story: Hidden Alienated Feelings

One of those Hidden areas in my own life showed up in 1962 when I was a high school senior working as a clerk at a local drug store. A middle-aged customer walked up to the cash register, lowered his voice, and asked for a new magazine called *Playboy*. I had no idea that the store carried them. He said he'd just tried to find the owner, who usually sold him a copy. "I'm in a hurry, young man. Can you help me?"

We scurried to the pharmacy area, and I looked in the stacks of shelves where he said the *Playboy*s were hidden. (In its early days *Playboy* was never displayed openly with other magazines.) I knelt down low and spied a stack of the magazines behind a pharmaceutical box. I grabbed a copy, and he thanked me, quickly paid for it, folded it inconspicuously, then left the store.

So it came to pass that I became part of the males-only,

don't-tell, wink-wink "club." I was no longer alone; older guys kept secrets too. Exposure to this new, grander network of grown men breaking rules and not getting caught (or not caring if they did) influenced me greatly. Secret keeping became more than my solitary stolen hours; it could now be a communal conspiracy. I felt seduced by this new source of shared intrigue and the underground nature of it.

Thus came the day when the group of classmates I hung out with sneaked off to watch X-rated movies. We had to lie about our age at the box office to get in, then we busted a gut laughing once inside because the ticket seller, an elderly woman, had "innocently" played along with our scam.

No longer was my discomfort as a Secret Keeper something to hide — at least the communal part of it. We guys were in this together, and I was starting to evolve as a "team" Secret Keeper. But, along with David, I still kept hidden from everybody my volcanic feelings about our family's outrageous home life. The developmental deficits in my life were adding to my Hidden area. Soon my home life was to become even more painful.

By 1965, three years after graduating from high school, I had returned from six months of strenuous National Guard active duty to find Dad in an extended coma. His relentlessly deteriorating health had made him more of a victim than ever. I felt three emotions: anger, anger, and anger. I smoked unfiltered cigarettes and drank more than my fair share of beer. I was attending college classes at the huge University of Minnesota campus across town and working thirty hours a week in a soap factory. I was dating an army buddy's sister in St. Paul and drove a used Chevy. And all the while I was visiting Dad in the hospital every other day.

Unconscious in his bed, Dad held on to life aided by a constant supply of oxygen. My feelings of powerlessness and free-floating rage overwhelmed me. In those quiet moments when I stared at his shrunken body, now hardly ninety pounds (down from three hundred fifty), I thought of his lifelong habits of overworking, overeating, getting too little exercise, and never sleeping enough. I reflected also on his unrequited love for Mom. No matter how much or how often he had tried to please her, she had demanded more. At fifty-nine, he'd finally given out.

On a dismal rainy Sunday — November 14, 1965 — nothing stood between Dad and death. Mom sat in a corner of Dad's room working quietly on her needlework, while I stood at Dad's bedside. Lately I hadn't seen so much as a blink, and I waited minute by minute for his final breath.

You can imagine my surprise when his head arched upward and his eyes opened wide. A smile even cracked his face as he looked straight up at something invisible to me but clearly not to him. I reared back, speechless, witnessing what seemed like a miracle. His eyes shone with a supernatural radiance, and his smile broadened. It looked as if he'd made contact with a divine, unseen presence, one that nurtured and welcomed him right at that moment: *Johnny, I'm going to a place of peace, rest, and comfort* his face seemed to say. I leaned closer, less than two feet away, and watched his eyes close in complete peace. His last breath came with a slow sigh.

I felt a fiery blast of emotions. Grief, pity, and despair coursed through me. *Dad, I never knew you! This can't be the end!* So much that needed saying had never been said. Seldom had we spent time together as father and son. Dad had been a man of very few words. He'd been there for my hockey games, yes, but I never *knew* him! And he never knew *me!* Now it was too late. Something inside me cracked, something escaped from the closed-in darkness of my Hidden area: fiery tears of resentment and a loud cry of "Unfair!"

At the funeral, a massive sense of loss weighed on us all.

While Mom greeted the dozens of close friends and television fans who paid their respects, I observed her as if through a haze. She had done so much to strain his health and, I believed, to prematurely end his life. His attempts to please her by building the Chippewa Hills house had never satisfied her; she just wanted more and more. He was her lowly footman, she was his lofty queen. I recalled the time when he'd followed her orders to have Dave and me haul the concrete paving stones for her patio on our birthday, and this time I felt the agonizing embarrassment he must have felt. Recalling times like these, I seethed like a volcano.

Death wasn't quite finished with the Prin family, however. In the weeks after Dad's departure, my secret murderous urges toward Mom kept boiling hotter and hotter. I chafed at any little thing she said or did. Medical and funeral bills meant we owed more than $35,000 (think $350,000 today). The sole remaining asset was the Parkside Circle house. The day came all too soon when she sold this cherished home and moved "down" to a smaller, more affordable rambler on the deceptively named Maple Ridge Avenue. Once again, more of Mom's decorating and landscaping projects plagued me.

Six months after New Year's, 1966, Mom got spring fever and insisted that I ignore my college homework so that I, her "fix-it" boy, could build shelves in the house's basement for her geraniums. "Mom!" I protested. "I just finished wallpapering your bedroom a week ago. I'm studying, okay?"

"Johnny, drop everything and come down here!"

But I would not. My murderous rage finally came to a head. It was time for a standoff. Mom came to my bedroom, where I sat at my desk, and demanded that I listen to her plans. So many times I'd tolerated her inflated sense of entitlement, her unreasonable orders, and she hadn't softened a bit, hadn't learned a thing since Dad's passing.

"Johnny, come downstairs *now!* Don't make me say it again!"

Enough was enough. "I'll hear what you have to say," I bargained, "but I'll get to it some other time."

"Okay," she replied. "Come and take a look."

I followed her downstairs to a damp corner of the basement where she rattled off instructions about building the shelves. I was weary and sick of acting one way (agreeable) while feeling another (vengeful), of holding back my pent-up fury in the Hidden area. This time my emotions blasted out of control. I "lost it." While her back was turned, I reached for a nearby folding chair and lifted it up high. I trembled, ready to club her with it. It wavered in my hands above her skull, ready to come crashing down. In a heartbeat, I "witnessed" her lose life and die. Death's door opened, and I saw Mom in her casket.

Suddenly, *my* future flashed before my eyes. I grasped the idea that *by destroying her I would be destroying myself*. By killing her I would be putting to death my hopes for a happier life. Before she turned around, I lowered the chair and charged up the stairs to the back door.

"Where are you going, Johnny?" she demanded. "I'm not done talking to you!"

"Oh, yes, you are! I hate your guts, Mom, and I'm not coming back! I'm leaving!"

I never saw her stunned reaction, because the door slammed behind me on my way out. I drove away and came back a day later when I knew she was gone, then cleared out all my clothes and books. It would be years before I returned to that rambler.

But the fury in my heart burned fiercer than ever. Freaked out by the close call, I forced the still-secret revenge attempt back into the murky shadows of the Hidden area never to surface again. . . .

—ɯ—

As we have seen, the Hidden area can hold mighty secrets. To illustrate this further, I would like to share a poem by nineteenth-century American poet Edwin Arlington Robinson.3 In the poem Robinson writes about a pillar in the community at the turn of the twentieth century when automobiles were rare and telephones nonexistent. Imagine the street life of that bygone era, when horses clip-clopped on the pavement, and the fancy apparel worn by a wealthy CEO inspired admiration in passersby. Yet behind this veneer, in the Hidden area, this upstanding citizen secretly harbored intense pain.

RICHARD COREY

Whenever Richard Corey went down town,
We people on the pavement looked at him:
He was a gentleman from sole to crown,
Clean favored, and imperially slim.

And he was always quietly arrayed,
And he was always human when he talked;
But still he fluttered pulses when he said,
"Good-morning," and he glittered when he walked.

And he was rich — yes, richer than a king —
And admirably schooled in every grace:
In fine, we thought that he was everything
To make us wish that we were in his place.

So on we worked, and waited for the light,
And went without the meat, and cursed the bread;
And Richard Corey, one calm summer night,
Went home and put a bullet through his head.

Chapter 5

WHO ARE YOU WHEN
NOBODY IS LOOKING?

Be the master of your will and the servant of your conscience.

— MARIA VON EBNER-ESCHENBACH

*H*AVING EXPLORED the Hidden area in our relationships, let us turn to another hidden area that is personal to everyone — your character. Your character is who you are when no one is looking. Unlike your reputation — what other people think of you — it resides within you. We can put on a show for others, and we can influence the impression we make on others (as Richard Corey did). But character is who we *are* — not our successes, failures, achievements, or disappointments.

So who *are* you when you are alone? I ask this because it's our solitary actions that tell the most revealing stories.

Your answer to this question may determine the importance you place on your character. So far we've had glimpses of how Caroline, Brad, Tracy, Kevin, and I have behaved when nobody is looking. Each story, in its own way, contains the message: "When I'm alone, I'm a different person than the one I let the public see. Yes, I do the same things that everyone else does like cooking, paying bills, listening to music, and doing the laundry, but I do other things when nobody is looking that I'd rather not have anybody know about, so I keep them hidden. I would be embarrassed if anyone discovered these activities, so I never let anyone see me engaged in them." The height of crafty impression management!

One way to understand why some human beings indulge in these kinds of secretive habits and activities was offered by psychologist and philosopher Dr. Carl Jung. An early giant of psychology, in 1912 he theorized that human beings have a "Shadow side" within their psyches that contains repressed portions of the personality. The formation of a person's Shadow is an essential process of normal personality development that occurs as children grow up in "civilized" societies. Recall the child in chapter 1 who received a dreadful but well-intentioned birthday present from Grandpa. She was instructed not to appear disappointed but to smile and say thank you instead. The rule being taught to the child was, "Mask your real feelings when they will hurt someone you love; substitute a phony but less hurtful feeling."[1] (Think splintered mind-sets.)

Each time a child is told to substitute a falsehood for the truth, it's as if she is standing in the middle of a tipsy seesaw; the child's Shadow grows, becoming "slimier," and the persona, to compensate, becomes "shinier":

To stay balanced, the Self regulates the actions, impulses, and drives of both the (shiny) persona and the (slimy) Shadow, allowing neither to dominate. In a healthy personality, the see-saw tips up and down, as seesaws by definition do, but neither side controls or dominates the other side.[2] A balanced rhythm develops. But in a Secret Keeper's personality, the *appearance* of balance is presented to observers (the shiny persona, i.e., the "presentation of self") when in reality the Shadow/id/child dominates — except nobody perceives this because the solo activity is done secretly and shrouded in clever cover-ups.

Jung believed that human beings are constantly adapting to the demands of society — of authority figures such as parents, teachers, and police officers. They are coached or coaxed to behave in certain ways. It is as if they are riding a seesaw, simultaneously feeling opposing impulses based on their own desires, wants, and needs and those based on the contrary desires, wants, and needs of those around them. It's a balancing act each of us performs every day, from infancy to old age, regardless of our culture or ethnic origin. And it's something most people largely remain unaware of and therefore remain at the mercy of.

Refer back to the Unknown area of the Johari Window: acts that are unconsciously motivated belong here, unlike acts that are consciously hidden (secret-keeping activities), which belong in the Hidden area.

During a secret-keeping episode, the inherent tension between the persona and the Shadow becomes especially intense. This balancing act generates self-alienation as well as an increase in guilt and shame.

The persona, as Jung defined it, refers to the mask we put on when relating to others whether or not we are Secret Keepers (the word *persona* means "mask" in Greek; ancient Greek actors wore large masks onstage). When we comment on someone's "*persona*lity," we are commenting on how much we like or dislike his or her "mask." To Jung, the persona was the "packaging" others see and observe[3] — what I call the shiny side. It is responsible for advertising to people how we want to be seen and reacted to. Alienation occurs when the Shadow is viewed as a treacherous enemy, intruder, or stranger. Then it rises to the surface within the individual and acts beyond his or her control in the form of dirty jokes, slips of the tongue, unintended cursing, or aggressive gestures — what I call the slimy side. Observers of these behaviors will remark that the person is acting "out of character" or being "totally unlike themselves." These behaviors often surprise the person as well, who is left saying, "That's not like me."

Similar to Freud, whom Jung followed in his early career, Jung believed that conflict and duality in a person's psyche were universal struggles that everyone deals with. It's a process, when successful, that he compared to biological *homeostasis*.[4] Jung postulated that the Self (which means the same as the term *ego*, as used by Freud) regulates or governs the positive/light and negative/dark forces that are in *dynamic opposition*, as a healthy way to achieve *psychic equilibrium* (similar to biological homeostasis). Jung identified health as a state of harmony existing between human beings, their vital forces, and their environment.

Sadly, Secret Keepers are doomed never to find this harmony.

For the Secret Keeper, these dynamics provide several cautions. The more "successful" Secret Keepers are, the more they release their Shadows in *controlled and solitary settings*. Without others' knowledge or awareness, their Shadows act out — sometimes in harmless ways, but not always. When harmony eludes Secret Keepers, it is because their two worlds are as far apart as two ends of a seesaw. With their actions compartmentalized by impenetrable walls of their own making, many Secret Keepers' only strategy is to spit-polish their personas, so that they can fool others and appear above suspicion. Achieving wholeness is impossible.

The sorts of things that Secret Keepers so carefully hide fit Jung's concept of the Shadow as the collection of unacceptable characteristics that an individual rejects and stores in the psyche. The Shadow is an isolated splinter personality, largely beyond one's awareness and often denied expression. It's the very thing that defines Secret Keepers — a spurious, hidden, disowned personality that hates suppression and loves acting out — secretly acting out.

> Gaining awareness of the Shadow and dealing with it is ultimately so powerful an experience that it can transform the whole person. *Unless* a person deals with his or her Shadow (recognizes it, exposes it, owns it, embraces it), wholeness (psychic equilibrium) is unattainable.

The paradox for Secret Keepers is that this dynamic actually offers much hope! These concepts, when understood and applied, can help heal them and transform their characters (we will examine how in greater depth in part 2). The polarities Secret Keepers face when leading double lives, and the healing that is available if they choose, were well expressed by Jung:

> Here and there it happened in my practice that a patient grew beyond the dark possibilities within himself... an experience of foremost importance to me. [Facing one's Shadow was] useful and essential for personal growth and therapeutic healing. Only when this charade becomes too costly in terms of energy, guilt, or anxiety may it give rise to neurotic misery and require therapeutic intervention.... The stories of Jekyll

and Faust, like the biblical story of Adam's fall, are cautionary tales which illustrate our theme: in each case a virtuous man decides to rebel against the prohibitions of the superego in order to liberate the Shadow.[5]

Only Secret Keepers who become "masters of their will and servants of their conscience" can begin the journey toward wholeness and healing. While secret keeping is a form of releasing the Shadow and giving it its due (the third splintered mind-set, *stealing hours to do what feels better*), this inner experience of the Secret Keeper requires an outer expression, or our fourth splintered mind-set: *walking a tightrope between two opposing worlds*. Thus, Secret Keepers strive to have their cake and eat it too. They want life to be two different ways: first, they want the taboos of the Shadow to be released from captivity so that it can play freely and make mischief in solo sessions (kept Hidden in the Johari Window), and second, they want a persona that sparkles in the eyes of others who are fooled and rarely, if ever, suspect anything (the Open area of the Johari Window).

By developing ever more clever cover-ups, alibis, excuses, and hiding places, the Secret Keeper expresses nonconformity and hopes for a whole identity. If only all this effort didn't require endless superhuman energy, calculated hair-splitting, and highly developed cunning, leading to elevated stress and high blood pressure.

So let's return to the question, Who are you when nobody is looking? As mentioned earlier, some people belong in the first category on the Continuum, those with simple secrets. If this is you, congratulations. For the remainder who aren't as fortunate, self-examination and an analysis of your options are a must.

Dr. Jung believed that neurosis results from "self-division. The sick personality is a house divided against itself."[6] The healthy personality is whole, albeit still composed of three balanced

components. Although often a disagreeable task, the healthy assimilation of the Shadow can radically improve a Secret Keeper's situation. First you must recognize that the Shadow exists. Then you
must realize its myriad powers. Then, the more Shadow that you
can assimilate, the more your inner division can be healed.

In other words, you *can* move from living a *secretive, closed,
risky* life based on *fear expressed during hidden solo sessions of
shadow activities* to living an *honest, open, transparent* life based on
courage *expressed by healthy assimilation of the Shadow into your
character.*

Because your shadow can play such a large role in your behavior, and because it can act so forcefully on its own, you need to ask
yourself, Just what *do* I choose to do in solitary hours when I have
full freedom? What *is* my character, as measured by my actions
when nobody is looking? Your self-examination and analysis
should supply answers. If your secret keeping includes harm to
others, your need for outside help becomes immediate and critical.

Below are the stories of two more everyday individuals who
have each walked the tightrope between two opposing worlds,
whose stealing hours to act out secret habits plunged them into
an examination of their character and their future options.

MITCH: SECRETLY ENSNARED IN DEBT

A white-collar professional, married for eighteen years, and the
father of a teenaged son and daughter, Mitch traveled worldwide
for his corporate manufacturing company based in the Midwest.
"Ensnared" is how Mitch described his once highly hidden life of
credit card folly. "I thought of myself as a really good person, a
person of high character, with a walled-off part of me that held
really bad garbage," he says. Over a five-year period he embezzled
$2,000,000 dollars from his employer. He used the money to pay

off his seventy-three credit cards, at times facing minimum charges (plus late fees and penalties) as high as $18,000 a month.

It all started innocently years earlier when nobody was looking. Recently married and on his way up the corporate ladder in the 1980s, Mitch wanted to provide his family with "the many nice things they deserved." As his salary grew, credit came easily. "We had nice cars, nice clothes, ate out at restaurants, belonged to a country club, paid for private schools, and traveled a lot on my frequent-flyer miles," Mitch says. Every so often another credit card would come in the mail with $5,000 to $10,000 of additional credit. "That became my high," he adds. "Like a drug addict getting a fix, I loved the new funds." Mitch quietly handled the family's finances and told no one about the extra credit lines.

"More debt started piling up, and I was getting buried. But I didn't want to cut back on our lifestyle, or say anything to my wife, Donna. I kept her in the dark about it and secretly panicked every time more credit statements came in the mail."

Still more credit cards arrived. Mitch used the new limits to pay off old balances. "I was working twelve-hour days as usual, so there was no time to keep close track of everything. Basically, I just acted like nothing was wrong and kept right on going."

The first falsified invoice Mitch submitted to his employer, for $800, helped make ends meet. His son had applied to an expensive Ivy League college. "The invoice slid through with no problem, so I upped the amount and sent through another one." Because he was the vice president of his worldwide division, Mitch's authority to submit invoices went unquestioned, and his boss routinely okayed them. Mitch submitted more false invoices for amounts as high as $15,000, and "every time a check arrived with no questions asked."

But keeping all this a secret became his "private, personal hell." Donna and the kids had no clue.

Months passed, bringing more late fees and higher balances. "Now I was truly getting desperate." His daughter learned that a prestigious college on the West Coast had accepted her — annual tuition $34,000. Mitch couldn't say no to her, so another huge payment was necessary. After a three-week business trip to Europe and Asia to develop new business, Mitch returned home, and the company's CFO and HR director were waiting in his office for him. They informed Mitch of "certain discrepancies" in his bookkeeping, clarified the legal penalties facing him, and, by ten that morning, security officers had escorted Mitch to his car in the parking lot.

"Sitting there in my car, I panicked. By now I'd cashed in all my stock options and hadn't paid state or federal taxes for two years. I was completely alone and couldn't drive home so early in the day. I was facing felony charges, had no credit left, and no cash except a few bucks in my pocket." Driving aimlessly, Mitch faced the ugly facts of his secret keeping and pondered suicide, even writing a note. When he reached a large bridge spanning a river, Mitch decided this was the right place and time. After four stiff drinks at a nearby bar, still wearing his suit and tie, he jumped.

In the twilight he landed in the swirling water feetfirst.

Like Troy's in the last chapter, Mitch's worldview centered on attaining as many nice things as possible at the expense of level-headed money management. He lived a delusion, a "fixed, dominating, or persistent false mental conception resistant to reason with regard to matters of fact."[7] Despite his own high estimate of his character, externals such as prestige, social status, and privilege dictated his frame of reference rather than internals such as ethics, morals, and personal values — that's the essence of the fifth splintered mind-set of Secret Keepers: *living from the outside in.* Mitch's downward spiral also demonstrates the fourth splintered mind-set, *walking a tightrope between two opposing worlds.* Struggling to maintain his highbrow lifestyle, he suffered alone and in secret. His character was the last thing on his mind before he jumped.

LILA: SOMETHING FOR NOTHING

At eighteen, Lila started cosmetology school ninety miles away from her farm home in the hills of Kentucky. Lila lived alone, and loneliness and homesickness soon crept into her uneventful life. So she found a way to fill the emptiness. The first thing she recalls stealing from a store was a swimming cap: "I just walked out with it, and it was mine. I thought, 'Wow, I got away with it!' "

A year later, Lila moved to a larger city and found work in the beauty salon of a department store. There, her shoplifting continued. She dared herself to take supplies and cosmetic products from the store and, the third time she did it, staff members confronted her. She faced swift dismissal from her job. Lila then found work in a bank. In just weeks she had figured out two schemes that allowed her to cash fraudulent checks. "During this time I was also stealing heavily from the shops and stores in the downtown area," Lila admits. "At lunchtime I would steal huge bags of items each day — bedding, clothes for myself, household items. I was taking anything I could possibly get away with, and nobody ever stopped me."

At first it seemed easy to keep her compulsive shoplifting a secret because no telltale physical symptoms followed, as they would with drinking or drug abuse. "It felt so seductive," Lila continues. "Getting something for nothing gave me a feeling of power. Subconsciously I was probably trying to make up for something missing in my life, although my three younger sisters and I enjoyed growing up on the farm." But she says her emotions went wild in stores — before, during, and after a stealing spree. "The thrill of getting away with it made my day."

Lila couldn't keep the merchandise itself a secret, though. By now married with kids, she discovered that her husband liked the things she brought home. Many times, though, he disapproved of her illegal behavior. Lila recalls, "I didn't know what was driving me. I really had no idea. I always believed I was a good, respectable woman of high character who would never dream of breaking the law."

Lila's secret money schemes at the bank began to fray, and her superiors investigated. Very scared, she resigned, but too late. The felony charges against her meant she had to hire an attorney. She ended up serving probation for one year and paying high legal fees. Regardless, Lila kept everything a secret from her kids and continued stealing from stores until she was arrested again. Much worse legal trouble resulted that led to a divorce. "My parents supported me in the divorce, even though they felt ashamed of me, with good reason. I felt I carried an awful stigma."

Part of her legal obligations was seeking therapy. She learned about shoplifting from classes, hypnotists, therapists, and court-ordered groups. "But secretly I really never put a total stop to my behavior. I just couldn't quit completely." She realized she was losing control of her life, of her future, and she knew she was addicted and that only a disaster could stop her.

But is shoplifting really an "addiction?"

The answer is yes, very often. Recently some psychologists have concluded that shoplifting is as much an addiction as it is a crime, that people do it for misguided emotional reasons.[8] The majority of shoplifters can afford to buy what they steal, and they often don't even need the items. They are usually law-abiding citizens in every other way, and they invariably know what they are doing is wrong. Secrecy is the prime component of it all. One out of eleven Americans are shoplifters like Lila and steal for reasons other than financial hardship.[9]

Lila's urges required her to *walk a tightrope between two opposing worlds.* In one world she was a seemingly hardworking wife and mother, and in the other she was captive to unacceptable, contradictory behaviors. Her deeds illustrate low self-awareness and shiny-side statements such as, "I always believed I was a good, respectable woman of high character." For decades even her Christmas gifts were stolen merchandise. Hers is another example of *living from the outside in.* Lila tried to use outer *things* to substitute for inner *longings.* She tried to make outward *appearances* make up for inner *emptiness.*

Both Lila and Mitch fell victim to what I call the Lie of Addiction: *Something outside me can fix what is wrong or missing inside me.*

My Story: Secret Keeping Away from Home

The whiskey flowed from the brown bottle and tumbled over the ice cubes in my glass, making a cheerful clug-clug-clug sound. I lifted the glass to my lips and swallowed the amber fluid, swirling it over my tongue and savoring its musky flavor. A blast of liquid fire descended down my throat. My face and scalp tingled pleasantly. All these sensations were a healing tonic to my jagged nerves.

I was alone. I was edgy. I was drunk. Again.

My slide into addiction didn't feel like another dimension of secret keeping at first. It was easy to keep my drinking a secret because nobody was present to observe it or disapprove of it. I was twenty-four, it was August 1968, and drinking wasn't yet the compulsive ritual that it would become in the years ahead. I'd recently graduated from the University of Minnesota with a bachelor's degree in English and Theater Arts and had hitchhiked five hundred miles south to start my new film career in Kansas City, Missouri. Nobody knew me there. A perfect recipe for indulgence.

Inspired by my dream to make movies and by my ambition to succeed in a film career, I'd landed a job as a 16 mm film editor at an industrial film studio for $72 a week. The company produced promotional films for firms like John Deere and Bell Telephone. Having sold my Chevy, I walked the streets carrying my suitcase until I found a "Room for Rent" sign. The elderly widow who lived on the main floor of the large, three-story home welcomed me when I rang her doorbell. We climbed up three flights of stairs, and she showed me the tiny space. Clean and quiet, it contained an easy chair and lamp, a sink and refrigerator, and a bed. I agreed to pay the rent of $10 a week, and we shook hands.

Jubilant, I bought a quart of Jim Beam whiskey at the corner liquor store to celebrate my good fortune. The pain-numbing effects of alcohol and the ritual of drinking alone became rooted in the weeks ahead. No longer did my pain center mainly on Mom, but on the haunting loss of Dad, old hurts suffered at the hands of army drill sergeants, my recent breakup with my fiancée, and the nagging sense that I was ill-equipped for life.

During the long evenings by myself, a pattern developed: in my attic refuge I drank a bottle of whiskey every two days and smoked cigarettes. Although I worked diligently every weekday at my editing desk, I repeated the process of indulging in solitary excess each evening. No constraints. No keeping up appearances. No one to please but myself. The whiskey offered an escape for a few hours and waves of euphoria that helped me to stuff any unwelcome emotions. In this manner, my initiation into the Lie of Addiction took place when I reached, night after night, for something outside myself to fix what was missing inside me.

After working hours, I went barhopping occasionally with the crew of editors. We alternated paying for rounds of drinks. What nobody knew when we said good night was that my drinking did not end there. Back in my attic flat, I poured myself another stiff drink to increase my intoxication. Drinking in private both elevated my joys and numbed my distress, a dual benefit.

Looking back, these fundamentals of addiction gradually became habits:

- *Resentment.* I was reliving all my past hurts. I nursed grudges. Another thirty years would pass before I could face these resentments and rid them of their corrosive power.

- *Isolation.* My drinking intensified whenever I spent time alone. Solitary time was to become the riskiest situation for me to be in. When I became a counselor years later, I found that it was also true for most Secret Keeper clients whom I helped.

- *Drama and crisis.* Overreacting, partly learned from Mom's open displays of temper, partly due to my brain's overly sensitive conditioning, ruled me. Exaggerated emotions became my way of responding to life.

- *Delusional thinking.* My choice of a high-profile film career had already hatched a larger dream to make movies in Hollywood and — why stop there? — to win an Oscar. Excessive boozing inflated these unrealistic expectations.

Unwittingly, I fell into the trap of *living from the outside in.* Accountable to no one, losing my bearings, I cared little about my character development yet easily became a slave to the ambitious pride that had aroused me. My slide down this slippery slope sped up when I took in a roommate who loved smoking pot. A kindly soft-spoken long-haired hippie, he introduced me to "grass," and soon ingesting one more mood-altering drug became a daily pastime.

About this time, a new young woman crossed my path and changed — really, *really* changed — the direction of my life. Within two weeks Susan and I were dating regularly. Cute and attractive, Susan amused me with her whimsical wit and subtle humor. I learned about her formative years in New Jersey as well as her recent breakup with her fiancé. Four months of courtship followed: we took long walks together, went to movies, ate and drank in restaurants. On October 18, 1969, Susan and I got married in her hometown church in New Jersey. Her patient and gentle ways were so unlike Mom's, something I admired. In time I discovered her parents' good behavior masked a rat's nest of secrets they'd spent a lifetime keeping and that belied their respectable facade.

The new Mr. and Mrs. Prin relocated to Minneapolis. That meant seeing Mom again. I'd barely been on speaking terms with her since slamming the door behind me four years earlier. Yet this occasion gave her the opportunity to host a reception for us in her home. Susan's own history of craziness fit right in with our family's. She adjusted quickly to the new environs, and we rented a small house a safe distance from Mom.

By now pot smoking had become the norm for both Susan and me (and compulsive for me). It also reflected an us-versus-them family dynamic; no one accepted this behavior, so it developed into a double life for both of us. Yet by the dawn of the

1970s, my double-mindedness lay dormant, and I sensed that my secret keeping was firmly behind me. I thought I was acting the same way I was feeling, that our walking a tightrope was harmless. My character seemed to grow stronger every day. Despite numerous unresolved inner tensions, I felt poised to soar into a bright future.

Chapter 6

MAXIMIZING PLEASURE, MINIMIZING PAIN

Life is a battleground. It always has been, and always will be; and if it were not so, existence would come to an end.

— CARL JUNG

*I*N THE LAST CHAPTER, we explored the Lie of Addiction — something outside me can fix what is wrong or missing inside me — that distorts and damages the lives of so many Secret Keepers. Maybe you believe that pornography will replace the lack of excitement and adventure in your love life, that indulging in ice cream and cookies will compensate for your loneliness, or that beating the odds at casino games will make up for being overlooked for a raise or promotion.

You get the idea. The habit of changing one's moods at will, avoiding painful emotional states, battling duality at every turn, and escaping reality (real or perceived) by keeping secrets becomes repetitive. The strategy of *maximizing pleasure and minimizing pain*, the sixth splintered mind-set, becomes the Secret Keeper's response to everything. Of course, we can all relate to this way of coping, and it works fine for many of us, provided our activities don't become compulsive or addictive or secretive. What sane person doesn't want to spare the hurts and compound the comforts? Yet it is just this lie that so easily lures the Secret Keeper down a destructive path.

So why *are* some people susceptible to secret keeping and others not?

Well, that's like asking, Why are some people susceptible to heart attacks, cancer, or diabetes while others aren't? Scientific answers to this question are still few and far between. Very little research has been done; therefore, what follows are my own theories.

BIOLOGICAL BASICS

We all use different classifications to define people, such as race, sex, gender, religion, and culture. The ancient Greeks categorized people by naming them *sanguine, choleric, phlegmatic,* or *melancholic.* But while helpful in some ways, these ancient descriptions do little to help us in the twenty-first century. They don't help us, for example, to determine who is most likely to develop into a Secret Keeper.

We can also examine the question in terms of personality, something we all possess. Here is a good definition: "Personality is the combination of characteristics, inherited and learned, that make up a person's physical and mental being, including appearance, manners, habits, tastes, temperament, and moral character."

Describing personality in this manner allows some measure of predictability. (Note the inclusion of "moral character" in the definition.) A person with an outgoing personality, for example, is someone we can expect will start a conversation with a stranger or enter a crowded room feeling comfortable. Other definitions limit the characteristics to those that distinguish one person from another. Describing personality in this manner means a person with an outgoing personality is different from a person who is more introverted, and we can list behaviors typical of each personality to distinguish the first individual from the second, and so on.

So just how does a healthy personality differ from a secret-keeping personality?

Recently some scientists and researchers have focused on the additional component of *temperament*, a person's predisposition to responding to events in certain ways; it is a person's style rather than the content of his or her behavior. Psychologists believe that temperament is present at birth and that it remains stable throughout one's life. Ultimately, nature and nurture are intertwined, and individuality is formed when a person of a particular generation, race, and gender (nature) grows up in a particular home environment, religion, and culture (nurture) and expresses his or her temperament in daily interactions.

In *The Roots of the Self*, psychologist and neurobiologist Dr. Robert Ornstein explains two of several ways in which temperament can be determined.[1] Both of these ways could apply to Secret Keepers. In the first case, an individual either *sits quietly alone*, or *he or she seeks excitement*. For the individual who sits quietly alone, the world is loud, intrusive, and noisy, unlike for people at the opposite end of the spectrum who seek excitement (potential Secret Keepers), for whom the world is too subdued and quiet. In the second case, an individual either *plans their actions carefully*, or *he or she acts spontaneously to new experiences*. For the person who plans their actions carefully, the world is disorganized, scattered, and chaotic, unlike the individual who lacks stimulation and seeks out variety, activity, and "noise." The latter person actively looks for something outside her ordinary experience, something daring, risky, or dangerous.

Regarding planning carefully versus acting spontaneously, some individuals map out their priorities, regulate their actions, and do things in an orderly sequence, while those at the opposite end of the spectrum are open to new experiences, have fluid boundaries, and act before thinking. Since these two temperaments pertain to those who may be biologically predisposed to secret keeping, it appears that budding Secret Keepers tend toward *both* polarities on this dimension: they plan their double-life activities carefully and deliberately (to avoid suspicion and getting caught) *and* they stay flexible and fluid while indulging in solo thrills and risky extremes. Thus, Secret Keepers *carefully plan* new and exciting experiences in secret, then they *act spontaneously* while living out their double lives (another instance of Secret Keepers wanting to have their cake and eat it too).

"Most people experience a good deal of emotional arousal both before and after they commit a transgression,"[2] writes Ornstein. "We feel our heart beating, for example, when we are about to do something bad."

No doubt biology has something to do with the reasons certain people are susceptible to secret keeping and others are not. Neurologically, the brain's "pleasure circuit," or reward pathway, gets "rewired" by pleasant behaviors that reward you for repeating them again and again. We want to repeat what feels good. In the case of abusing chemical substances in order to maximize pleasure, the brain gets easily hijacked by drugs or alcohol because these boost the levels of neurotransmitters like dopamine and serotonin, which stimulate the pleasure circuit. In the case of pleasurable activities, the brain can easily be affected by such activities as reading pornography, eating favorite foods, gambling, or shoplifting, which trigger the same neurotransmitters. The net result is that the Triad of Secret-keeping Emotions — *excitement, pleasure, and delight* — gets reinforced, and one's urges soon develop into cravings. Extremes and excessive use reinforce the strategy of *maximizing pleasure and minimizing pain*, and Secret Keepers are off to the races.

ALTERED STATES

In my counseling office, I've observed many secretive people who are dissatisfied with their lives. They dislike their everyday reality so much — because something feels wrong or missing —

that they seek to alter their mental states by numbing themselves or somehow escaping reality. This is not so hard to understand for people who have grown up lacking essential nurturing or who have suffered direct abuse and systematic neglect, that is, anyone who has suffered from developmental deficits.

Abuse and neglect during childhood breed confusion, doubt, low self-esteem, and a torture chamber of painful emotions. From birth, human beings are meant to connect with nature, parents, family members, friends, classmates, teachers, and the wider community, including colleagues and those from other cultures. All people develop in stages, and each of these stages requires an essential "task" to be completed before passage to the next stage will be successful.

The chart below depicts one way of viewing these stages:[3]

HUMAN DEVELOPMENTAL CHART	
STAGE	TASK
Infancy, 0–1	Trust
Toddlerhood, 1–3	Autonomy/independence
Early childhood, 3–6	Initiative
Middle childhood, 6–12	Competence
Adolescence, 12–18	Identity
Young adulthood, 18–40	Intimacy
Middle adulthood, 40–65	Legacy/care for others
Late adulthood, 65 on	Integrity/fulfillment

Note that *five* of the eight stages occur before age eighteen, making childhood an extremely significant period. Problems arise when the time frame for a task passes before an individual has mastered the essence of the task. In other words, these tasks are *basic needs*. To be a capable, functioning, thriving person, an individual must "own" each task within the time frame for it. When one or more of these needs goes unmet or is actively thwarted during the time frame for that task, the child grows older chronologically but *enters the next stage disadvantaged or ill-equipped developmentally* because the previous stage's need went unmet.

Think of a newborn baby. When it cries, it signals a caretaker to meet its needs for food, water, a clean diaper, or cuddling. When the caretaker responds consistently and in a timely manner, the child learns *trust*. When the child turns one and begins walking, it passes into the toddler stage where it learns — with the help of nurturing caretakers — to assert itself (*autonomy*). The toddler learns words such as *no* and *mine* and displays the confidence to explore its surroundings and its capabilities; it *trusts* in the safe environment, in its caretakers, and in itself. Later, when the child turns three, it relies on its well-learned trust and autonomy to seek its next challenge, *initiative*, and so on.

Now think of another newborn. When it cries, it signals a caretaker to meet its needs for food, water, a clean diaper, or cuddling. But what if the caretaker responds inconsistently and seldom in a timely manner? The child eventually learns *mistrust*, including toward people, its environment, and even itself. When the baby turns one and begins walking, it passes into the toddler stage *lacking*. There it learns — without the help of nurturing caretakers — not to assert itself (to gain *autonomy*) but rather to withdraw, cower, and throw tantrums. The toddler is likely to be punished rather than encouraged; its confidence goes undeveloped. The child lives in a confused, chaotic state. It feels frustrated, and its distress signals are ignored. Its needs go unmet, and the essential tasks remain uncompleted. Perhaps painful spankings and loud, harsh words are its daily reality — or the opposite, utter silence and long periods of neglect.

Later, when the child turns three, it flounders when trying to meet its next challenge, *initiative*. Ill-equipped to meet life's challenges, it pays ever-worsening consequences. Failure, grief, and pain become a way of life. By age five, the child's brain circuits have become wired into a distorted, convoluted, hostile worldview.

Do you see the link here between developmental deficits and basic unmet needs?

Writing about those who have experienced tremendous suffering, Viktor Frankl, a survivor of Auschwitz and renowned philosopher, said, "An abnormal reaction to an abnormal situation is normal behavior."[4] It's no wonder some people with histories of victimization are ready to try drugs or other medicating escapes by puberty! They dislike their daily lives so much that they strive to dwell in altered realities. Consider the payoffs: excitement, adventure, momentary stress-reduction, illusion of power, self-soothing, novelty, and variety. If they get caught, the costs may be sky-high, but risk is part of the escape from their miserable routine. Once a person is saddled with developmental deficits — costly deficiencies in character formation caused by environmental pressures — secret keeping becomes an attractive outlet. Whether they appear in kids involved in inner-city violence or in bored school dropouts in suburban subdivisions, for multitudes of youth these deficits never seem to be addressed.

When one or more developmental tasks/needs goes unmet or is actively thwarted during the time frame for that task/need, the child grows older chronologically but enters the next stage disadvantaged or ill-equipped, destined for failure, frustration, and a going-nowhere future.

Fortunately, our brain circuits *can* be rewired. But help is needed before an individual can rescript his or her reality. Although young Secret Keepers like those we've observed in this book may not have been treated as badly as the second baby in our example, the same principle still applies. Imagine the thoughts of such children who say to themselves these kinds of things over and over:

THOUGHT/SELF-TALK	FEELING/RESULT
"I'm a loser."	Shame, inadequacy
"Everything I do gets punished."	Self-pity, bruised pride
"I'll never amount to anything."	Self-doubt, low self-esteem
"Nothing I do matters."	Depression, frustration
"Life sucks, then you die."	Despair, suicide risk

The deficits evidenced by distorted thoughts and painful emotions get carried forward in a person's life, often unsuspected or glossed over. In the case of Kevin, whom we met in chapter 3, his sense of identity as a four- to five-year-old became confused owing to a home life of abusive teasing and the belief he was "damaged goods." Wanting to be a girl, he carried this belief forward into the later stages of his life, resulting in many conflicts and struggles as an adult. Children with histories of developmental deficits, therefore, are more susceptible to psychological issues and behaviors they must mask and keep secret.

SOME HELPFUL CLUES FROM BRAIN SCIENCE

Neurologically, the brain's *alarm system* remembers traumatic events by forging highly charged negative memories as a way to survive, thereby hoepfully preventing future similar situations from harming the body. Over time, recall of these negative events fades and becomes part of one's *implicit memory*. "Implicit Memory is experienced by the individual in the present without awareness of the impact of information and energy embedded in the memory from an earlier time," notes Terry Fralich, a trainer in mindfulness.[5] The pain in the past hijacks the present, activating reactive behavior to current events. These negative emotional states dampen the pleasure circuit's *excitement, pleasure, and delight* cycle, unless conscious awareness and therapy aimed at learning new mind-sets interrupt the vastly quick cycle of reaction.

At the moment a reaction in the alarm system occurs, the neocortex (our thinking brain) has to catch up to the alarmed emotions, which are instantaneous. Before our thinking can modify the impulse to act, instantaneous behavior like fighting, fleeing, cursing, or blaming occurs (fight-or-flight responses). The emotionally charged behavior happens *before* the neocortex can evaluate, regulate, or terminate it. The emotional brain is so much faster than the thinking brain. How often have you said, or heard someone say, "I wish I could take back what I just said" or "I wish I had counted to ten"?

What all this is leading to is the prominence of our emotional brain when secret keeping arises. Secret Keepers *indulge*. Indulging means to go beyond healthy limits here and now, to gratify one's desires *beyond sane limits*, frequently irrespective of harmful consequences. Indulging in unsafe, unprotected, secretive sex with total strangers can lead to HIV-AIDS or other STDs. Hitting the bar patron sitting next to you with your beer mug when you're drinking too much on the sly can lead to medical emergencies and jail time. These types of extreme behaviors may expose your secret keeping. Be warned!

Think of the woman who conceals her excessive binging on sweets or other types of carbohydrates or the man who spends extra hours eyeing cyberporn and playing violent video games.

These people are seeking an altered consciousness here-and-now in order to evade distressing feelings. Compounded by feelings of guilt or anger at themselves afterward, the Secret Keeper's original painful feelings persist. And the person's moods are often made even worse by hangovers, weight gain, financial ruin, jail time, and so forth. The altered mentality that allowed escape into *excitement/pleasure/delight* provided only momentary distraction. The remorse and shameful feelings remain raw and festering. Consistently masking and sidestepping imbedded, troubled feelings by indulging in solo, hidden excesses merely traps a person and magnifies self-alienation.

In other words, shortcuts to altered states are not a solution. To deal squarely with troubled feelings, what would a healthy individual do? He would phone a relative and talk openly about them, or meet a friend over coffee and ask for advice. She would discuss a book she is reading on the topic with a counselor, listen to soothing music while catching up on household chores, or any of a number of productive outlets. Don't we all need to take a nature walk or spend a few hours at a favorite hobby occasionally?

But, in contrast, secretly indulging in shortcuts to altered states requires the intentional concealment of what is shameful or discreditable. Invariably, the real culprits — the deep developmental deficits influencing secret keeping — go scot-free. Realistic and effective solutions such as surrender, sobriety, mindfulness, and its cousins, *high-level thinking* and *increased consciousness*, also go ignored. Assistance that could offer logic, compassion, science, spirituality, and even love, goes unsought. The Secret Keeper's behavior prevents him from finding legitimate ways to resolve his developmental deficits and to effectively reverse stubborn secret-keeping habits (more on this in part 2).

Here are two stories of individuals who lost their way in search of altered states.

EARL: INTIMACY GONE AWRY

By all appearances, Earl, thirty-six, appeared to be happy, successful, and a well-adjusted businessman, husband, and father. His financial planning company had paid for a sporty BMW and a suburban home on a lake. His income allowed his wife, Sandra, to volunteer in their Oregon community while raising two teenagers. However, behind Earl's cheerful smile lurked a sadness that strangers often missed.

Earl grew up in a working-class home, where his dad, a strict disciplinarian, ruled the roost. Earl suffered regular beatings, once with a two-by-four aimed at his head by his enraged father. His mother swallowed tranquilizers and took secretive sips of brandy from a bottle hidden in her kitchen cupboard. She was incapable of empathy. Despite the fact that he had two younger siblings, Earl felt lonely. He never remembers receiving any kind of affection or caring from his parents, never remembers experiencing intimacy. "I grew up starved for warmth," he says. "We had food, but no love." He made up for this lack by applying himself as a student and excelling in math, but with people he remained reserved and insecure.

After fourteen years of marriage, still starved for love, one evening he stood outside his daughter's bedroom door and made a life-changing decision — for himself and for her. Tiffany, twelve, sat tucked into bed reading a book. Desperate for intimacy, Earl pondered entering her room. With Sandra out late at a PTA meeting and his ten-year-old son playing video games at a friend's house, he was free to make his move. Earl sat down on Tiffany's bed and began stroking her hair. At first Tiffany suspected nothing, until his hands moved gently down her shoulders and . . . the rest became a tragedy in the making. "I longed, longed, longed for a loving connection," he admits. At the time he only vaguely recognized the danger this longing posed to Tiffany.

Earl's secret keeping around his sexual intimacy with Tiffany filled him with shame and self-loathing. After each monthly episode he could not bring himself to admit the incest to anybody. Raised a Catholic, he believed "if I asked God to take something away, He would." Although Earl prayed again and again over the next two years for the incest to be "taken away," sometimes praying while standing outside Tiffany's bedroom before commencing another episode, "God took nothing away," says Earl. "Nothing. Even when I told the priests during confession, all I ever heard was, 'Say five Our Fathers, five Hail Marys, and promise to never do it again.' "

What compelled Earl's misguided search for intimacy? His actions stemmed in part from developmental deficits, and he *mistook intensity for intimacy*, another symptom common to Secret Keepers and addicts in general.[6] Gradually Earl realized he was becoming mentally ill. He lost weight and felt depressed; his business suffered, and Sandra began hinting that he needed to see a doctor — or a psychiatrist. Meanwhile, Tiffany started skipping classes, and her grades plunged. Earl's having committed the taboo of violating his daughter added immeasurably to his bleak emotional existence, despite his misguided attempt to maximize pleasure and minimize pain.

In Earl's case, his secret keeping began as an effort to cope with difficult, frozen emotions. While consciously abusing his daughter and keeping it a secret, he saw past the harm it was causing her and thought ahead to the betrayal his wife would one day feel. Thinking about the shame he would bring to his family and the harm to his business reputation that a disclosure would cause — the tarnishing of his shiny image and the stable reality of their lives — paralyzed him. Could he ever face the hard work of confronting the powerful negative feelings from his youth? In his paralysis, Earl couldn't find acceptable ways to soothe his wounded, childhood heart. So living an honest, open, transparent (H.O.T.) life was impossible. (We will learn more of Earl's plight in part 2.)

Now let's observe how another person's developmental deficits led her in large part to seek an altered emotional reality.

BONNIE: GROWING UP INVISIBLE

Bonnie's small hometown was about two hours from a major city on the East Coast. As one of six kids, in the middle, she was raised to be a good girl. Her father, the mayor, was highly social, and alcohol played a role in every activity, at home and in the community. He loved their local church and embraced its activities more than its theology. At home he was critical of the kids and was seldom available. Bonnie became a recluse, like a "lost child," while her dad was always onstage and her mom tried to cope with the responsibilities at home.

Bonnie saw her mom fly off the handle at times "because she didn't know how to manage six kids." Often her dad just avoided coming home. As his alcoholism worsened, her mom became more controlling; Bonnie believes it was her way of organizing a completely disorganized family. It was very hard for her to watch the friction between her parents. Secretly she wanted to be happy-go-lucky like her dad and not end up uptight like her mom.

Bonnie's fear of authority developed while she was attending Catholic school. "What I learned was, don't question authority," says Bonnie. "I learned to keep my thoughts secret. I can think of so many times when, as a young girl, I clearly called out for help but nobody caught on." Later, a couple of high school teachers took her under their wing and tried to bolster her self-esteem, but it never lasted. "When you have secrets, you wish that someone would hear you or somehow find out about them."

When Bonnie was around eight, her older cousin by five years started to abuse her sexually. This manipulation, which occurred whenever he visited, went on for years. "My sister and I both experienced this and tried to come up with a battle plan. Any time we tried to enact it, though, he smooth-talked us out of it — he charmed us. I told my mom about it, but nothing changed."

Bonnie's way of dealing with the abuse was to stuff her feelings and to become a perfectionist. She refused to fail at anything. She became a straight-A student, lettered in several sports, and was a team captain. "I was the good girl. I excelled at everything I did. My competence proved I was okay. But I was too scared to be popular, scared of talking to people, especially boys." Because boys were off-limits psychologically, Bonnie never went to proms or other school dances, even though she wanted to do "those girly kinds of things."

In college, she discovered that alcohol could be a real stress reliever. It helped her be the person she wanted to be. "I felt I had to measure up and be a party girl. That meant drinking a lot. Anything to change my sour moods." Eventually she developed an eating problem. It came on the heels of her getting pregnant (an ectopic pregnancy). "I totally denied it was happening until I got very, very sick. They told me I was lucky to be alive because I'd let it go so long. I needed two surgeries to stay alive." So she dropped out for a semester to recover and experienced long bouts of low self-esteem. "I'd let everybody in the world down including God, so I just stopped eating." Bonnie felt she needed to control something in her life, and food was a good candidate. Eventually she tried wacky diets, and binge-and-purge cycles developed, which she kept secret.

"Basically, life seemed to trap me in so many ways, big and small. I was a prisoner to so many secret habits that owned me," she says, "and I desperately wanted to be free."

Naturally, everyone seeks as much pleasure and as little pain in life as possible. Healthy people are not masochists. Unfortunately, Secret Keepers take this natural desire to extremes. When hiding their indulgence in habits or rituals that relieve tension, they escape the pain and injustices of life by chasing the fleeting pleasures of a "parallel universe." By avoiding the deeper dilemmas in their lives, like the stored pain in their implicit memories, they fall prey to altering their moods in the one way they know how, by *maximizing pleasure and minimizing pain*.

But at what cost to themselves and to others?

Earl's violation of Tiffany certainly broke relational boundaries and ethical/moral standards, and it definitely crossed the line into breaking the law and perhaps into some form of temporary psychosis as well. In others words, he had crossed the line from category 3 in the Continuum of Secrets to category 4, *Crime/Psychosis*. Bonnie's search for an acceptable altered state led to perfectionism, alcohol abuse, depression, and a life-threatening pregnancy that she didn't even recognize because of blinding denial. Both Earl and Bonnie suffered overt abuse in their youth, and such histories proved to be deeply detrimental to their development as adults. For both, any hope of integrity or authenticity in their lives seemed unattainable. They discovered that the Lie of Addiction was just that — a lie. It turned out that nothing outside them *could* fix what was wrong or missing inside.

In the next chapter, we'll go on a quest for authenticity. We'll investigate the boundary between normal and abnormal behavior and discover what it means to be true to oneself.

Chapter 7

THE QUEST
FOR AUTHENTICITY

We are all, simultaneously, normal and abnormal.

— ELTON MCNEIL, *THE QUIET FURIES*

SECRET KEEPERS ARE PRIMARILY FOCUSED on seeking thrills and, at the same time, avoiding responsibility. The goal, as we learned in the last chapter, is to maximize pleasure (which can take many forms such as getting high on drugs and other escapes) and to minimize pain (responsibility, work, study, sacrifice, a victimized past). Secret Keepers do this by choosing shortcuts — easy, quick highs gotten on the sly — rather than applying concentrated effort toward longer-term goals, such as seeking therapy and the kinds of help explained in part 2.

Goals that involve learning, study, and perseverance, like earning a master's degree or succeeding at a singing career, create self-worth and authenticity but also impose the "pain" of responsibility and delayed gratification. Some Secret Keepers remain deluded that by secret keeping they are being true to themselves. I thought this myself for decades. Scratch the surface, however, and you will find the Lie of Perpetual Youth: "So that I can avoid adult responsibilities and prolong playing like a kid, I'll do what I like alone, so that nobody will ever know."

Yet this isolating and withdrawing, meant to protect the Secret Keeper, tends to backfire. In the last chapter, we read about how human beings are meant to connect from birth with parents and caregivers, siblings and peers, teachers and employers, and the larger community. Some say we are also designed to connect with nature itself and a divine presence. At all times, though, we are meant to connect with our one true Self, the only ongoing relationship we have from cradle to grave.

Shouldn't we, then, be our own best friend? And shouldn't we forge all these relationships in an honest, open, and transparent way with nothing to hide or make excuses for?

Whenever we isolate and withdraw as a way to guard our secrets, we enter a lose-lose situation: we lose touch with others, and they lose touch with us. While secret keeping may begin as a harmless game, in time loneliness creeps in. There's a difference between solitude and loneliness. Loneliness is the emotional pain of being apart from cherished companions or loved ones and being separated from your Self. Solitude is the emotional connection you make with yourself when you choose to be alone rather than with others. Loneliness repels, solitude invites. For Secret Keepers the novelty of their lonely activities wears off, and inevitably what remains is stale repetition, or even bolder risk-taking and brash boundary breaking. On top of their fear of losing power, control, protection, and pride, they also learn to greatly fear loneliness.

No wonder Secret Keepers grow so weary!

Let's return to the question asked just above (and throughout these chapters): Are you willing to live a secretive, closed, risk-filled life *based on fear*? Remember that fear breeds insecurity. And the insecurity of leading a double life — "doing what

I like alone, so that nobody will ever know" while fearing getting caught — multiplies with each added risk and entanglement. Fear runs the show. And fearing the effort it would take to transform one's psyche into a healthy state of worry-free authenticity keeps many Secret Keepers from taking positive action.

Secret keeping is always *appetite*-based. And our appetites can drive us to extremes.

Consider the difference between food that satisfies one's craving and food that satisfies one's hunger. Feeling insecure, we may raid the refrigerator for chocolate cake at three in the morning. Eating meals simply because we're hungry has almost become an antiquated custom. Other cravings may drive us to buy extra lottery tickets while fantasizing about winning the big jackpot, to order double cocktails and to drink them faster, to add newly advertised cosmetics to our shoplifting list, to play that video war game three more hours, to look at dozens more naked bodies in sexual bondage — the list of actions driven by appetite rather than true need is endless.

But keeping secrets only satisfies our momentary human appetites, only what's here and now. Gratifying one's temporary pleasure preferences rather than one's real-life needs creates a merry-go-round that twirls ever faster but never stops. Unless you jump off.

Adhering to the Lie of Perpetual Youth, Secret Keepers assure themselves that as long as nobody knows about their activities, nobody is the worse for it. Well, actually, the *Secret Keeper* is the worse for it, as should be more than obvious by now. It comes down to a guessing game of "How long can this go on?" Plainly, it's a question of immaturity: "Will I ever grow up?" or "Will I ever stop avoiding responsibility?" go unanswered. Others may suffer, yes, but the Secret Keeper will suffer the most. If you are serious in your quest for authenticity, ask yourself: "Can I achieve it stealthily by secret keeping, or openly by H.O.T. living?" And if you're not serious about being authentic, ask, "Why have I read this far?"

THE SEGMENTED SELF

The parts of ourselves that we compartmentalize represent the segmented self. From Freud and Jung to modern neuroscientists and psychologists, the various experts' notions of the Self have one thing in common: the Self is not one, but many. Their portrayals of human personality and behavior show human beings torn in multiple directions.

As every parent knows, infants arrive in this world with an inner sense of self that governs them throughout life. As we grow up, we face both the *internal* problem of orchestrating and balancing the contending segments of our id, ego, and superego (or Shadow, self, and persona) *within* our psyche, and the *external* problem of making favorable impressions on other humans in order to elicit positive opinions and responses. When the self is segmented inwardly, it is vulnerable to psychic disorder. When it is segmented outwardly, it is vulnerable to disapproval from others.

Consider the psychological structure of King Arthur and the knights of the Round Table. Putting aside the romantic fantasy of the Camelot legend, imagine the inner contending segments of self as (1) Arthur, who manages the separate and often conflicting interests of his knights, and (2) each knight, who is loyal to the king but argues with rivals at the table for his share of the kingdom. Arthur arbitrates as necessary to keep peace and harmony. But should the intrigues and threats to Arthur's kingdom by France or Spain interfere, the knights will close ranks quickly around King Arthur and show a strong and united front against the foreigners. The self that is segmented outwardly does much to impress outsiders, even when the domestic affairs of the inner self may be in disarray.

When it comes to the secrets we keep, whether we disclose them, and to whom we disclose them, matters greatly. We are sovereigns over our domestic affairs (our inner self) and foreign policy (our outer self), and these decisions matter less when we sit next to strangers on an airplane or bus who have no stake in our revelations. The same goes with telling them to paid listeners, such as bartenders, barbers, taxi drivers, or even prostitutes. But when it comes to parents, spouses, children, or relatives — those with a high stake in knowing us for who we really are — the revelation of secrets leaves us feeling vulnerable. We avoid telling stigmatizing information to them and shy away from exposing our flanks.

"The essence of secrecy creates...exclusion and denial," writes Mark Wexler. "To exclude others is to generate hostility. Exclusion breeds conflict."[1] And conflict leads to betrayal. It turns people close to us into outsiders. The risk, if we divulge our secrets, is to suffer loss and unbearable embarrassment. Anyone who wants to be seen as authentic finds it of strategic interest to act as if she were not role playing — even while she is! The strategic (and segmented) self, then, conceals not only information itself but also the act of concealing it.

"Whether one has a disorder of the self is a delicate question since the 'dividing line' between normal and abnormal is not absolute," writes Ornstein in *The Roots of the Self*. "Conceptions of normality change with the times, and disorder is often in the eye of the observer. A century ago it would have been considered

abnormal for a woman to have premarital sex, and she might
have been locked away for it. Now it is not. Homosexuality used
to be classified as a disorder; now it is not. Cultures change and
standards change."[2]

Along with the blurry dividing line between culturally perceived normal and abnormal behavior, there's the common
divide between being vulnerable (exposing who we really are
and meeting with approval) and being judged (exposing who we
really are and meeting with disapproval). "We long for a world
in which others can know us fully, yet as others begin to, we
fret," states Wexler. "We fear betrayal. We fear criticism. When
strangers criticize us, we have little to fear. After all, they do not
really know us. But when intimates to whom we have shown our
inner room display their criticality, we wound rather easily."[3]

One of my clients felt afraid that his openness could result in
criticism and calamity. Kurt, who was thirty-seven and married,
reluctantly attended treatment for his drinking, but nothing
much happened until he came clean during a private meeting
with me. Risking disapproval, he spoke about the two hundred
or so porn videos he'd kept hidden in the ceiling tiles of his basement: "*That's* my real addiction." As Kurt explained his secret
addictions openly with me and ultimately in group therapy, the
truth met the bright light of day, and extensive healing became
possible. My job was to empathize and not to criticize.

The turning point for Kurt came when he admitted his secret
sex habits to another therapist and faced the intimacy issues in
his marriage. Now he is living in the healthy here and now and
no longer in the fear-filled past of repetitive secret keeping
and debilitating shame and remorse. Once he took responsibility, his segmented psyche began to unify — like King Arthur's
knights closing ranks — and both his inner and outer Selves
started growing in authenticity and wholeness.

EXISTENTIAL DEPRESSION
AND LOW-LEVEL THINKING

Clients who come to me for help frequently exhibit symptoms of depression, anxiety, and a deep sense of "lostness" that blank, eyes-down look of profound confusion. The term I use for this mental wasteland is *existential depression*. I've learned that this beleaguered state is brought on by a crisis of meaning or a lack of purpose in one's life. It may also result from what is called "low-level thinking"[4] or being severely alienated from oneself.

Some people remain willfully ignorant of their needs, motives, and conflicts all their lives. When the deepest questions of life arise, they intentionally ignore them and look the other way. Another name for this process is *denial*. Denial is a key ingredient in low-level thinking, says psychologist James Pennebaker. He puts it this way: "High-level thinking is characterized by a broad perspective, self-reflection, and the awareness of emotion. Low-level thinking is the relative absence of these attributes. When people are mindful, they are active problem solvers. Low-level thinking and mindlessness [lead to] letting others do our thinking for us, watching television, and being in uncontrollable settings where we think that nothing we do can make a difference. In short, low-level thinking usually serves as a mental Band-Aid."[5]

When we stay in denial we are attempting to evade the anxieties and ambiguities spawned by the awareness of our emotional complexity. Denial leads to self-delusion, but never to self-examination. Secret Keepers who wish to bury their heads in the sand *want what they want when they want it*.

That means they will do almost anything to *get their way in any way possible*, the seventh splintered mind-set. This mind-set is an offspring of low-level thinking. The battle cry of this mind-set is, "It's my way or the highway!" To insist on getting one's way, however, is to live inauthentically. Bill Wilson, the founder of Alcoholics Anonymous, noted that selfishness and self-centeredness are "the root of our troubles": "Any life run on self-will can hardly be a success. [We are] driven by a hundred forms of fear, self-delusion, self-seeking, and self-pity. Our troubles are basically of our own making.... they arise out of ourselves, and the alcoholic is an extreme example of self-will run riot, though he usually doesn't think so."[6]

Substitute "Secret Keeper" for "alcoholic" and you have a clear picture of where denial gets us — nowhere. It's the charming deceiver's way out. Add in the power of the Shadow, that depository of things dark and dank, and the lure of secret keeping starts to make sense on certain levels. Recall that the Shadow — what is frequently called the dark side — can, and will, erupt in awkward and troubling ways and at embarrassing times. It will not be put down or ignored; it will get its way in any way possible.

As we observed in chapter 1, psychological *incongruence* occurs whenever we substitute what is false for what is real, whenever our feelings are not congruent with our facial expressions or body language. In a similar way, *existential* incongruence occurs whenever we substitute addictive secret-keeping habits for genuine inquiry into who we really are, whenever our anxiety and ambivalence stymie our need for genuine authenticity. The word *existential*, after all, means "related or pertaining to existence." Because they lack the courage to face the questions "Who am I?" "Why am I here?" "Am I alive for a purpose?" many individuals will escape into the hidden parallel universe of secret keeping to avoid the painful negative emotions evoked by such existential questions, which by definition elude clear-cut answers.

The despair inherent in such single-minded avoidance fuels existential depression. So what is the cure? The answer is: to determine your own answers to the basic "human existence" questions, to accept any difficult emotions that arise, and to choose what attitude you need to take — a basic human freedom. Doing so will sap your secret-keeping urges and illusions. Coming to grips with your authentic Self frees you to become whole. So if you're weary of avoiding responsibility, get ready for a wholesale change on the journey toward wholeness. Don't wait until your secret keeping goes too far one day and change proves too difficult, too late, or too little. Exert your one last human freedom and choose!

NEUROSCIENCE TO THE RESCUE

It used to be believed that our brains remained stubbornly fixed entities unable to replace dead nerve cells or old neural circuits established in youth. Not so. Experiments by neuroscientists since the mid-1980s have demonstrated just the opposite. The human brain can indeed regenerate cells and create new circuits up until old age. The scientists call this our brains' *plasticity*. This plasticity holds out great hope for Secret Keepers who are motivated to change. Change *can* and *will* occur at the cellular level in that chemical and electrical masterpiece of engineering, your brain, if you want it to.

"We know physiologically that nerve cells that 'fire together wire together,'" states Joseph Dispenza, interviewed in the movie *What the Bleep Do We Know!?* When we practice something over and over again, nerve cells develop a long-term relationship. "If you get angry on a daily basis," he adds, "if you get frustrated on a daily basis, if you suffer on a daily basis, if you give reasons for the victimization in your life daily, then eventually those neural nets will develop a long-term relationship with all the other nerve cells we call our identity."[7] Fortunately, the opposite is also true: nerve cells that don't fire together will no longer wire together. They lose their long-term relationship with each other over time whenever we choose to *respond* rather than *react* — whenever we use our freedom to choose what attitude to take in any given circumstance.

So what does all this boil down to? There are no excuses. If you decide to change, your own biology will help you do it! Let's return now to Kevin's story. Kevin's belief that he was born into the body of the "wrong" gender meant dealing with existential incongruence at the deepest level of identity. I will leave it to you to decide the sincerity, or delusion, of his quest for authenticity.

KEVIN'S STORY: LIVING AS A WOMAN

Kevin's desire to dress up as a woman in secret came to mean taking three-day weekends, during which he could escape family life and "live as [he] was born to live." Safely away from his wife and five kids, 170 miles from home in a motel suite with a balcony overlooking a courtyard, Kevin shaved his legs and underarms and the rest of his body hair, slipped into silk ladies' underwear, nylons, and high heels, donned a real-hair wig with long blonde curls, then applied mascara and lipstick in sexy shades of black and red.

Stepping onto the balcony, where wandering eyes could see and appreciate "her," Cassandra, as Kevin had named this alter-ego, strolled to the railing and struck the casual pose of a woman of leisure. At times men whistled, and Cassandra responded in a feminine voice, something Kevin had practiced secretly for months. "Out there in view of the world is where I felt alive and unconflicted," says Kevin. "Nobody, absolutely nobody back home knew what I was doing. I'd tried to discuss this part of me with my wife, Amy, years before and learned to never, ever bring it up again." Only here, in his makeup and wig and bra, did Kevin no longer feel like damaged goods; instead, he felt admired and appreciated. Kevin also took rolls of photographs of Cassandra in every possible pose and state of dress and undress.

With a woeful shrug, he recalls playing the part back home of the "good husband" and "good father" for nineteen years as sincerely as possible. "That means I loved, really loved, Amy and the kids for their special qualities. I worked long hours, we built a suburban home, and went to church like everybody else."

But the day came when Kevin quietly sought the counseling services of a large university's sexuality clinic. He submitted to lengthy interviews and questionnaires, all with the idea of determining whether he was "sick" or "perverted" or if the world around him was. "I came to the conclusion that the world was sick and wrongheaded."

During one of his motel excursions, Kevin/Cassandra ventured out to a restaurant for supper. After a few cocktails, his male voice became detectable, and one of the cowboys in a group of men called his bluff. Insulted, the man dragged Cassandra into an alley and roughed her up, tearing her dress off and shouting names. Cassandra, now Kevin, swung savagely at his attacker. The brawl attracted the police, who arrested both combatants and held them overnight in jail. Charged with indecent exposure and disorderly conduct, Kevin returned home the next day — having concocted a flimflam story for Amy and the family — but he had to go back days later to face a judge. The disorderly conduct charge was dropped but not the indecent exposure count, which became part of his record. A background check a year later, along with the information that he'd dressed as a woman in public, killed Kevin's bid for a new, better-paying position within his telecom company. It also created a scandal with his family and relatives when they found out. Kevin sought new employment, but things never quite worked out for him.

Did Kevin's quest for authenticity backfire? Or did he stand true to his deeply held identity in the storm of controversy? His risky secret-keeping pretense triggered events that became public knowledge, a legal record, and costly career-related consequences. Today, more than three years after Amy divorced him, Kevin lives alone in a trailer in the desert fifty miles from civilization.

Like millions of others, Kevin became trapped in stealing hours to indulge in secret habits. Perhaps his quest for authenticity was sincere, and existential depression played a role. For some years, at least, he exhibited the seventh splintered secret-keeping mind-set: *getting your way in any way possible.*

Secret Keepers like Kevin confuse intensity for intimacy. They hope that the intensity of risks and thrills will replace the missing contentment and fulfillment in their lives. While gender dysphasia is a recognized identity disorder, and he did attempt to deal with it by seeking professional help, Secret Keepers like Kevin with these kinds of severe disorders act out rituals in isolation to reduce inner tensions based on the belief, "If I must do it, it's worth doing to the hilt." Stealing hours to push the limits in secret serves the need to feel authentically alive. But this pleasure only lasts a short while.

Was Kevin being true to himself, or was he in denial? How can anyone get inside his head and really know?

As a therapist, here's my take. Kevin was in denial more than he was being authentic. I base that statement mainly on the fact that he experienced developmental deficits very early in his life, especially during the toddler and early childhood stages of the Human Development model (see chapter 6), when he first became attached to wearing dresses and girls' shoes. Because he received acceptance and approval at that time for identifying with the opposite sex, I believe he developed an attachment disorder early on — no thanks to his brutish father, his insipid mother, and the encouraging influence of his older sister. By anchoring his self-worth to the opposite gender (by getting approval and acceptance for who he was *not*) and by never uncovering this flip-flop decision later in life when he was an adult — but clinging to it at all costs — Kevin doomed himself. He fell prey to a long history of secret keeping and, after he was so rudely exposed, he isolated himself even more. The story of his life became a double tragedy: victimization as a child and alienation as an adult.

In the next chapter, we will see further evidence of how secret keeping's seductive ways can lead to destructive results when those who are sliding down its slippery slope don't, or won't, act to save themselves.

Chapter 8

WHEN SECRET KEEPING
GOES TOO FAR

If you can't control your emotional state,
you must be addicted to it.

— JOSEPH DISPENZA, *WHAT THE BLEEP DO WE KNOW!?*

*A*S WE SAW FROM KEVIN'S STORY, the line between secret keeping and going to disastrous extremes — getting caught and being publicly exposed (the number one no-no for Secret Keepers) — can be razor thin. Many do end up crossing that line, sometimes when they don't mean to.

Until now we have focused on secret keeping, the third category on the Continuum of Secrets, where most of you reading this may fit or may know someone who does. Yet some of you may be at risk of crossing over into the fourth category, crime and psychosis. Generally speaking, if your hidden behavior ends up as a headline story in a newspaper or on the TV news, then you can be reasonably certain that you've crossed that line.

Remember the pastor whose extramarital love affair became news? The one who had to leave his ministry at the megachurch he built? Although his affair did not result in a court case or a jail sentence, because he did not commit a crime as defined by law, the media ran headline stories for weeks that left his wife and family devastated.

In what I think is a textbook case of crossing the line into crime, the 2002 movie *One-Hour Photo,* starring Robin Williams, depicts a lonely clerk working at a big-box suburban store who "loses it." Williams's character, Cy Parrish ("Cy the Photo Guy" to customers), takes orders for film processing from customers who want their prints back in an hour. One family in particular becomes the focus of his obsession. They are the perfect suburban husband, wife, and son — the family he never had but fantasizes he could have. Secretly he reproduces his own sets of prints from every roll the family brings in. In his private moments, he studies each photo longingly, wishing to be a member of this loving family. At a restaurant where he eats alone, he tells the waitress he is the uncle of the nine-year-old boy seen in birthday party snapshots.

Several scenes follow that demonstrate a Secret Keeper's hidden life to a tee. Then comes the moment when Cy discovers shots of the husband having a torrid sexual affair with a young woman. Outraged, he broods about the injustice of the husband's betrayal and the harm to his (Cy's) family, whom he has "adopted."

Cy is still solidly in the secret-keeping category so far, not having broken any laws or acted as a criminal. He is leading his secret life strictly by himself. But soon he takes matters into his own hands and begins stalking the husband and his mistress, following them to a hotel. There he breaks into their room, and things get scary. Finding them undressed, he brandishes a knife in outrage, then terrorizes them in an attempt to make them repent. Cy has crossed the line into crime, with tragic results for everyone, including himself.

His downward plunge, along with displaying the seven mindsets we've explored so far, demonstrates the eighth splintered mind-set of a Secret Keeper: *thinking of oneself first and others last.* The Jekyll and Hyde parts of his psyche, the sincere Self and the shadowy Secret Keeper, wage a constant battle for supremacy, but inevitably Cy's authentic Self loses out. His slide into psychotic derangement begins as the movie fades out.

Then there's the real-life story of Mel, the nicest guy you'd ever hope to meet. Mel retired from his job as factory supervisor in the rural South and he and his wife, Gladys, cherish their eleven grandchildren. At first, retirement allows him more time to spend with them and his buddies, but eight months later, having grown bored, Mel ducks away from home while Gladys visits her sister in another town. He drives to a casino across the state line and plays the slots for the first time in his life. He wins $75.

Fully aware of Gladys's disapproval of gambling, Mel also knows the members of the Southern Baptist church they have attended faithfully for fifty-six years consider it an abomination. But the novelty of daily freedom from scheduled work hours has worn off, and one more round of golf with his buddies makes Mel feel restless. How he spends a quiet summer afternoon, he tells himself, is nobody's business.

Until his first gambling foray, Mel was in the second category, the silent secrets stage on the Continuum. On his second trip, with Gladys unaware of his intentions, Mel is grateful he doesn't have to fib when he sets off for another win. On subsequent trips, Mel tells Gladys he is going to play golf, then drives to the casino to boost his earnings. This time, however, having to fib to Gladys makes him irritable. But once inside the heady universe of blinking lights, flashing neon, and bells and whistles, he experiences a small winning — then losing — streak. After dropping a $50-bucket at a double-slot machine, he chooses another "luckier" machine and becomes mesmerized by the rhythm of feeding it. He wins a $100 jackpot and goes home undetected.

In the days ahead, he returns again to the casino with other alibis (outright lies). Mel tries blackjack, only to see his losses soar to $600. Now squarely in the secret-keeping stage on the Continuum, he spends his spare time developing a system for beating the odds. Gladys and his pals at the local coffee shop notice that Mel seems frequently distracted and is no longer his jovial self. When the grandkids visit, though, Mel becomes his old self again — but in his quiet moments he fantasizes about the thrill of winning big.

FROM FANTASIES TO FELONIES

So far Mel's story is really rather innocent. He represents those who come late to the secret-keeping game. But as we have seen with stories of Secret Keepers using the Internet, fantasies can blossom into felonies. The Internet's ability to provide anonymity to fantasizers or curiosity-seekers is as potent as it is for stalkers and predators. Whether by way of intentional online deception or the clumsy crossing of real-life boundaries and thresholds, the kinds of progression to crime typified by Cy — and the downfall Mel is headed for — can happen faster than you can snap your fingers. The tragedy is that progressing to stage four, crime and psychosis, violates both the Secret Keeper as well as innumerable blameless victims.

But if you're thinking, "It could never happen to me," think again. Mel had exactly the same thought!

MEL'S STORY: ACT 2

Six months later, Mel's losses have piled up to over $2,800. He has invaded their retirement savings for "loans," and, with Christmas coming up fast and the eleven grandchildren to buy presents for,

Mel enacts his new and improved beat-the-odds plan. On a snowy day in early December, he tells Gladys a made-up story about an eye exam and drives to the casino. Hours later, every penny is lost. Despondent, Mel drives away slowly, berating himself for having no money with which to purchase presents.

While passing rural farms, he sees a home lit up with brightly colored Christmas lights. Mel makes a snap decision. He turns up the lengthy driveway and parks. He heads for the front door, rings the doorbell, waits, and hears nothing. He sees the Christmas tree through the patio door and admires the many brightly wrapped presents piled around it. Moments later, using a tire iron, he pries open the patio door and grabs an armful of packages, loading them into his car. He makes another trip, grabbing another armful. On the third trip, he climbs inside for the last remaining gifts.

Click! He hears a metallic sound and a voice saying, "Hold it right there, mister!"

Mel turns and sees a man in pajamas aiming a pistol at his head. Rubbing sleep from his eyes, the man phones 911. Police arrive minutes later and arrest the intruder. In handcuffs, Mel is hauled away to jail.

When Mel gets back home, Gladys's horror and stark sense of betrayal pain him severely. Their joyous Christmas festivities shattered, he stares at the floor for hours. Mel — the decent husband, father, grandpa, and church member — can barely face his loved ones and his church buddies, who can't disguise their confusion. Even with the passing of months and seasons, and even with Mel acting like his trustworthy old self again, the effects of his secret keeping can never be fully forgotten.

As I said above, Mel's errors are beginners' mistakes. He only crossed the line from secret keeping to crime *once*, for no more than ten minutes, before getting caught and branded for

life. Perhaps you're having a hard time swallowing the fact that
Mel would stoop so low. Perhaps you're thinking that you could
never do such a thing. But have you never done anything rash in
a moment of passion? Or regretted having hurt someone's feelings when you were in too much of a panic to stop yourself?

Accomplished Secret Keepers rely on far more advanced
tricks and wiles than Mel. They either cross the line into crime so
cleverly that they escape detection time and time again, or they
never permit their activities to go too far in the first place. In
short, although many experienced Secret Keepers have developed high levels of criminal thinking, they avoid crossing the
line into crime itself.

REAL CRIMINALS, REAL CRIMES

Scrapes here and there with the law like Mel's are one thing.
Rape, white-collar fraud, leading pornography rings, and murder
are another thing entirely. The rogues' gallery that follows is a
small sampling of crimes committed by Secret Keepers, all of
whom pretended to be "regular folks." I took each story from
published news accounts widely circulated and have described
each briefly to show how easily the lives of these regular folks can
erode from years of secret keeping. Notice how the individuals'
profession, title, status, and "shiny" persona help to dispel suspicion, as discussed in chapter 1. (For updates and more commentary,
check my website, www.johnprin.com. You'll find the monthly
"Secret Keepers in the News" featured on my home page, along
with brief stories about many Secret Keepers there.)

Boy Scout Porn

Douglas Sovereign Smith Jr., chairman of the Boy Scouts' Youth
Protection Task Force in Forth Worth, Texas, pleaded guilty to
keeping thousands of images of child pornography on his work

computer.[1] Smith stored and distributed these images of children in sexual poses, mainly boys of twelve years of age, to others in the porn ring as far away as Germany. His "shiny" side? He was a longtime, high-ranking executive in the Boy Scouts. His "slimy" side? He fed his hidden appetites by looking at images of boys the same age as those he "protected" in an organization devoted to boys' welfare.

Duo of Deceit

Al and Joan Porro of New Jersey left prison in 2005 after nine years for looting children's trust funds.[2] Known as the "duo of deceit," they went to federal prison for nineteen counts of fraud and tax evasion but today are lecturing college students about ethics. "I did much worse than what I was charged with," says Mr. Porro, a former seminary student who owned a strip club that amassed enormous wealth. Porro "cast himself as devoutly religious" but lived a lifestyle of "hypocrisy and self-indulgence." Along with his wife, he has renounced their secretive, self-indulgent lifestyle.

Fraudulent Public Servant

Dino Guerin, a county commissioner paid by taxpayers in St. Paul, Minnesota, gambled away $35,500 obtained from writing bad checks in a desperate bid to pay off his casino debts.[3] His slide into addiction, deceit, and despair started years earlier when he began leaving his office secretly during working hours. Donning disguises at casinos, he gambled his own funds on the taxpayers' time clock. Fired for dereliction of duty, Guerin made a bid to run for mayor of the city months later and lost in a resounding defeat.

Death by Internet

A sixth-grade altar girl in Danbury, Connecticut, flirted online with a married restaurant worker and paid the ultimate price:

death.4 Christina Long got good grades, led the cheerleading squad, and, it was discovered, used provocative screen names to set up appointments to have sex with partners she met in chat rooms. Until she dated Saul Dos Reis, twenty-five, that is. He left her body in a remote ravine and later confessed to law officers to having murdered her. Christina's teacher observed that she was a very good student but also "streetwise and very spirited." Hearing about the murder, the teacher added, "It's clear she was very torn in both directions."

One more case study awaits your attention, this one about a person whose secret keeping danced on the edges of public awareness and who displayed the eighth splintered mind-set, *thinking of oneself first and others last.*

TED: EXHIBIT A — HIS NAKED BODY

Ted prided himself on his he-man, movie-star physique. Nothing excited him more than wearing as little as possible during nonworking hours, especially in public, like when he mowed the lawn without a shirt in the skimpiest of shorts or when he sunbathed in the nude "where nobody could see" (but in clear sight of adjacent apartment building windows). Married for the fourth time to a woman he'd met in a 12-step recovery group (her second marriage), Ted, thirty-nine, saw no reason to limit his sex life to the bedroom.

Before the arrival of the Internet, Ted's exhibitionist urges found expression via videos. With one buxom lover, he used hidden cameras to make tapes of their lovemaking in daring places, including his own living room and her patio garden. Later, the Internet proved a rich venue. He downloaded photos of naked women from websites and digitally blended nude images of himself into these photos to create personal porno picture albums, which he masturbated to.

These and additional secret activities would have gone unnoticed had his wife, Shelly, not clicked on a digital image mistakenly. What she saw floored her. She insisted on their going to counseling. Just two years into the marriage, she complained that the dream man she'd wedded had "changed from a caring friend into a callous stranger." Since her discovery of his secret, Ted had turned hostile and threatening toward her. He felt irked that Shelly "whined" so much, that she kept bringing up the "rigorous honesty" part of the 12-step program with their counselor. He also disliked that she reminded him of his promises that their marriage "would operate on the same kind of principles." He sat back in the counseling sessions, withdrawn and quizzical, polite but indifferent. She pointed out to the counselor Ted's opposite behavior at home, where daily outbursts of angry criticism and blaming rage made her fear for her safety.

Between counseling sessions, Ted turned a cold shoulder to Shelly and spent more time at work — his job as a roving office machines troubleshooter "required" long hours and overnight stays within a large region. Long ago Ted had mastered the secret-keeping mind-sets of *appearances first, reality second; maximizing pleasure, minimizing pain; getting his way any way possible*; and currently he was in the process of mastering *thinking of oneself first and others last.* On one overnight trip while driving his repair van, he just could not imagine how paranoid Shelly's behavior had become. Ted wondered how long the marriage would last and whether he should divorce her sooner rather than later. Sooner, he reflected, as he stopped his van at a motel that advertised X-rated adult movies on cable television. . . .

—〽—

Sadly, the list of criminal and/or psychotic offenders could go on forever. Whether cold and calculated Secret Keepers like Ted or naïve and amateurish ones like Mel, such divided individuals slip from engaging in sly solo activities that break ethical, moral, and relational boundaries into committing crimes that directly and grievously harm others. Whether it is perverse or petty, an element of criminal thinking (at the malignant level on the Continuum) is inherent in the deceptive nature of this type of secrecy. The consequences of crossing this line lead to disaster and devastation. Lawbreakers like Lila in chapter 5, who compulsively shoplifted, have often been heard to say, "I don't know what came over me. I always believed I was a good, respectable person of solid character." If you believe the same about yourself but are caught in the downward spiral of a deceitful double life similar to those of the individuals featured in this book, then now is the time to take action.

Today is the day.

Why wait any longer?

If you're a Secret Keeper, ask yourself whether you really want to stay on the slippery slope of deception-by-omission that your double life demands. Turn to the chapters in part 2, "The Journey Toward Wholeness," to learn ways to end your slavery and your destructive habits. Make fresh choices *now*.

If you suspect you are living with or otherwise involved with a Secret Keeper, ask yourself if you intend to continue looking the other way or going further downhill emotionally. If the answer is no, then you're in luck. Part 2 will also help you find ways to deal squarely and cope more effectively with the Secret Keeper in your life.

Empower yourself. Be decisive. Begin right now.

PART 2

THE JOURNEY TOWARD WHOLENESS

Solutions and Rewards

Chapter 9

SEEKING THE HELP
YOU NEED

Power is the ability to achieve purpose ... to effect change.

— MARTIN LUTHER KING JR.

*N*OW THAT WE'VE EXAMINED THE PROBLEM, with all its devastating consequences, let us turn our attention to the solution. For the truth is, no matter how desperate you may feel, you can have a happier and more fulfilling life. The essential motivation you will need is to believe that you can break free from the captivity of secret keeping to the freedom of recovery. In this second part of the book we ask, How can my true Self reassert itself and vanquish the Secret Keeper? How can I reduce the Secret Keeper in me to a fading flicker of a distant memory?

Changing your thinking is what really makes recovery possible. As your thinking changes, so will your personality and your character. Your moods will improve as your thoughts transform. The six stages listed below comprise a blueprint for successful recovery, for *gaining* freedom over harmful secret-keeping habits. I call these the Blueprint for Gaining Freedom:

1. *Surrender* secret-keeping habits and attitudes (covered in chapter 9),

2. *Accept* your duality and start understanding it (chapter 10),

3. *Prepare* to state the true facts (chapter 11),

4. *Disclose* secrets (true facts) to somebody (chapter 12),

5. *Trust* in a new worldview (chapter 13), and finally,

6. *Account* for present and future behavior (chapter 14).

THE FREEDOM OF RECOVERY

In the following chapters, you will learn how each of these six stages can help empower you to live a happier and more fulfilling life. To start this process, consider the information about your own life that the diagram below, The Four Squares of Life, will help you to uncover.[1] Think of this diagram as a lens through which you can view new insights into your personal healing that will promote your growth. We will be revisiting the "squares" of this helpful diagram in upcoming chapters. Spend a few moments now to become acquainted with it.

THE FOUR SQUARES OF LIFE

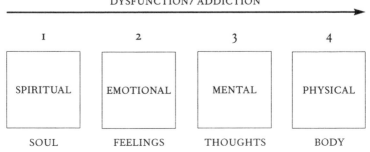

DYSFUNCTION / ADDICTION

1	2	3	4
SPIRITUAL	EMOTIONAL	MENTAL	PHYSICAL
SOUL	FEELINGS	THOUGHTS	BODY

These four squares represent the major areas of our lives from cradle to grave. Like the four seasons or the four directions, these areas represent how every human being of every culture and generation experiences life.

Starting at the Spiritual square (1), we arrive on earth as needy human beings. Food, water, shelter, and clothing are vital. We also require nurturing and close contact with parents and caregivers in order to grow up as healthy people. Our need to belong is strong, as is our need to connect with siblings, peers, relatives, and the wider community. Spiritually, small children are ready to believe in anything — from angels to Santa Claus to ghosts to talking animals. Although they are spiritually open and curious as toddlers, many grow up to believe that *spirituality exists outside themselves*. The day inevitably comes when kids no longer believe in things such as angels or talking animals. Sadly, the divine spark within them flickers and fades. In time, as children age, *disconnection* occurs in the Spiritual square.

In the Emotional square (2), children feel both loving and nurturing emotions as well as painful emotions from the hard lessons and difficult experiences of growing up. All children strive to be liked and to fit in, but siblings or bullies may taunt and tease them. They may fail in some important area of development or suffer neglect and outright abuse. Children may experience kindness and encouragement at school and mayhem and neurosis at home. Kids in elementary school aspire in avenues such as academics, arts, and athletics. Popularity and praise follow their achievements, or frustration and inadequacy dog their failures. Sooner or later life seems to turn unfair, and tender emotions experience *damage*. Painful feelings generate wounded hearts and minds. Environmental disparities and developmental deficits (explored in chapter 6) can lead to a steady stream of hurtful feelings that destabilize children. When these conditions persist, such individuals may easily turn to secret keeping as a way to escape, or to numb and medicate, their stressful existence.

In the Mental square (3), healthy and affirming experiences generate positive self-talk and hopeful attitudes toward life, resulting in an optimistic worldview. At the same time, damaged emotions and disconnected spirits generate *distorted* thoughts and doubts, resulting in a pessimistic worldview. These kinds of thoughts can become ingrained through negative self-talk, such as: "I'm a loser," "I'll never measure up," "Everybody else is smarter than me," "I should never have been born." Distorted thoughts undermine and drain the child of energy and initiative, producing a downward spiral of underachievement and low self-esteem.

The buildup of a person's disconnected spirit, damaged emotions, and distorted thoughts can start to make any means of escape appear attractive. By the time a child reaches puberty, drugs or dysfunctional habits like secret keeping enter the picture, and he or she experiences a "high," an altered state of consciousness, pleasant and sometimes ecstatic. Escapist behaviors become more frequent, resulting in an addictive cycle. Invariably, these activities — like sneaking away to the woods or partying all night at a friend's house — require hiding the frowned-on behavior from disapproving parents or teachers or police officers.

In the Physical square (4), the individual's body, gripped by stressful habits rooted in disconnection, damage, distortion, drugs, and dysfunction, starts showing symptoms of breaking down, owing to the toxic effects of substances to the liver, blood, lungs, and brain. Endless hours spent playing computer games, or injuries incurred from thrill-seeking, further weaken the body. Many kids develop impaired immune systems and ignore trouble signals, refusing to alter their feel-good habits. The pleasure centers of their brains trump the alarm systems and cognitive functions. Teens who get drunk, for example, do daring things that defy reason — driving too fast, picking fights, and becoming the victims or perpetrators of date rape. The dysfunction-addiction cycle deepens and intensifies, leading to medical *disease* or *disorders* like high blood pressure, insomnia, and damage to the liver or lungs.

Risky or ever more dangerous activity levels and medical impairments worsen until *disaster* looms. Research has established that self-concealment, or the general tendency to keep secrets from others, is related to a variety of physical and psychological symptoms, including depression, anxiety, headaches, and much more. The ultimate disaster is *death*. Besides physical demise, death can also mean divorce, termination of custody rights, a career crash, massive depression, and so on.

Let's look at the diagram again:

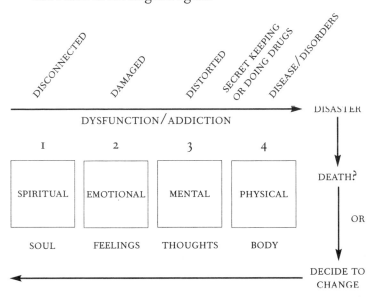

Now follow the progression of stages 1 through 8:

1. *Disconnected* spiritually in childhood (divine spark separated from Self).

2. *Damaged* emotions (hurts, betrayals, shame growing up).

3. *Distorted* thoughts (lies and misperceptions from hurts, betrayals, shame). When we add to that *drugs, drinking,* or *dysfunctional habits* like secret keeping (age ten to eighteen) as a means of numbing or escape, we get:

4. *Diseased* bodies (from stress, toxins, anxiety, and a self-defeating cycle of use, abuse, and dependency), until *disaster* looms in the form of injury, insanity, or even actual *death*.

Before it's too late a *decision to change* is required!

You have two choices: (1) Recovery, which leads to health, balance, and sanity, or (2) Refusal, which leads to more dysfunction, illness, injury, insanity, and *disaster*. Obviously the first choice makes the most sense. Recovery occurs in the *reverse direction* of Dysfunction/Addiction, starting with the *decision to change*:

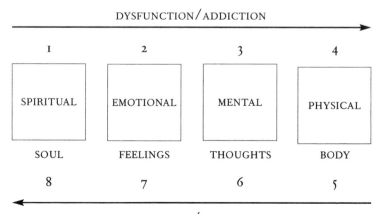

Notice how the diagram looks now when the Wholeness/Recovery arrow is added. Let's see where your choice of Recovery takes you. The *start* of any recovery program is to stop the pathological behavior and to take a 180-degree turn. Immediately (see 5 on the bottom arrow) you will begin to experience:

5. *Relief thanks to feeling physically better* because stress, anxiety, and toxins decrease and no longer deplete or disease your body. Note: a brief period of uncomfortable withdrawal often occurs.

6. *Realistic thoughts replacing distorted thoughts* because lies, exaggerations, and victim-centered thoughts from your growing-up years are reinforced less and less.

7. *Restoration of positive feelings* because identifying and facing troubling emotions (applying numerous therapies) disempower the old damaged feelings and encourage positive energy and moods.

8. *Reconnecting with your spirituality* because your trust in a revised worldview will empower you from within (that is, transform your psyche) and open your eyes to new possibilities (the divine spark returns).

The final square, Spirituality in Recovery (8), is where the benefits of living with a new purpose and rejuvenated energy come together. It's the place where meaning increases in your life, where your goals and interests and gifts unite, where gratitude and serenity follow from serving others, where partnering with a higher power equips you to tackle each challenge facing you, and where you will become *you* to the fullest, brightest, happiest extent ever.

Where does the power come from to act — and to benefit from acting — in these new ways? It comes from the freedom of Recovery, which you can experience through following the Blueprint for Gaining Freedom, from filling in the Four Squares of Life with events from your own life, and from living a reawakened lifestyle aimed at wholeness.

So let's get started on the exciting adventure before you by looking at the first item on the Blueprint, *Surrender*.

THE REWARDS OF SURRENDERING

Surrendering to the truth is one way of resigning control. Admitting to having reached your limit is another. Together these mean taking responsibility to change. Taking responsibility requires:

- admitting powerlessness
- admitting the unmanageability of our lives
- breaking through isolation
- ending the internal debate within ourselves.

Above we talked about deciding to change. Change depends on surrendering the old and embracing the new. Surrendering means deciding you need help and asking for it. *Surrender*, by its very definition, implies a *loss* of power. Soldiers fighting in combat consider surrendering to their enemies to be the absolute last resort. Ironically, when it comes to moving from the captivity of secret keeping to the freedom of recovery, admitting your lack of power is actually empowering. That's because you have a new purpose (changing your personality and your character), but double-mindedness fogs your thinking. Fortunately, many paths and strategies are available to you. Your job is to select from the options and tailor a recovery plan that works for you.

Most people find it very difficult to surrender and to admit to needing help. We want to be strong and self-reliant. We don't want to impose on others. We want to run our lives successfully and not have to admit to failure. Asking for help seems like weakness and cowardice. We don't want to give up the fight. Like war-worn soldiers, we think that abandoning our cause will make us traitors. We hang on to the idea that, "I'm still functioning, so how can I really need help?" But our secret keeping has drained us and divided us, has alienated us and held us captive.

Surrender is the essence of what millions of out-of-control people in 12-step support groups have done for decades. Doing so, they have reaped the blessings of authenticity and the rewards of recovery. Alcoholics and drug addicts, pathological gamblers and food junkies, porno zealots and chronic shoplifters all have come to admit that they were "powerless" over their addictions and that their lives had become "unmanageable."[2]

The act of surrender, of admitting the truth, can help Secret Keepers turn their lives around as well. Admitting powerlessness and facing one's unmanageability can bring benefits. Think of the German soldiers in World War II who surrendered to the American Army. They traded their weapons for a truce, hungry stomachs for a hot meal, wet uniforms for dry blankets, and days without sleep for nights of long rest.

You have probably experienced the feeling of caving in to cravings many times. Most likely you have tried to balance your secret life — with mounting stress and nail-biting close calls — with your public life. The irony? Once you admit your powerlessness over secret keeping (your inability to stop, your lack of control), you *gain* a small degree of power. Admitting the truth has the power to reduce what's false about your life to a speck. I've seen this occur again and again in recovery and treatment groups, both those I attend as a recovering alcoholic, addict, and Secret Keeper and those that I lead as a trained professional counselor.

Herman was a client of mine who sought treatment for his alcoholism. But he never disclosed his cocaine use. That was his secret, one of several. When I learned from his probation officer of his positive urinalysis for cocaine, I raised the issue of dishonesty with him. He broke down in tears — grateful tears. Herman admitted that keeping this secret, and the deception that doing so required, felt far worse than now having the secret be known. He was weary of chasing the coke high and dodging his wife's suspicions and lying to authorities when asked about drug abuse. He pledged to fight his addiction to cocaine and to stay abstinent. I decided to give him enough rope either to hang himself with or to tie up his Secret Keeper in knots with. In group, co-members emphasized the additional need for Herman to pledge "rigorous honesty," as the Big Book of Alcoholics Anonymous urges. He did so, staying cocaine-free with such passion in the weeks ahead that his nickname in the group became Honest Herman.

Overcoming his entrenched pride wasn't easy for Herman. Our egos fight fiercely to prevent any sign of weakness, of surrender. But in truth, self-sufficiency is a hoax. People like Herman who swallow their pride and surrender to compassionate helpers experience unexpected heights of freedom. They feel affirmed after having done so — and in this case the "knots" won over the "noose."

To use a fictional example, in *Indiana Jones and the Last Crusade*, "Indie" takes a similar risk. He faces the deadly choice of whether to leap across a deep ravine in his search for the Holy

Grail. His choices are either to rely on his own limited understanding (jumping the impossible distance meant sure death) or to have faith in a power he couldn't see that would provide an invisible bridge across the ravine. Empowered by the importance of his goal, he looked up, sighed the word *believe*, and stepped forward into the empty void. At that instant, when his weight shifted into the empty space and his own strength could no longer save him, the promised bridge appeared, and he walked safely across to claim the treasure.

Both Indiana Jones and Herman demonstrate this principle: "Faith is when we reach the end of all the light we know and must step into the darkness... and we realize that when we jump we will either land on something firm or have wings to fly."[3] So said William James, the great nineteenth-century American psychologist and philosopher.

Your act of surrender can be just like theirs. Be adventurous!

After surrendering and admitting powerlessness, it can be another stretch to admit all the ways in which your life has become unmanageable. Not sure your life really is unmanageable? Look again at the challenges faced by those we met in part 1, such as Brad, Kevin, Lila, and Bonnie. Measure their circumstances against your own. If doing that doesn't convince you, then consider the high-wire acrobatics you've been engaged in — con games, alibis, cover-ups, lies, tricks — to keep secret keeping alive in your divided world. Don't these stressful acrobatics equate to life being "unmanageable"?

If you need a bit more convincing, try rating yourself on the Eight Splintered Mind-sets: When have you acted under their control? How often? To what degree? Then take the quiz on the next page. Think of the time period when you've been *most active as a Secret Keeper*, or, if you're thinking about another person, when she or he has.

QUIZ
Am I a Secret Keeper?

Do the following secret-keeping statements apply to you? Answer *True* or *False*.

_____ I engage in private activities, behaviors, or rituals that I keep secret from the people I care about in my life.

_____ I have left work or home in order to engage in my secret behaviors and activities.

_____ I feel angry, ashamed, or depressed after I engage in secret fantasies or activities.

_____ I have done things in my secret life that are against my personal morals or values.

_____ I use private fantasies and behaviors to get away from the problems in my life.

_____ I spend time and energy keeping others from finding out what I do in my private life.

_____ My life has been in crisis because of my secret behaviors or activities.

_____ I worry that others will find out what I think about or do in private and that it will get me into trouble.

_____ I have tried to stop doing the things I keep secret, but I keep going back to them despite the problems my secret life is causing me.

Add up the *True*s and *False*s. Were you completely honest? What do your responses tell you?

If all of your responses were *False*, you can rest assured that you or the person you rated fit in category 1 or 2 (simple and silent secrets) of the Continuum of Secrets. Go ahead and feel satisfied with what these responses tell you.

If you have any *True* answers, especially more than one, then read on. The chapters in part 2 address the kinds of issues and concerns reflected in these statements and will offer several options for you. The suggestions and exercises in part 2 are designed to help you deal with your hidden habits or feelings about being a Secret Keeper.

> To take a more comprehensive quiz, go to
> www.secretkeepingquiz.com.

The challenges of taking responsibility can seem overwhelming. Facing your habitual lies and your betrayal of loved ones stirs up guilt and remorse. Thinking of the disgrace to your reputation, career, family name, and your position in the wider community may prevent you from coming forward. But all these obstacles to surrendering melt away once you commit to a plan of action, just as athletes and coaches develop a game plan to win games, then conference titles, then championships.

When leading group therapy sessions, I regularly coach clients about taking responsibility by using sports analogies. "So what wins the game?" I'll ask. Then I'll answer my own question: "You have to put points on the scoreboard to win, that's what."

Someone might suggest that a good defense can win games too. "Yes," I will reply, "defense can prevent a loss, but it's the total points your team makes on offense that *wins* games."

Like sports, recovery is not just about avoiding losses. Being sure you pay your court fines or remembering not to skip probation meetings are defensive maneuvers. They can keep you from getting into deeper trouble, but only offense keeps you *out* of trouble. Offense means not secret keeping *in the first place*. It means not living a double life that requires you to keep secrets. It means harboring no shame or guilt *to begin with*, because you haven't snuck off by yourself and shoplifted when nobody was looking, or gotten drunk alone again, or crossed the line and done something criminal. It means acting lawfully from the get-go. Offense sets the pace of the game; it doesn't mean struggling to keep up with the opponent's pace.

Every day that you don't secret-keep, every day that you live a H.O.T. life, you're putting points on the board. You're winning. Every time you say no to cybersex or gambling on the sly or to whatever form your secret keeping takes, you're also saying yes to health and sanity and to everyone's best interests, especially your own. You're saying yes to life, yes to honesty, yes to loved ones, and yes to being a winner.

Playing defense matters, but it's offense that wins the game.

So the first offensive move you should make is to surrender your secret-keeping attitudes and habits. Admitting openly that you've been secret keeping begins the recovery process. Simply saying "no" to secret keeping, however, while certainly part of recovery, is only the start. It's the change in your character that wins the game. Saying no to secret keeping is defense; saying yes to *changing your personality and character* is offense.

CAROLINE: A CRY FOR HELP

This is how Caroline described her surrender stage:

By my late thirties I was married with kids, and rituals for everything dominated me. I had to turn the washing machine dial exactly sixteen times to start a load. I sorted clothes so that certain clothes never touched other clothes. The idea was, "If I somehow do the laundry wrong, something might happen to one of my family members who wears those clothes."

I also had all sorts of rituals around food. Like I wouldn't want my children to eat Cheerios three days in a row because on the third day something bad might happen. My whole life was encompassed by these things.

With my car, there were more rituals. Often I'd have to circle back around and around the block — and finally, finally somehow force myself to get on my way wherever I was going. If the door latch on the garage door didn't look perfect, exactly perpendicular, I'd have to go back and fix it. I don't know how I survived, and I don't know why I didn't commit suicide. I felt miserable every day.

Now, the interesting thing is that I was also a community leader at the time with major responsibilities. I was successful in everything I did, but at a huge cost. Somehow, as chairwoman of the school board, I would run a great meeting but get to the meeting barely on time. I kept hearing, "Caroline, you do such a great job," but they didn't know the half of it.

One day a good friend who knew me well confronted me, very gently, and helped me see that mental health problems like mine had to be addressed. She convinced me that these kinds of problems don't often lead to being hospitalized or institutionalized for life, but without help they do take a major toll on you.

I finally went to a professional when I was thirty-nine, thanks to taking that good friend's advice. I learned I had obsessive-compulsive disorder. My life would've been very different had I learned about it and been treated sooner, because OCD is very treatable. The problem with many mental health disorders, in my case anxiety disorders, is that you do tend to *hide* them, because you know what you're doing and thinking is really weird. But when you give up trying to deal with them on your own, you can get past the secrets and make great progress.

I learned I had five mental health problems: anxiety, agoraphobia, panic disorder, OCD, and depression. The world to me was a scary place. I avoided crowded shopping malls. I didn't go grocery shopping for fourteen years because of panic attacks. I was afraid of running over a child in the street when driving. On top of all this there was the secrecy, the shameful hiding. And so I was depressed. My constant frown and downcast posture sent a cry for help to a friend who had the courage to beg me to locate a professional therapist. Despite my initial resistance, I found professional therapy to be the beginning of the freedom I feel today.

Caroline finally surrendered and sought help. Surrendering made possible a slow and steady personality change, a process of months and years that included applying her insights to dealing with her disorders. Her husband and kids attended family sessions, where they learned about her challenges, while Caroline underwent extensive behavior-modification therapy. Caroline's childhood also yielded some helpful insights into what had started her down the path to secret keeping in the first place:

When I was a little girl, I was terrified of monsters. Every night I went to bed panicky. I would have to look under all four corners of the bed, but if I didn't quite do it right, I'd have to do it again, over and over. My sisters became so annoyed with me that I learned to hide my actions, which led to my mastery of keeping secrets. Nowadays I know that early intervention can make a difference, so I hope my story helps somebody suffering right now. The difference between my life today and before surrendering is enormous.

Today Caroline volunteers as a spokesperson at conferences and conventions for other sufferers with OCD, having turned her fear-based behavior into service to others. By tailoring, and following, her own program of recovery, Caroline lives a far less anxious and secrecy-enslaved life today.

THE FOUR SQUARES OF LIFE AND YOU

Now it's your turn. As described above, The Four Squares of Life is a tool you can use to help surrender your secret-keeping habits and begin the process of changing your personality. To review, once you are *disconnected* spiritually, *damaged* emotionally, thinking *distorted* thoughts, and reliant on *drugs, drinking,* or *dysfunctional habits* (like secret keeping) to cope, medicate, or escape, you feel the ill effects of a *diseased* body. Sooner or later *disaster* looms in the form of injury, insanity, or *death*. A *decision to change* is required, and let's assume that you've made it! Now let's look at the diagram once more:

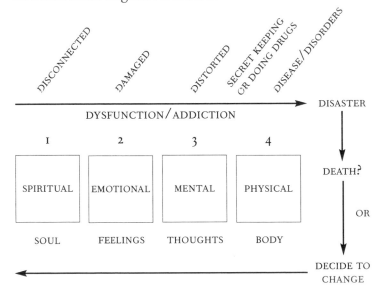

EXERCISE

Referring to this chart, zero in on the key events of your life's
history. Record your answers in your journal or notebook:

1. When did I experience *disconnection?* _____

    _____

    _____

    _____

    Here are some examples from my own history: The
    night my mother announced our move to a new house,
    the day we boys transplanted the grove of birch trees.

2. When did I experience *damaged* emotions? _____

    _____

    _____

    _____

    _____

    Examples from my history: Playing the Getting Lost game
    to cope with my hatred of and aversion to Mom, my homicidal
    urges brought on by rage about Mom's work projects and Dad's
    poor health.

3. When did I experience *distorted* thoughts? _____

    _____

    _____

    _____

    _____

    Examples from my history: While collecting patio stones on
    my birthday, I thought, "My mother hates me," "I am her slave";
    while selling the man a *Playboy*, I thought, "Now I'm 'one of the
    men's club.' "

4. When did I experience *diseasing* my body?_____

_____

_____

_____

_____

Examples from my history: Running naked in the woods caused injury to my skin and feet; my intense homicidal rage caused high blood pressure, headaches, and heartburn.

Once you have identified several events from your life for each square, then start playing offense by designing your own recovery plan. Your first points in the tournament ahead of you will come from following the Blueprint for Gaining Freedom and *surrendering your secret-keeping habits and attitudes.*

Congratulations for choosing Recovery, with its benefits and successes, over Refusal, with its battles and defeats. It's your life. And you're winning.

Chapter 10

FINDING YOUR
MOTIVATION

Matter is not what matters most.

—— MESSAGE IN A CHINESE FORTUNE COOKIE

*D*ECLARING BANKRUPTCY. Getting fired. Being arrested for drug possession. Sitting in jail after a DUI. Being hospitalized for an eating disorder.

Sometimes a Secret Keeper's double life is disclosed to the world through these kinds of events. Secret-shattering crises that go public motivate anyone in this kind of a bind to seek help. I call this process "being motivated by external pressures." The Secret Keeper's response is *compliance*, or making outward behavior changes in response to the precipitating event.

Other Secret Keepers, those who have not been caught engaging in blatantly risky behaviors, keep the details of their lives hidden successfully. Almost anyone who fears being exposed will actively resist spilling the beans, so heavily invested are they in their secret keeping. The thought of disclosing their stigmatizing habits makes them cringe. Because the pressures of external circumstances don't force the issue, they need to *find* the motivation to change, preferably one that comes from within themselves and makes changing much easier. Rather than allowing us to avoid losses, it encourages making gains. Rather than forcing compliance, it empowers transformative choices. Rather than helping us play defense, it sparks offense. Why? Because it draws on human beings' internal powers rather than relying on their knee-jerk reactions to external forces.

What exactly is this inner source of motivation? It is based on one's *voluntary altered perspective* — one's decision to see life, and one's identity, differently. I call it "being inspired by internal motivators." A Secret Keeper's response to his predicament can be a *choice*, reflecting an inward change that emanates from his deepest desires. And this inner change starts with acceptance.

Here is where the second stage of the Blueprint for Gaining Freedom comes in: *Accepting* your duality and starting to understand it. Since Secret Keepers are often emotionally intelligent and experts at self-discernment, their ability to tune in to their duality offers them the advantage of discerning what internal impulses to curb, and one day to cease entirely the cycle of destructive secrets.

How do you start accepting and understanding your duality? By identifying the "internal motivators" within your character that define who you really are. By understanding the duality at work in you and letting it work *for* you. Secret Keepers who commit to whole-mindedness soon realize that they must do more than abstain from secret keeping; they find that they will succeed only when they follow a program of recovery tailored to their needs. As a bonus, their self-understanding will lead to improved moods over time and will benefit their loved ones as well. The general term for this in alcohol and drug recovery is *sobriety*, but for Secret Keepers a slight twist is in order — so let's use the term *authenticity* instead, a concept we've touched on already in earlier chapters.

My definition of authenticity is "consistency and wholeness, soundness of moral principle and character, and unimpaired or uncompromised integrity." So while *abstinence* means putting an end to secret keeping (just as an alcoholic stops drinking liquor), *authenticity* means enjoyable abstinence (most former alcoholics will testify that they are far happier, more authentic, and less fearful once they are liquor-free). For more about the joys of authenticity (enjoyable abstinence), see chapter 14.

Recovery, then, *is a daily program of authenticity.*

When you choose to use your duality to your benefit, your heightened awareness of human duality will provide the powerful motivation needed to overcome difficult, overwhelming challenges. Your process of honoring the values you hold dear *within* you will fly in the face of your secret keeping. If you say, for instance, that you love your children but your focus remains on your career (during work hours) and on your secret keeping (during leisure hours), then the time and energy you *don't* invest in your kids smells like hypocrisy, which it is. When you don't live in accordance with the values you profess, like loving your kids, you are merely paying lip service...and your kids undoubtedly know it! Only when you're authentic will you be able to achieve congruence. Your public and private selves will match once more; you will be acting the same way as you are feeling, turning the first splintered mind-set on its head.

Here's another example. The abstaining alcoholic knows that liquor, beer, and wine are available almost anytime or anywhere she wants it. Liquor stores, bars, and cocktail lounges abound and, during business hours, they have no locks on their doors to keep customers out. (For drug addicts, cybersexers, gamblers, shoplifters, or food addicts, the same thing applies — the supply is there for the taking.) As the abstaining alcoholic benefits from the awareness of her duality, she decides not to drink. Her *voluntary altered perspective* guides her. It frees her of having to follow the old pattern of being a slave to her cravings and entering a liquor store, bar, or cocktail lounge. By *choosing not* to enter such establishments or to drink again anywhere, she shows she is motivated internally. She now benefits from the knowledge that abstinence is healthier for her in every way: medically, financially, emotionally, and relationally. Understanding her duality has equipped her with these insights and the motivation to stay true to them.

FINDING EXTERNAL AND INTERNAL MOTIVATION

So how do these two forms of motivation, internal and external, compare? Let me first say that both forms can work together, if you act on them intentionally as part of your self-tailored recovery plan. Events like declaring bankruptcy, being fired, and getting arrested can certainly motivate a person. External pressures oblige the offender to consider changing the problematic behavior that led to these sorts of crises. Sitting in jail or lying in a hospital bed allows for time to think and reflect: "What made me break the law? What am I doing to my health? Am I headed for financial ruin? Why am I making so many people — my spouse, my kids, my parents, my boss, myself — crazy?"

Pressures can also come in the form of the overwhelming consequences of our activities: court fines, probation, driver's license suspensions, legal convictions on your record, DUIs, anger management classes, hospital fees, spousal ultimatums, loss of credit cards and penalties, job loss, and so on. Basically, these circumstances that you "acquire" (from your own self-defeating actions) just generate more pressure until real change occurs. Do you really want even more pressure? If the answer is no, then learn to use the pressure to put an end to your secret keeping.

What if you were to become motivated by something more effective than external pressures that force you to comply with others' demands and conditions? Besides merely pretending to change or putting on the appearance of having changed, which will just lead to even more "impression management," what if you were to try genuine *inward reform* rather than phony *outward* compliance? External pressures create inner resistance. If you are dead set against changing, then the pressures of "being told to change" will only feed your Secret Keeper's already crafty set of skills and splintered mind-sets: more *placing appearances first and reality second*; *living from the outside in*, and so on, like a broken record. Simply put, outside pressures make you play defense rather than offense. It will take something internal, something truly empowering, to convince you to change.

For perspective on what kind of motivation works best in the long run, look carefully at this chart:

DUAL MOTIVATION	
COMPLIANCE TO EXTERNAL PRESSURES (*force*)	INSPIRATION FROM INTERNAL MOTIVATORS (*power*)
Impaired health	Improved health
Job loss	Job promotion
Being trapped: no choices	Growing: new choices
The need to repair damage	The chance to build self-esteem
Spousal/family threats	Spousal/family support
Weariness of saying I'm sorry	Keeping promises you made
Debts, financial ruin	Prosperity, financial gain
Playing defense	Playing offense
Avoiding what's worse	Gaining what's better

The factors in the left column drive you to take healthy action so that you can keep things from getting worse, while the goals in the right-hand column encourage you to make healthy choices so that you can gain what's better. In other words, external pressures drive you to take healthy action in order to *avoid* what's worse. Internal motivators encourage you to take healthy action in order to *gain* what's better. At its simplest, it's the old carrot and stick concept: poke a donkey with a stick and it will react, but dangle a carrot in front of the donkey's nose and it will move forward to eat it. I think it is clear which kind of motivation is stronger in the long run.

Fortunately, as I stated above, both sources of motivation can, and will, work together — if you allow them to. External forces will "push" you in a positive direction, while internal motivators will "pull" you in a positive direction. I think we would all agree, however, that being pulled is a more positive experience than being pushed! Would you rather obey a judge who is telling you what to do and informing you of the penalties for not doing it (force, avoidance), or would you rather choose to do what is best for you and others while enjoying the rewards for doing it (power, gains)?

I use the terms *force* and *power* to help clarify the source of energy behind each kind of motivation. Coined by David Hawkins in his book *Power vs. Force*, the terms designate the difference between coercive manipulation (force) versus one's free choice (power).[1] To illustrate, Mahatma Gandhi relied on power to gain independence, while the British military relied on force to squelch it — and look who won!

Ask yourself: Would I rather comply with penalties or be empowered with benefits?

Since both kinds of motivation have their merits, you don't have to make an either-or choice; you can make a both-and one.

External pressures can prompt sudden awareness and break-throughs. Internal motivators can provide ongoing strength and perseverance. When only external pressures are in effect, once the heat is off, you may revert quickly to old patterns. Although internal motivators are better in the long run, when only they are in effect, your intentions may be worthy but effective solutions may come slowly or seem too delayed. Together, they will serve you well. Consider baby birds. While sensing the pull to fly into the big world beyond the nest, they may need a nudge from mama or papa to push them on their way. In the beginning of any journey of growth, both "push" and "pull" can prove equally handy.

TAKE THE LEAP

Secret Keepers committed to authenticity need to grow up, to act maturely, and to accept responsibility for their lives — the task of adopting new beliefs and realigning their emotions. It is time for them to leave the nest as well. Like Peter Pan, the boy who chased his own shadow, Secret Keepers often don't want to grow up. Regardless of their age, many of them are housing an inward adolescent who is hollering, "Let's party, let's fool everybody, let's have fun now!"

But personality and character changes demand tough (yet nurturing) lifestyle choices — and sustained internal motivation. Tapping the powerful source of that motivation requires removing the barriers erected by one's secret-keeping history and ingrained attitudes. Basically, finding sustained motivation starts with taking an Indiana Jones leap of faith and landing in a place where you can start anew. Then the power of fellowship with people like you in support groups (anonymous support groups, church groups, and the like) will help open your mind to solutions that encompass the spiritual as well as the practical.

By surrendering and accepting help from others, your days of "I"-solating will taper off. No longer must you be alone in a parallel universe. Becoming part of a support group is one way that the "we" of recovery works (the first of the 12 steps reads, "*We* admitted we were powerless," not "*I* admitted"). Picture a lion waiting to pounce on a lone elk or antelope straying from the herd. Once you are associating with others and no longer isolated, you are safer. You aren't in as much danger of being "pounced on" by your secret-keeping urges. Because those in such groups have already made the same kinds of confessions that you will, judging or condemning is frowned on — everybody knows where you're coming from. They know all about the kind of insanity that secret keeping can cause. The details will be different, but the stories will be the same. You can let your inner defensive walls down and allow more of you to show.

TURNING TO SPIRITUALITY

Taking this kind of a leap is a very tall order indeed. If you think it's too much to handle alone, you're correct. That's because our human limitations are so much greater than we realize. That is why, as stated earlier, self-sufficiency is a hoax. And it's why steps 2 and 3 of AA exist: "Came to believe that a Power greater than ourselves could restore us to sanity." "Made a decision to turn our will and our lives over to the care of God *of our understanding*."

Here's where your willingness to partner with an invisible divine power comes in. Here is where doing it alone will no longer work for you. Our strength to recover successfully requires both our own power and a higher power ("a Power greater than ourselves," "God of our understanding"). The authors of *The Spirituality of Imperfection*, Ernest Kurtz and Katherine Ketcham, acknowledged this need: "We seek help for what we cannot face or accomplish alone; in seeking help, we accept and admit our own powerlessness. And in that acceptance and admission, in the acknowledgment that we are *not* in control, spirituality is born."² Rather than our imperfection being an obstacle to spirituality, it becomes the doorway to divine partnership — not a detour or a dead end, but the *doorway*.

For some former Secret Keepers, spirituality comes easily; for others, it's a daily struggle, a puzzling enigma, a stumbling block. For the individual who struggles with believing in "a Power greater than ourselves," or with the term *God*, partnering represents a major leap. This is true especially for those who were disappointed by organized religion as children. However, while it is easy to confuse spirituality with religion, they are not the same thing. Religion can be the portal to spirituality, but sadly, it often proves to be a dead end. The reasons for this can be debated endlessly. Reflecting briefly on all of humankind's wars, both ancient and current, reveals the devastation wrought by fanatics fighting in the name of *their* God. It's understandable why people are put off by the thought of religion.

But the truth is, God cannot be owned by any one group or individual.

I often address this issue with my clients, using the chart below to aid discussion:

SPIRITUALITY	RELIGION
Experience-based	Truth-based
Rooted in relationships	Rooted in doctrine
God is unnamed	God is named
Embraces diversity	Sometimes accepts diversity
Everyone welcome	Seekers and converts welcome
May unify	May divide

As you note the differences and similarities, consider that "[s]pirituality is a lot like health. We all have health; we may have good health or poor health, but it's something we can't avoid having. The same is true of spirituality: every human being is a spiritual being."3

Perhaps you are turned off by the terms *God* and *higher power* because you don't think of yourself as religious. Or perhaps you just can't believe in something that you can't see. But just because we can't see God, that is no reason to disbelieve. If I held up a pen and asked what would happen if I let it go, you would reply that it would drop to the floor. Why? Because of gravity. Just because gravity is invisible doesn't mean it doesn't exist.

For those struggling with this question, John MacDougall, former supervisor of Spiritual Care from Hazelden, offers this:

The suggested minimum standard for a higher power is:

1. It is not us.

2. It is greater than us.

3. It wants to help us.4

What a clear and concise way of describing the indescribable! My colleague and friend from Hazelden, John Driscoll, director of Recovery Services, draws the following analogy for those who question God's existence: "What is one thing that is so important to us that if we don't get it, we can't last five minutes without it? The answer is simple. Air. Air is what every one of us needs to survive. If something is choking us or we can't get air, we fight like crazy to get a breath. And if we don't get that breath in five minutes, chances are, we are dead or going to die."5

Driscoll goes on to say that although we didn't make the air ourselves, we rely on it to stay alive. We realize that whatever made it is greater than we are. In other words, we don't need to be religious to have a belief in a higher power: "We just need to believe that we can't live without help and that since we are alive, then something must be helping us.... Truthfully, in the beginning of our recovery, this is all we need to believe."[6] Carrying this idea further, he claims that we don't have to understand how or why there is a higher power. Because air is always there, we take it for granted. It's only when it's not there that we become aware of it. Acutely. Most of us, most of the time, rarely think of God. We don't become aware of God until we are in crisis. But God, like air, has been there the whole time.

John Driscoll also makes clear that God doesn't love us more when we believe in God or are not paying attention to God. God's love is constant. It never changes. God, just like air, doesn't play favorites. God is a loving, caring power that is always there for us. Connecting to divine power helps us do what we cannot do for ourselves. But first, we have to believe that God exists and wants to partner with us.

Perhaps the following list will help you to clarify your thoughts on the subject.

A Recovering Secret Keeper's Thoughts

- A divine power is willing, and waiting, to help me.
- I have a serious problem due to keeping secrets and hiding harmful habits.
- Because the problem is so serious, the best decision is to quit.
- Quitting will mean making some major changes in my life.
- Making a commitment to personal authenticity, recovery, change, and growth benefits those dear to me and myself.
- Successful recovery means managing the obstacles to my recovery in order to prevent relapse. Obstacles are both external and internal.
- God is always present and available.

MOTIVATING YOURSELF TO CHANGE

The founder of Alcoholics Anonymous, Bill Wilson, also struggled with the question of God. He admitted freely to his skepticism and to being one of the worst drunks ever known. Prior to starting AA, he wrote: "With ministers, and the world's religions, I parted right there. When they talked of a God personal to me, who was love, superhuman strength and direction, I became irritated and my mind snapped shut against such a theory."7

Then one day a former drinker came to visit Bill. "My friend sat before me, and he made the point blank declaration that God had done for him what he could not do for himself."8 As they talked, Bill felt a profound change occur within him: "I stood in the sunlight at last. *It was only a matter of being willing to believe in a Power greater than myself. Nothing more was required of me to make my beginning.* I saw that growth could start from that point. Thus was I convinced that God is concerned with us humans when we want Him enough. At long last I saw, I felt, I believed. A new world came into view.... I have not had a drink since."9

By following these tips, you can tap into the powerful motivations available to you — internal, external, and *eternal*:

1. Understand the dual roles of motivation, both external and internal. Then allow eternal power to help.

2. Admit that you can't succeed alone.

3. Accept God or a higher power as your partner.

4. Join others like yourself in recovery; it's more rewarding to cooperate than to white-knuckle it alone.

5. Realize you are heavily invested in secret keeping and that your worst fear is being exposed. Be ready for resistance!

6. Consider your only options: continuing on your current path and risking graver consequences to yourself and

others, or changing to a way of life that is honest, open, and transparent (H.O.T.).

One Secret Keeper who became motivated to improve her life by partnering with God is Bonnie, whom we first met in chapter 6. To move on, she had to uncover emotional injuries she sustained in her childhood that had damaged her personality.

Bonnie's Story of Healing

When we last saw Bonnie, she was attending an all-girls' college and struggling with alcohol, an unwanted pregnancy, binge eating, and perfectionism. Let's hear her story in her words. But first I want to make clear that while Bonnie turned to Jesus, the God you choose to accept may not be a Christian God, and that's perfectly okay.

> In college it dawned on me that my upbringing didn't have anything to do with God's love. I remember being so angry about that. I'd heard you could go to hell for your sins, but nobody had ever said, "God cares for you and is willing to walk next to you in everything you do." It didn't matter how good I was in everybody's eyes or whether I tried hard; he just wanted to love me.
>
> After college, I got into the Bible for myself. A co-worker helped me understand how to walk closer with God. I asked Jesus into my heart and immediately felt at peace. The world didn't seem as scary anymore. Three months later the desire for alcohol just disappeared, and then I learned about food the way the Lord sees it: as something to sustain you but not something that runs your life. I opened myself to the wonder of the world. He became my guide in life. I felt his love, and it took my pain away.
>
> I got married two years later, and we had our first child.

By then we were part of a community that met in a storefront
in the inner city, and the pastor was incredible. She really
helped me deal with shame. I read books and heard people's
stories and eventually joined a powerful group of six women
who met once a month. Thanks to the security I felt with
those women, I stood up for myself and expressed my opinions more often. I took charge of my emotions and actions.
Gradually I let them in on some of my secrets, especially the
childhood sexual abuse, and felt waves of healing. Attending
this group inspired me. It was the exact thing I needed — by
associating with others, I no longer withdrew as much or isolated like I always had.

These changes served Bonnie well in the months after her
parents' difficult divorce, when her mother fell apart and her dad
hit bottom from alcoholism. Her brothers and sisters didn't offer
much help, so she stepped in. "I really think that without the
group to turn to, without God to pray to, and without a couple
of work friends who listened to me, I would have come apart at
the seams." Bonnie told her mother about some of her childhood
secrets, and doing so brought them closer together. Months later
she disclosed to her dad some of her painful memories growing
up. Since then her internal motivation to "say [her] truth" has
remained strong. Lately Bonnie has started her own group for
women needing inspiration and a listening ear.

Bonnie created a recovery program for herself tailored to
her needs. Although she did not attend 12-step support groups or
seek professional counseling, she did find effective ways to surrender, to confess, and to find community. She learned how to
reject secret-keeping habits around food and drinking, as well as
how to deal assertively with the emotional discord and relational
and spiritual conflicts in her family of origin. She adopted a *voluntary altered perspective.* "Somehow, I have the strength today

to live more in the open," she says. "I've never had a drink or stuffed my face with food or been deeply depressed since giving to God what used to divide me, what used to secretly pull me down."

Identifying internal motivators means saying yes to what you know is right and is in your best interests, to what you value. And it means saying no to what you know is wrong and destructive, to what is harmful to your best interests.

Instead of wasting time and money gambling on long-shot lottery games or casino schemes, change strategies and invest your money in bona fide securities with trustworthy, legitimate returns. Instead of sneaking off to purge yourself of another meal, stand up to your eating disorder and seek help and healthier ways to live for you and your family.

When a once-active Secret Keeper seeks authenticity, thinks of others, and lives a H.O.T. life, he begins to lead a life characterized by growth, empowerment, and lasting satisfaction. Positive behavior changes beget positive personality changes. Sustained internal motivation results in ever more authentic character change.

The following poem, by Portia Nelson, shows the power of internal motivation and one's voluntary altered perspective. Note how the narrator made the "leap" to a new choice.

AUTOBIOGRAPHY IN FIVE SHORT CHAPTERS

I

I walk down the street
There is a deep hole in the sidewalk
I fall in
I am lost...I am helpless
It isn't my fault
It takes forever to find a way out.

2
I walk down the same street
There is a deep hole in the sidewalk
I pretend I don't see it
I fall in again
I can't believe I am in the same place
But it isn't my fault
It still takes a long time to get out.

3
I walk down the same street
There is a deep hole in the sidewalk
I see it there
I still fall in ... it's a habit
My eyes are open
It is my fault
I get out immediately.

4
I walk down the same street
There is a deep hole in the sidewalk
I walk around it.

5
I walk down another street.[10]

You too can walk down a new street. Don't wait for the worst to happen. Decide to use external, internal, and *eternal* motivations. Rather than allowing your duality to get the upper hand, take control of it, accept and understand it, and use it to honor

your true values. Harness its power. Play offense. Your willingness to climb out of the dark cellar of the Hidden area and into
the sunny Open area is the measure of your motivation. Join
forces with God. Aim to gain what's better, not to avoid what's
worse.

Chapter 11

PREPARING TO LIVE
AUTHENTICALLY

A slave is one who waits for someone else to come and free him.

—— EZRA POUND

*A*SSUMING THAT YOU HAVE surrendered your secret-keeping habits and learned the vital importance of finding and staying motivated, the next step is to examine your history. Your challenge will be to explore your secret-keeping behavior and to understand what motivated it. That will lead you to the third stage in the Blueprint for Gaining Freedom: *Preparing to state the true facts.* During this stage you will get ready to communicate to people what you've done and why. Another way of thinking about this phase of the process is "preparing to come clean."

The essence of coming clean is *telling others what they need to know that will show them the real you.* If you want to improve your relationships with others, it takes honesty and openness. It also takes motivation, timing, and plain old guts to face tough and uncertain outcomes. No one can predict how another person will react to difficult news, and this uncertainty may lessen your eagerness to prepare. Another description of this preparation phase comes from the 12 steps: "Made a searching and fearless moral inventory of ourselves" (step 4).

But before you can reveal the truth to others, you must first reveal to *yourself* the information that will show *you* the real you, a key topic of this chapter. As you begin viewing the past with new eyes, remember that you are now acting in *others' best interests* as well as *your own* — and that this combination holds the promise of a stronger, healthier life for everyone. Looking back on your life while planning your strategy to disclose means that you have arrived at stage three and are considering how to state the true facts.

The goal of this self-examination is twofold: (1) to increase the benefits to those who will hear your faithfully prepared story and (2) to increase the benefits to you before you say a word to anyone else. In the process of coming clean with yourself, you will find that you are practicing new ways of seeing — perceiving old events in new ways. The days of seeing things through the lens of early trauma, victimization, developmental deficits, or drama and crisis are behind you.

Coming clean consists of four substages. The first two, which will be covered in this chapter, are solitary activities (A and B below), and the last two, to be covered in the next chapter, are dialogue activities (C and D below). All four substages are essential.

COMING CLEAN

S

O   A. *With yourself*: Make a fearless and searching moral inventory of yourself *by* yourself.

L   B. *With God*: Express to your higher power the true facts of your secret-keeping and addictive behav-

O   ior; ask for divine help and the guidance you need.

D
U
O

C. *With strangers*: Express to counselors, clergy, healthcare professionals, and/or support group members what you have done and the conse-quences

D. *With loved ones*: Express to your spouse, parents, siblings, older children, and/or relatives (those you care about and share the future with) what you have done (but are no longer doing) and the consequences.

Beginning at A, here are some tips and pointers on ways to write out your secret-keeping history. "Write out?" you ask. Yes, write out. I've heard this reaction innumerable times in my counseling practice; writing seems to strike terror in most people's hearts. Sorry, but it's essential to put pen to paper when taking this kind of self-inventory. I have observed scores of clients struggling with this assessment step because it takes some discipline. Think of it as another opportunity to mature and take responsibility.

But relax, I am not asking you to write a book-length autobiography.[1] Instead, you will need to write down key phrases and make lists describing the turning points and main events of your life, including your feelings about them and any self-talk associated with them. Like a map to your destination — which is lasting satisfaction in recovery that exceeds the happiness you once sought by secret keeping — it needs to be visible on paper.

Because feelings color our memories so powerfully, let's start with them. Begin right now by using the sheet below, which I've included to help you name key feelings. Follow these simple directions:

EXERCISE

1. Check off the feelings you associate with your secret keeping, choosing approximately thirty to forty. Don't stop to ponder each one; just check off any that strike you as relevant at the moment. Be sure to place yourself in the frame of mind when your secret keeping felt the most intense, dire, pleasurable, strongest, and so on.

FEELINGS			
abandoned	cheated	ecstatic	glad
accepted	comfortable	elated	graceful
adventurous	compelled	embarrassed	grateful
afraid	confident	empathetic	great
alone	constructive	empty	guilty
ambivalent	contented	encouraged	gutsy
angry	cowardly	energized	happy
anxious	daring	envious	hateful
ashamed	dazed	exasperated	helpless
awed	defeated	excited	hesitant
awkward	defensive	exhilarated	high
bitter	defiant	exploited	hopeful
bold	desiring	fearful	hopeless
bored	despairing	foolish	hostile
calm	disappointed	forlorn	hurt
captivated	discouraged	free	impatient
caring	disturbed	frustrated	indifferent
cautious	eager	full	inferior

FEELINGS (CONTINU			
irrational	overwhelmed	remorseful	
irritated	pained	resentful	
jealous	patient	resigned	
joyful	peaceful	satisfied	un⟨ ⟩le
kind	playful	secure	understood
listless	pleased	selfish	uneasy
lonely	possessive	self-pitying	unhappy
loved	proud	shy	unloved
lovely	pushed	sick	unsure
miserable	put out	stupid	unworthy
natural	rational	successful	used
nervous	refreshed	suffering	vengeful
numb	regretful	superior	weary
obligated	rejected	surprised	wonderful
overcome	relieved	suspicious	worried
overjoyed	reluctant	sympathetic	worthy

2. Next, mark with a dot or other symbol the feelings you associate with your *recovery* from secret keeping (what you expect to feel one to five years from now). You can mark the same word twice. If you felt eager when secret keeping, for example, and you also feel eager to recover from secret keeping, it's okay to mark the word both times. *Place yourself in the frame of mind in which you would feel the potential rewards and benefits of recovery as well as the feelings that you would have about them.*

Next, select the top-ten feelings from the first round (checks) and list them, then select the top-ten from the second round (dots), with each list including the strongest, deepest, longest-held feelings. Your lists might look something like this:

FIRST ROUND	SECOND ROUND
adventurous	awkward
anxious	anxious
disturbed	constructive
eager	eager
exasperated	encouraged
hopeless	hopeful
irrational	obligated
playful	pleased
resigned	relieved
suffering	worthy

4. Now determine the predominant theme of each list, based on whether the feelings you've chosen are mainly positive (POS) or negative (NEG). In the sample lists above, seven are negative from the first round, and seven are positive from the second round.

In this manner, you can see for yourself, based on your own choices, what feeling states you have experienced (NEG) or what ones you would like to experience (POS). Look at the remaining words from each round and verify these themes, then choose which ones you prefer to live with long-term: the feelings of round one or those of round two. Think about it: without anyone telling you *what* to decide, you have just informed yourself about your own feelings and your "gut sense" about how to better direct yourself. (*Note*: If your top-ten's are clearly reversed, with round one being POS for secret keeping and round two being NEG for recovery, then you're satisfied with the way things are and are unlikely to change. But even if that is the case, the fact that you have read this far suggests that you are at least weighing the option of changing.)

PUTTING YOUR LIFE ON PAPER

Now let's add to your personal assessment by taking a careful look at the important events in your life. This vital step consists of jotting down major emotional turning points, starting from early childhood. Use the Four Squares of Life diagram from chapter 9 for this step. Turn to page 131 and reread the information about the Emotional square (2). Think of events, joyous or traumatic, from early childhood to adolescence, then list them. Take all the time you need. Identify the hard lessons and difficulties you experienced growing up. What memorable triumph or failure occurred in some important area of your development? Did you suffer neglect and outright abuse? Did life seem to turn unfair? Describe the damage your tender emotions experienced. Name the developmental deficits you've lived with all these years. Then ask yourself:

What followed from each?

Did it shape my thinking or behavior?

Did I gain confidence or lose it?

Did it help clarify my identity or make me doubt it?

Go to the next indelible event you remember on your list and ask the same questions, then do this with the next and then the next.

Let's use my own narrative as an example. There was the time when I stole cookies as a five-year-old and first experienced the triple whammy of *excitement*, *pleasure*, and *delight*. When I did my own inventory I listed several key moments in my happy childhood until age ten, but for purposes of this book let's skip to the night when I was eleven and my mother announced that our family was moving from our beloved home to what became (in my experience) the House of Horrors. That announcement was the turning point in my life when everything changed for the worse and numerous traumatic trials followed, such as the grueling work projects I was forced to do, especially the one on my fourteenth birthday. I focused on how those particular trials shaped my secret-keeping behavior like playing Getting Lost and running naked in the woods. I then experienced the first of many splintered mind-sets that I fell prey to, *feeling one way while acting another*. Thereafter, I also recorded all the other incidents that you have read about in earlier chapters and that I purposely selected to show you how I fell into the trap of secret keeping and subsequent addictions.

One way to jog your memory is to follow the progression outlined in the Developmental Chart from chapter 6. Flip back to page 91 to refresh your memory. Try to view the events and influences in your growing-up years in terms of these stages and the tasks the chart describes. Recall that for every positive outcome like Trust or Autonomy there can be an *opposite negative outcome*:

HUMAN DEVELOPMENTAL CHART	
STAGE	TASK
Infancy, 0–1	Trust vs. *Mistrust*
Toddlerhood, 1–3	Autonomy vs. *Doubt*
Early childhood, 3–6	Initiative vs. *Guilt*
Middle childhood, 6–12	Competence vs. *Inferiority*
Adolescence, 12–18	Identity vs. *Role confusion*
Young adulthood, 18–40	Intimacy vs. *Isolation*
Middle adulthood, 40–65	Legacy/care for others vs. *Stagnation*
Late adulthood, 65 on	Integrity/fulfillment vs. *Despair*

The more you view your life history developmentally, and the more you understand the patterns, both positive and negative, the more motivated you'll be to face the challenges ahead of coming clean and staying on the path of recovery. For example, when you were six to twelve years old, in what ways did you learn "inferiority"? Were you a poor student? Not picked for an athletic team? Not popular with the opposite sex? Abused at home? Such experiences would have provoked painful emotions at the time, and these would have spawned vivid, often virulent, self-talk.

Now, connect these damaged feelings (review your choices on the Feelings Chart) to the specific distorted thoughts you can identify (review the description of squares one, two, three, and four on the Four Squares of Life diagram).

Let's see how this process plays out. Say you played a clarinet solo when you were nine. You got stage fright, and the large audience of students and parents snickered and booed you off the stage. Perhaps you sobbed and chided yourself, saying, "I'm a failure! I hate music! I'll never go on stage again!" More than likely you've been repeating those thoughts all these years until they have become beliefs. And what seemed like wise protective measures back then today seem like harsh constraints that have limited your opportunities. Basically, you sense your life has suffered for it. You've held yourself back too often. If so, that's vital information to jot down in your inventory.

Of course, you could have had quite the opposite experience with your clarinet solo. Then the question your memory might prompt would be, In what ways did I learn "competence"? In what ways has my life benefited from such a richly rewarding experience? Yet it's the negative experiences of our lives that shape the darker, more hidden, less noble alchemy we are dealing with here. In chapter 13 we will deal more with this topic, but for now take a fresh sheet of paper and make headings like those below, using the entire page:

EXERCISE
My Early Childhood: Birth to Age Six

Experiences (positive and negative) _____

_____

_____

_____

My *self-talk* resulting from above experiences _____

_____

_____

_____

My *beliefs* (or *worldview*) resulting from above self-talk _____

_____

_____

_____

My *behavior(s)* resulting from above beliefs _____

_____

_____

_____

If you'd like to use a separate page for each developmental stage, the next sheet would be "My Middle Childhood: Ages Six to Twelve," and so on. This is what my sheet looked like:

EXERCISE

My Middle Childhood: Ages Six to Twelve

Experiences (positive and negative):

· *Move from first home to new house in Chippewa Hills.*

· *My fourteenth birthday ruined because Mom wanted patio stones hauled.*

· *Watching Dad heading toward premature death.*

My *self-talk* resulting from above experiences:

· *"Do we have to?" "I feel like Mom's slave." "How can I escape?"*

· *"This is outrageous! Unfair!" "My friends don't matter." "I feel like Mom's slave again." "How can I escape?"*

· *"I feel powerless to stop it." "Dad has never talked to me; we've never had a conversation." "I love him. Does he love me?" "I hate my life!"*

My *beliefs* (or *worldview*) resulting from above self-talk:

· *Something good for one person (Mom) is bad for every-body else. I only matter when the projects Mom requires me to do are completed.*

· *Life is unfair. I am only a puppet, not a person. My parents abuse me; it hurts.*

· *Life sucks. I dread seeing Dad die and can't stop his dying. If God exists, does He care?*

My *behavior(s)* resulting from above beliefs:

· *Hiding angry feelings, avoiding Mom, inventing game of Getting Lost.*

· *Shunning Mom, despising Dad. Thinking of ways to kill Mom. Running naked in the woods.*

· *Blaming Mom, hating her even more. Trying harder (but failing). Shaking my fist at God in protest.*

Notice that the three items listed under "experiences (positive and negative)" are all negative. This is extremely common. While you have the option to write down positive events, ask yourself: "Which do I remember most? Which define me most? The difficult and troubling turning points in life? Or the positive and triumphant turning points?" Clearly, both can and will define us. But for the purposes of this exercise, I believe we learn more from studying adversity than we do from recalling our successes. One reason may be that in order to protect us from adverse similar experiences in the future, our brain burns into our memory the protective preventive measures we used during such powerful events that either worked or didn't. The memory of these events reinforces the attitudes and behaviors that will help us survive in the future. With your own data and lists, notice how the events you've chosen translate into the categories above and become useful for understanding decades later when recovery becomes possible.

YOUR LIFE HISTORY "BUILDING BLOCKS"

As you record key events and what followed, realize that the self-talk messages you learned can be unlearned or reprogrammed. In the same way, the predominant character traits you developed (strengths such as patience and loyalty or defects such as impatience and stubbornness); the worldviews you've come to hold; the harms your secret keeping has caused you and others; and the hard feelings, resentments, and other emotional or mental distortions that shaped your beliefs and moods: all stemmed from your history of developmental deficits or assets.

Refer back once more to the Four Squares of Life diagram on page 133. Reviewing the squares will help you to define the "skeleton" on which you can hang the prominent elements of your life history that spell out who you really are. To the bones of this skeleton, you will add the "muscle and tissue" of your life's specific events and turning points.

Be patient. This kind of inventory takes days and sometimes weeks to do fully. Rushing it or skipping parts of it is doing a disservice to yourself. The time and attention you give it now will pay off richly. What you learn about yourself will serve to fuel your recovery.

Earnie Larsen, longtime master trainer and veteran of recovery techniques, says: "All of us have been affected by our past, but none of us has to be a victim of our past. We need to spend the time necessary to 'discover' before we 'recover.' The better your discovery, the better your recovery. To begin with, we need to understand the nature of Habit and how unhealthy habits cause destructive patterns."[2] A big part of a "better discovery" is making careful notes about your life history, which at this early juncture may trigger the same overwhelming sense of nausea you feel when you enter a messy house.

Many of us are familiar with that feeling we get when walking into a dirty house — especially our own. We may have a good job and great life, but when we go home to a big mess, suddenly all those good things don't seem so good. Why? "Because we are back in the same mess we left earlier that morning," writes John Driscoll.[3] "When our insides are all messed up even a good day doesn't feel good. We carry the nagging thought, 'If they only knew.' " Before we can begin to clean our house (by preparing to state the true facts), we must first admit that it is messy. Also, we must want to change it. Once we take responsibility for cleaning it, we need to recognize that we do not have to clean it alone. We can get help from a higher power, a subject we examined in the previous chapter and one we will turn to again shortly.

We've been using the term *personal inventory* a lot. In business taking an inventory means counting and evaluating the items of merchandise on the shelves. This is referred to as "a fact-finding and a fact-facing process."[4] One reason for taking an inventory "is to disclose damaged or unsalable goods, to get rid of them promptly and without regret," Driscoll states. "Therefore, this is where we go into the house and see what is trash and what is not, what clothes are dirty and what clothes are clean, what dishes are dirty and which ones are clean, what is broken and what is useable and so on until an inventory is made."[5]

Ask yourself, What cover-ups, alibis, lies, and deceptions

have I used? How have I harmed myself and others? Basically, identify those things in your house that need to be changed, replaced, cleaned, fixed, and thrown out. Using your journal or worksheets, write down what in your past needs to be:

- Changed _____
- Replaced _____
- Cleaned _____
- Fixed _____
- Thrown out _____

What's God Got to Do with It?

Above I made clear that you do not have to clean your house alone. With that in mind, let's move on to the next solo substage of coming clean: *with God.* Coming clean with God means expressing to your higher power the truth of your secret-keeping actions and clandestine motives. At first asking for divine help and guidance can feel unfamiliar and awkward. Remember that a higher power is "not us, is greater than us, and wants to help us." Think of this power as a loving, generous, forgiving Presence that is with you, and *for* you, at all times. It's a Presence dedicated to your growth, your health, your relationships, and your recovery.

Let your higher power gently lead you into remembering all essential events, emotions, and self-talk that have stuck with you throughout the years. Claim this promise, "God is doing for us what we could not do for ourselves."[6] It's really about pausing long enough and slowing down your busy thoughts to say to yourself, "I'm worth taking a few hours, even a few days or weeks if necessary, to make sense of my life. If I don't do this now, I'll just keep making poor choices and living in a messy house and staying trapped in low-level thinking, addictions, and more secret keeping."

In my own life, this process of partnering with a higher power led me to attend weekly Emotions Anonymous meetings in my forties (while I was still actively secret keeping). I became friends with other normal high-functioning folks on the "outside" who admitted to painful and disabling extremes of emotions on the "inside": corporate managers, housewives, insurance adjusters, single working moms, and construction workers. Some were as volatile and overreactive as I was, some were the opposite, disengaged and under-reactive — yet each of us sought aid and solace from the fellowship of others who admitted to sharing our afflictions.

EA sayings like "I will not compare myself with others" and "My happiness does not depend on what happens outside me; it results from being at peace with myself" reflected *my* inner landscape. When I told EA co-members about the stresses in my career and marriage, more precisely about the stresses in my psyche from long-term secret keeping, which I hinted about disclosing at the time, I heard myself describing many unmet expectations. My companions helped me understand that I was describing *unrealistic* unmet expectations. What I judged as reasonable they judged as unrealistic, exaggerated, and inflated.

I sensed that God was talking through them, so I listened. I felt the gentle nudge to trust these folks, which meant one day telling them about my secret keeping.

It was scary, damn scary. But telling them about my hateful, murderous emotions toward Mom aroused not disgust in them but empathy. Confessing to running naked in the woods provoked not their aversion but their compassion. I sensed, through them, that God was doing for me what I could not do for myself. With the divine guidance of a higher power, I expressed to these H.O.T. people some truths of my secret-keeping history and the emotional damage incurred from it. They neither condemned nor ostracized me. Instead, they helped prepare me to clean house (to come clean) and to speak authentically. At last, finding a new voice, I was able to confess to God and show somebody the real me. And I'd survived!

As the wise old philosopher Socrates said, "The unexamined life is not worth living. 'Know thyself' is the key to happiness." So take the plunge and tell your higher power all that you've learned about your life. Say it plainly and simply. Experience the feelings of release and relief. Unburden yourself of those shameful and discreditable actions that you have intentionally concealed, and *feel the freedom of it*. Great risks bring great gains!

Now let's catch up with Mitch and see how taking an inventory and preparing to come clean helped him.

MITCH'S RECOVERY FROM CREDIT CARD DEBT

When we last observed Mitch in chapter 5, he was jumping from the bridge into the river, landing feetfirst in the dark water. To his shock and surprise, he floated to the top. He tried many things to drown himself, and each failed. Amid noisy sirens from the squad cars on the bridge and a sheriff's boat on the water, he was lifted, gasping, to safety. Sped to a hospital, Mitch came to about midnight and learned that a passerby had seen the suicide note in his car and had called 911. He also learned that Donna and their daughter had been notified. His son, away at college, heard the news by phone. When Donna arrived at his bedside, he saw from her shocked expression her crushing awareness of something gone terribly wrong.

Mitch says, "About all I remember telling her was: 'I've done some bad things at work. I've had some major financial problems,' "

The hospital put Mitch on a seventy-two-hour psychiatric watch. He hired a lawyer, and Mitch kept his mouth shut, as the lawyer advised, even with family members. For the moment only the attorney knew his secrets. As a condition of his discharge, the hospital psychiatrist referred him to a two-week outpatient program. This exposed him to other people with debt problems. "Attending the group really opened my eyes. At first I thought it was dorky, but then I realized I wasn't the only one who schemed like I did, but here were others just like me in major denial and debt." Humbled, and in some ways comforted, Mitch continued going and, instead of returning home, he moved into a friend's spare bedroom. This further befuddled Donna and the kids. She demanded details, and Mitch still provided only sketchy information.

Twice a week, as another part of his discharge agreement, Mitch also had to visit a psychotherapist one-on-one. At the therapist's urging, Mitch wrote out in his quiet hours the basic facts of his life history and his fall from grace. In this way he discovered times when he'd made choices based on unexamined assumptions — for example, the illusions that his increasing credit limit would never end, that he somehow would never have to pay back in full the thousands he'd borrowed, and that his kids needed to attend expensive private schools. Based on his upbringing in a home where "nice things" mattered and his mother belittled his father for failing to meet her "country club expectations," Mitch says, "I developed a fear of not being well thought of as a husband and a provider."

While waiting to go on trial, Mitch began sweeping floors as a church custodian for minimum wage. He also volunteered his spare hours at a homeless shelter. "These jobs were the first really honest work I'd done in years." According to the priest at the church, Mitch was "experiencing God's forgiveness and resurrection power" — and Mitch came to believe that too.

When Donna confronted him about her deteriorated trust in him and her doubts about his "real" identity, Mitch finally doled out the full details to her, and she went numb with shock and disbelief. Facing bankruptcy, forfeiture of their house, criminal charges by the FBI and IRS, jail time, fines, and restitution, he simply could not sugarcoat the consequences. He also could not assuage her hurt feelings about being fooled. Once she realized the full extent of his secret embezzling, Donna wasted little time in applying for a divorce. Later his kids told him, "You hid it so well. We never knew who you really were. It's scary to think that all that time you were like two people."

In Mitch's case, getting arrested prevented him from adequately preparing ahead, forcing him to give Donna vague generalities. Shamed and disillusioned, as well as captive to an adversarial legal system that advised him to remain tight-lipped with everybody, Mitch endured a long period of uncertainty that descended on him like a black storm cloud. This kept his loved ones in the dark and hobbled their capacity to actively support him.

Intuitively Mitch followed two of the four substages of coming clean. First, assisted by group therapy and one-on-one counseling, he faced his past behavior patterns and motivations *by himself*, listing them and pondering their meaning. In this process he broke through many illusions and saw things more realistically, although the process was of little benefit to his wife and family. Second, he talked to *strangers* and learned to confide his secrets in therapy groups and to treatment professionals.

Regarding substage B, *with God*, Mitch slowly opened up in

tiny ways to a higher power over the months and a new spiritual bond began to strengthen him. "Slowly I felt the reality of God's grace and redemptive power happening for me," he says. Still in recovery support groups today, Mitch says his connection with a higher power has helped him deal with the divorce, a court trial, and paying off debts as part of his restitution.

—∿∿—

Given that you are taking steps to "fess up" to yourself and to your higher power, what is your plan for telling others? What will show them the real you? Are you taking the risk of getting caught unprepared like Mitch? What self-talk messages can you identify and unlearn? The more you can view your life history developmentally and understand the patterns, the more motivated you'll be to face the changes ahead and to stay on the path of recovery.

Think of the harm your secret keeping has caused yourself and others. Now consider the hard feelings, resentments, and emotional or mental damage you can still prevent if you prepare a plan now to disclose wisely — sooner rather than later. Instead of getting caught red-handed, admit to yourself the true facts of your double life *and* avoid having to do more damage control.

Why deal with more hostility, conflict, and hurt feelings? Tell the people close to you *what they need to know that will show them the real you.*

The next chapter will help you do just that.

Chapter 12

COMMITTING TO COMING CLEAN

Confession is good for the soul.

—— ST. AUGUSTINE

*I*N THIS CHAPTER we learn to verbalize *"to another human being* the exact nature of our wrongs" (from step 5 of the 12 steps). If you feel nervous about taking this step, that's normal. What will happen once you open up is anybody's guess, and your feelings of vulnerability may skyrocket. But planning your strategy ahead of time is the single best way to calm these qualms.

Does the idea of being vulnerable with another person seem intolerable? Does the thought of revealing your secrets to someone make you want to run screaming? If so, try writing in a journal. The surest way to build your self-confidence is through systematic self-discovery.

Self-disclosing your thoughts and feelings *to yourself on paper* can do wonders, as we saw with Mitch in the last chapter. When I was taking college English courses, I often heard the phrase, "Writing is catharsis." The word *catharsis* comes from the Greek word for "purging," for cleaning out and making pure

— for coming clean. It's the relief of emotional tension we all feel when we watch a good play or movie or listen to a favorite song. For Secret Keepers who hope to disclose their secrets, the thing to remember is: *Catharsis happens naturally whenever you write down your feelings, either as you're feeling them, or later during quiet moments of reflection.*

"The release of pent-up feelings, or catharsis, discharge(s) psychic tension in the same way that removing the lid from a pot of boiling water slows the boiling," states psychologist James Pennebaker.[1] In his decades of studies and experiments at the University of Texas, Pennebaker has focused on the health benefits of self-expression compared to "active inhibition": "Actively holding back or inhibiting our thoughts and feelings can be hard work. Over time, the work of inhibition gradually undermines the body's defenses. Like other stressors, inhibition can affect immune function, the action of the heart and vascular systems, and even the biochemical workings of the brain."[2]

Secret Keepers take note!

Coming clean by disclosing yourself to others is serious business. It conjures up all sorts of contradictory feelings. In his "journey to find some answers concerning the nature of secrets," Pennebaker ascertained that "people who wrote about their deepest thoughts and feelings evidenced an impressive drop in illness visits to the doctor — a 50 percent drop in the monthly visitation rate." His volunteers reported "improved moods, more positive outlook, and greater physical health."[3] Adding to these findings, research psychologist Anita Kelly cited results from her studies of secrecy that revealing secrets offers several health benefits because "the revealer gains new insights into the trauma and no longer has to expend cognitive and emotional resources actively hiding the trauma."[4]

Insights flow from telling others about our secret keeping.

Bear this in mind: coming clean requires your *disclosing to others your deceptions and hidden habits — the facts of your secret-keeping double life.* Now that you have taken a thorough inventory and prepared *what* to disclose to others in the last chapter (substages A and B), it's time to strategize *how* to disclose to others. You have now reached the next stage in the Blueprint for Gaining Freedom: *Disclosing* secrets (true facts) to somebody.

Familiarize yourself once more with the C and D substages of coming clean:

C. *With strangers*: Express to counselors, clergy, healthcare professionals, and/or support group members what you have done and the consequences.

D. *With loved ones*: Express to your spouse, parents, siblings, older children, and/or relatives (those you care about and share the future with) what you have done (but are no longer doing) and the consequences.

How to Do It

Now that the *content* of what others need to hear from you is clear ("what you have done"), next you need to determine the *context* of coming clean — *who*, *when*, *where*, and *how much* to tell. When you do this part well, with the attitude of bringing about the most positive results and incurring the least damage, you will feel great! That's true power. This is your chance to move from that old secretive, deceptive self to a new honest, open, and transparent self.

If the alarm bells are still going off, remind yourself that what you are doing is "Opening" up the Hidden area from the Johari Window and letting out those stale secrets and tattered cover-ups — and letting in fresh air and nourishing sunshine. You are on the brink of leaping into the H.O.T. life. As you face the decisions around *who*, *when*, *where*, and *how much* to tell, you will no doubt ask yourself:

Will I be punished for my honesty?

Will the person I'm telling react in anger, despair, and shock?

How much is enough to say, and how much is too much?

Should I write a letter, make a phone call, or speak in person?

Where should I do the telling? In a restaurant, at home, with or without the kids, or in a counselor's office?

Take time to weigh these options carefully. Generally there's less at stake whenever you tell sensitive, stigmatizing information to a doctor, a lawyer, some other professional, or an outright stranger. Have you ever told your life story, or heard someone else's, while sitting next to a stranger on a plane or train? It's easier than spilling everything to your mom, dad, spouse, sibling, son, or daughter. And, this being so often the case, I strongly suggest that you open up to professionals or other "safe" individuals first before telling family members or anyone dear to you.

Let's take one of your options, to "spill all" (your personal life history inventory) in a comfortable, confidential setting with a savvy professional. Counselors, therapists, 12-step sponsors, and some clergy are trained to remain nonjudgmental and supportive. No matter what you say, or how long it takes, the person listening agrees to act as your guide and sounding board based on the understanding that you're taking big risks in speaking the truth. He or she understands how this process will support you in the personality and character changes that you desire to bring about. Having heard the content of your disclosure, that person can then help you strategize decisions about the *who, when, where,* and *how much* to tell to individuals closest to you who need to hear the truth.

In their helpful book *Disclosing Secrets,* Deborah Corley and Jennifer Schneider address these issues with seasoned advice: "It is safe to say that all disclosures are painful," they state.[5] And they conclude that couples who experience disclosure have a better chance of saving their relationship than those who do not. Both individuals feel relief, and partners often feel validated that their suspicions were correct or that they "weren't crazy." Reduction of anxiety and stress also frequently occur, allowing for the couple to begin healing. "Most couples (over 90 percent in our study) report that they are glad the disclosure happened."[6]

Barry Farber of Columbia University in New York adds his perspective: "The disclosure process initially generates shame and anticipatory anxiety but ultimately engenders feelings of safety, pride, and authenticity."[7] Farber's studies show that disclosing produces a sense of relief from physical as well as emotional tension. In other words, despite the risks we take and the vulnerability that comes along with revealing our deepest selves, the long-term payoffs are well worth it.

It should be clear by now that disclosure is a good thing. However, there are some definite guidelines to follow in terms of how *not* to do it. From the experience gained in their counseling practice, Corley and Schneider suggest some ways not to disclose, especially for couples. Here is one such account:

> John saw what seemed the perfect opportunity [to disclose] — a weekend workshop for couples recovering from addiction and co-addiction. He signed himself and Jody up, telling her it was a marriage enrichment program. During the two-hour drive to the retreat center, John told his wife about the hundreds of lies he had been telling her, the hours he

had spent at the race track, drinking and gambling, the hours spent on the computer at night when she thought he was asleep, the online risks he had taken, as well as about the young woman he met at the dog track who had offered him a blow-job for $20 after he had won.

When the couple arrived at the retreat center, Jody was in a state of shock. The two facilitators found themselves unexpectedly faced with a woman in crisis, in need of immediate one-on-one attention. Leaving the first group session to his associate, one of the facilitators ended up spending the entire evening counseling and supporting Jody. John had good intentions to disclose, but doing so put an unfair burden on the weekend facilitators and . . . also put Jody in a difficult situation."[8]

I've heard of cases like this more than once. At times my clients in treatment have asked others to act as go-betweens and speak for them because they couldn't, or wouldn't, summon the courage to tell their secrets face-to-face. Other times, their timing was way off, more suitable for them than for the person who was learning the long-hidden truth for the first time. Invariably, the person hearing the news in these situations feels cheated. One spouse reported:

[My husband] was safely away at the treatment center surrounded by nurturing caring professionals and fellow addicts. I was in our bedroom painting furniture, surrounded by our five small children. Laundry needed to be done, dishes from supper were waiting on me. [He phoned, and] I had to talk to him as though nothing was happening to my heart. It was horrible! I felt so alone and desperate! I was absolutely shocked by the seriousness of his addictions and the many years he'd been lying to me. I deserved better. He just went on and on. I didn't even hear half of it. I should have been given the same supportive environment as my husband, surrounded by other people in my circumstances. If I had not had those kids to take care of, I'm not sure what I would have done to myself.⁹

Years later, spouses or loved ones may still harbor resentment over the way impersonal disclosures were made. Clearly, neither of the men featured above had attempted the kind of planning or strategizing you are being encouraged to do here. In my own cowardly days early in my marriage, I failed at this approach with my wife, Susan, too. Occasionally I'd tape a note to the bathroom mirror that hinted at what needed saying, expecting her to read it in my absence. Or I'd give her a greeting card with a sensitive handwritten message — anything but talk to her face-to-face! More than once she tore up my notes and cards in anger, weeping in frustration.

Because this essential task is so important, here is a summary of some "don'ts":

- *Don't* disclose over the phone, by email, by letter, or from a distance — speak in person.

- *Don't* wallow in details, names, or other specifics — speak in themes.

- *Don't* save the worst for later or stagger information — say "the worst" sooner.

- *Don't* allow children to be present — speak to them separately after the key adults have been informed.

- *Don't* defend yourself or place blame — let the truth of the facts speak on their own.

- *Don't* argue, should emotions start to rise — remain patient, calm, cool. You have the knowledge the other person doesn't.

Sometimes the first disclosure happens precipitously when someone gets caught red-handed. Consider what happened to Mitch when he jumped off the bridge and ended up in the hospital bed facing his wife's questions. Typically, a Secret Keeper on the spot will attempt to do damage control by revealing as little as possible, most often only what he or she thinks their partner already may know or is likely to find out. Another example of this dynamic is the man whose credit card had been mysteriously denied, only to find, when he got home early one day, his wife at the computer, feverishly gambling online. Such situations demand immediate disclosure. And that often means disastrous reactions.

Do you really want to risk that level of harm?

Confessing the Truth with Love

Presuming that you are not caught in the act and forced to make an immediate confession, it's wise to anticipate the emotions both you and the person or people you're telling will experience. Keeping surprises to a minimum is the goal. Both parties involved, the teller and the hearer, will experience a variety of emotions throughout the disclosure process. Identifying those emotional states, and then managing them, is your task.

How can Secret Keepers ease the pain and shock for their partners while expressing the true facts of their hidden lives? "In the ideal world, disclosure takes place in the therapist's office," state Corley and Schneider, "after the addict and partner have both been prepared in earlier therapy sessions to go through the initial stages of this process and have been advised how much to ask and how much to disclose."[10]

Let's contemplate the following scenario. Armed with your personal inventory of your life history, aware of the health benefits of disclosing, and having disclosed to yourself, a higher power, and a professional the nature of your secret keeping, you are now ready to come clean — *to tell loved ones what they need to know that will show them the real you.* You are ready to take the Indiana Jones leap of faith and spill the difficult news. With motivation, timing, and fortitude you will make it safely to the other side.

Here's a basic list of "do's":

- *Do* meet with both a professional counselor and the "disclosee" if possible.

- *Do* meet with the "disclosee" in a quiet setting without distractions.

- *Do* speak face-to-face, sitting at eye level.

- *Do* write out what you will say, but don't read it word for word.

- *Do* allow the other person or people to vent feelings.

- *Do* listen calmly without defending yourself.

- *Do* have an "exit strategy"— a plan for where to go afterward that includes the "disclosee" and another plan that doesn't.

Most important, are you developing a plan of *who, when, where,* and *how much* to tell?

Let's see how one former Secret Keeper disclosed painful information to his loved ones and how things worked out.

EARL COMES CLEAN

In chapter 6, we saw how Earl's incestuous relationship with his teenaged daughter, Tiffany, victimized her and paralyzed him with shame. Although he believed that God would take away the desire for his wrongful behavior if he prayed hard enough, Earl says, "God took nothing away. Nothing."

Gradually Earl realized he was becoming mentally ill and changed his prayer. "I stopped asking, 'God, please remove this sin,' and started asking, 'God, please show me how to get the help I need.' " Earl still couldn't stop doing what he knew was detestable and wrong, but he also couldn't bring himself to tell his wife. He risked losing his professional standing, not to mention his reputation as a nice guy.

The day came when Tiffany, a high school sophomore of fifteen, broke down and confided to her mother about the sordid nature of her dad's relationship with her. Sandra sat stunned, horrified by the news of her husband's violations. When Earl arrived home that evening after another long day at the office, he saw the appalled look on Sandra's face and knew his secret was out.

Earl reluctantly confirmed his daughter's statements.

"The feeling was so awful I can still feel it now fifteen years later," reflects Earl. After Sandra confronted him, he felt overwhelmed and totally degraded. But he also felt huge relief, a sense of "it's over, and now I can face it." Sobbing, Earl admitted everything to Sandra, then drove to the local police station and turned himself in. Booked on felony charges, fingerprinted, and photographed for a mug shot, he sat in jail that night sleepless. "As awful as I felt sitting there in that cell like a convicted criminal, and I mean awful for Sandra and Tiffany more than for myself, it felt like my prayers *finally* were being answered."

Within a week Earl received the help he'd prayed for. Through referrals, he attended a family-renewal program at a local hospital, a two-year outpatient program that met three times a week. The group's premise was that incest is a problem involving the entire family, not solely the perpetrator or the victim. The program allowed patients like Earl to remain in their jobs while undergoing treatment, but it had a severe downside; it also meant total separation for twelve months from home and family for Earl. No visiting, no phone calls, no contact of any kind.

"Those first months were hell," Earl recalls. "I had to move out of the house right away and, to save money, I moved back in with my parents, who were the source of so many of my problems in the first place. The isolation, the absolute loneliness of being away from them, tapped into my anger toward my parents. I felt a mountain of rage toward both of them, topped only by that shame and guilt I carried."

Earl followed the counselors' instructions faithfully, telling his story to complete strangers in therapy sessions. "My story was so much like theirs. Hearing how similar the details were broke through my defenses. Others were just as troubled as I was." Earl also sensed at some level that "something spiritual was at work." He spent hours of solitary time looking out one special window and writing down on worksheets his weaknesses and strengths, his developmental deficits and distorted beliefs, his life history. He began a daily journal that he keeps to this day. The catharsis that he'd longed for finally came, the safe outlet for his pain. He "cleaned house." Better equipped to face his family a year later, he communicated to them his new understanding of his former behavior and asked for their forgiveness.

Much to his credit, Earl followed the four substages of coming clean:

A. He faced his past behavior patterns and motivations by himself, breaking through long-held illusions and seeing things from a new perspective.

B. He opened up a bit more to God every day until a new spiritual bond was forged that strengthened him to talk openly to others.

C. He talked to strangers and confided his secrets in ther-
    apy groups and to treatment professionals.

D. He communicated to loved ones as part of his therapy to
    (to Sandra, Tiffany, and his son), then made a list of
    friends who had been shocked by the news and prepared
    fitting ways to disclose to them.

Earl recalls a defining moment about eight months into his
program. As time ticked by during those long days and nights of
therapy, he "came to hear God's voice through people." Once
while Earl was lamenting that God had ignored him every time
he was victimized by his brutal father, his probation officer
placed his hand on Earl's shoulder and whispered, "Both you and
God know what horrible things happened to you as a child, but
from now on you can live the new story of your life."

Earl felt an immediate, uplifting change. "The moment I
heard him say that, everything for me changed. I'd been limping
through each day feeling hobbled and crippled, but now I could
start over." Earl has been living more fully and freely, less afraid
and resentful, ever since. "These days I believe that God answers
us and is actually there to talk to. I no longer think he's treating
me as a puppet without free will, but as his offspring who is capable of making healthy choices."

Although Earl may not have admitted his transgressions to his
wife if she hadn't confronted him first, once Tiffany spilled the
news he responded well to the crisis. He took responsibility for
coming to grips with his secret-keeping habits and the reasons
for them. With strangers, Earl learned that the stakes were lower
because no long-lasting relationships were at risk and no one
held preconceived attitudes about him. The months of his coming clean to people who were struggling like him allowed him

the time to reassemble his life according to his genuine values and goals. Earl became freed up to expose his hidden world and to examine his inner motivations. When ready, he reestablished communication with his family and with others.

As for Tiffany, today she is married with three children, lives in Florida, and works with disadvantaged youth who are socially and emotionally alienated. She and her father have reconciled, and they enjoy a fear-free, open relationship. Tiffany even trusts her father to babysit her children because the transformation to his authentic self has proven reliable and genuine.

In the next chapter you will learn about a totally different kind of trust.

Chapter 13

SEEING THE WORLD
THROUGH NEW EYES

We are born with needs but not the skills to meet them.

—— EARNIE LARSEN, *LIFE MANAGEMENT PROGRAM*

*H*AVING FACED THE CHALLENGE of doing one of the riskiest and most courageous things you will ever do, disclosing your secrets to fellow human beings, you now see the world from a radically fresh perspective. You have made the leap. Your feet have landed on new soil. As you look around, your mind reels from all the uncharted possibilities. You are now ready for the fifth stage of the Blueprint for Gaining Freedom: *Trusting* in a new worldview.

In my case, like Earl's, this meant heeding the call to authenticity and wholeness. It began when I examined my personal list of defects. I culled these from my journals and confessed them aloud numerous times during my early recovery, specifically *self-pity, resentment, hostility, impatience, irritability, insecurity, blaming*, and *envy*. These prevalent modes of feeling, behaving, and reacting were dragging me down. Over the years they had hardened into full-blown attitudes. As habitual negative traits that had shaped and warped my personality, they threatened to contaminate my entire character (real Self) for a lifetime. Unless I changed them. As difficult as it was to identify these attitudes while I was actively secret keeping, they became blatantly obvious once I heeded the call to wholeness. These intense feeling states had once fueled my urge to "steal hours" from my day-to-day life. Here's how the changes came about.

The downward spiral of secret keeping had continued well into my thirties and forties. For ten years I'd pursued a fledgling career in movies in Hollywood, where I became addicted to street drugs and heavier drinking. A stomach ulcer and insomnia plagued me. I flirted and philandered with several women, and my pornography habits intensified. Over the years I'd collected a pile of magazines with photos of beautiful nude women, a harem really, and occasionally snuck out on solo jaunts to X-rated movies or nude beaches. My wife got fed up and spoke of divorce. As I endured bouts of emotional turmoil and existential depression, I obsessed about suicide — believing that my life was devoid of meaning and any possibility of fulfillment.

In November 1977 I experienced a spiritual conversion. My worldview was turned upside down. I came to understand that I was a child of God. I felt perfect love and the generosity, forgiveness, grace, mercy, and belonging I'd longed for. I felt healing in my body, mind, emotions, and soul. Life became worth living again and, in trusting God and this new worldview, I came to appreciate the wisdom of giving up my many addictive habits and attitudes.

These outward changes reflected even more profound inward changes: letting go of bitterness, self-pity, impatience, rage, and bondage to ego. Because my dream of success as a Hollywood filmmaker and screenwriter hadn't come true despite my very earnest efforts, I'd labeled myself a "Frustrated Failure." In time I came to own, however, that I was really "Beloved of God." I went from gratifying myself to serving others, from bitterness to acceptance, from bondage to liberty, and I would one day go from secret keeping to freedom. I greatly prospered from the exercises, lessons, and principles of healing you are reading about here. I have lived every single one of them.

Until the mid-1990s, as a Secret Keeper with a solitary hidden life, I'd kept a journal for years. About every other day I would sit quietly and write down my musings in a spiral notebook, the inexpensive wire-bound kind that schoolkids use for class assignments. Now determined to recover, I found them a great vehicle for self-disclosure. In these notebooks I talked to myself and to God. Whenever I felt in the doldrums about my career, marriage, addictions, or sanity, I turned to my journal. While writing out my struggles and conflicts, I noticed certain words repeating themselves: *self-pity, impatience, rage, envy.* Gradually I realized that much of my pain resided inside me — from my long-held attitudes, feelings, and self-talk — rather than from external events or other people.

Starting in 1996, after having returned to my hometown of Minneapolis, I attended an Emotions Anonymous (EA) support group weekly for three years, as detailed earlier. It became much clearer to me that my own *negative habitual thinking* was most often the cause of my agitation and irritability. The repetition of negative habitual thoughts over the years had morphed into strongly held *beliefs* — about myself, my place in the world, and how the world works (my worldview). As part of my EA studies I learned to link these thoughts (such as my homicidal thoughts about Mom) to the developmental deficits in my upbringing. The patterns became clear.

I grew more aware and mindful every day. Later, while attending Alcoholics Anonymous in the late 1990s and while I was in college training as a counselor, my studies about addiction and brain disorders also opened my eyes. I noticed how my emotions often peaked and plunged daily, spurred by these habitual negative thoughts. The sudden urge to cry bitterly would come upon me, and I would pour out my soul in the hope that I would understand myself and my world better. I prayed that God would hear and answer me. Between attending support groups, journaling, praying, and reading self-help books on my own and psychology textbooks as part of my professional studies, I identified a list of character defects, especially my overreactive emotions. Doing so helped me to become ready to ask God to remove these shortcomings and, one day, I humbly asked him to.

Your own process of revising your worldview and trusting in a new one will develop once you: acknowledge powerlessness and unmanageability; ask for divine help and partnership; cooperate with a higher power; carefully review your life events and secret-keeping history; and disclose your full story to yourself, God, and another person. Following this process wholeheartedly is *how* you can come to *trust in a new worldview*. The continuation of this process is when you discover the wisdom of changing your old beliefs to new ones.

CHANGING OLD BELIEFS TO NEW ONES

Let's say that you, a once-active Secret Keeper now committed to recovery and seeking to trust in a new worldview, are abstaining from secret keeping and the addictive behavior(s) you were once hiding. Before moving on, let's clarify any confusion there may be about how the Blueprint, the Four Squares, and the 12 steps can work together.

Think of the Blueprint as the skeleton on which your recovery from secret keeping hangs. It is *specific* solely to secret keeping. Next, think of the Four Squares as the muscles attached to the skeleton. They are *specific* solely to your unique childhood development and individual life history. Then, think of the 12 steps as the fluids and various chemical elements flowing throughout your skeletal/muscular system that govern your wellness. They are *general* to everybody: the blood, lymph, oxygen, hormones, neurotransmitters, enzymes, and other essentials that nurture one's health. Acting together, these three offer you a winning path to recovery.

Look again at the Four Squares of Life (see page 134). As a recovering Secret Keeper you have already been following the Wholeness/Recovery arrow in the diagram! Your first benefit, according to square five, is *feeling physically healthier*. That means you are likely feeling less stress, have lower blood pressure and fewer anxiety symptoms, and may be sleeping better and enjoying life more (after some weeks of authenticity). That's a big step with big rewards. Your next challenge is to move to square six, *replacing distorted thoughts*.

Several methods for refuting old thoughts and beliefs and claiming new ones are at your disposal. Recall the discussion in chapter 6 about developmental deficits. Here, at square six, is where you can learn to turn them around, to refute them and remold them — specifically the old negative self-talk and accompanying self-definitions that have hounded you, like my old "Frustrated Failure" label that turned into the new "Beloved of God." (Are you ready for a change too?)

What do I mean exactly by self-definitions? "Our *self-definitions* are the center around which we organize and perceive our reality," says Earnie Larsen, recovery speaker and instructor. Two key principles, says Larsen, dictate the quality of our lives:

1. No one can outperform her or his own self-definition.
2. We do not see the world the way it is, we see the world
    as we are.[1]

Self definitions are the conclusions we draw about ourselves based on direct experiences. Let's use two nine-year-old kids, "Paul" and "Paula," who attend elementary school, as examples. In the classroom Paula either raises her hand and answers questions like other students, or she doesn't (academic comparison). Then the bell rings for recess. Paul either plays or doesn't play sports and games like the other kids, and he either throws or doesn't throw the ball the farthest (athletic comparison). Then the bell rings again. Paula and Paul either have members of the opposite sex approach and talk to them, or they don't (popularity comparison).

In these three everyday situations, kids like Paula and Paul arrive at conclusions about themselves over time. This is their own self-concept, not their parents' opinions of them or anybody else's. These conclusions are self-definitions. Every child decides where he or she fits, or doesn't fit, in class, on the playground, with the opposite sex, as well as in numerous other environmental situations like home, with siblings, on the school bus, and so on. Messages such as "I'm about average" or "I'm less than" or "I'm more than," based on every situation they encounter, get seared into children's psyches as they grow up.

Often these messages are self-fulfilling. A child who thinks "I'm poor at sports" may prove it by striking out easily at bat. A child who thinks "I'm great at sports" may prove it by hitting a home run. In either case, his or her mental attitude influences the outcome — at least sometimes. When the student goes home, the process repeats itself in terms of after-school activities, chores, and similar "performance" areas. At church or synagogue or mosque, the local swimming pool, at the computer, during holidays, and in any other social arena, the same process occurs over and over, until the child has come up with his or her self-definition. He or she may have a positive self-definition, what is called a PSD, or a negative self-definition, an NSD.[2]

At this point in the twenty-first century, almost everybody acknowledges that we carry on conversations with ourselves all the time. Everyone "self-talks." All day long. And these self-talk messages become the source of our worldview. Whether we view the world as friendly or hostile, gloomy or bright, exciting or boring largely depends on the things we say to ourselves day after day.

The problems start when NSDs dominate our thinking and our perspective on life. Nobody likes to live with negative self-talk or emotions, but few people even realize they are doing so. Very likely the NSDs began so far back in the past and became so imbedded that they are now largely forgotten. Few people realize that they can change these NSDs to PSDs. Although they owe it to themselves to do so, hordes of people never do. Below is the unfortunate progression many people live out daily:[3]

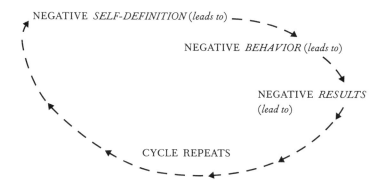

NEGATIVE *SELF-DEFINITION* (*leads to*)

NEGATIVE *BEHAVIOR* (*leads to*)

NEGATIVE *RESULTS* (*lead to*)

CYCLE REPEATS

It's no wonder that some people eagerly indulge in their addictions and secret-keeping activities to escape this cycle. Caught in a downward spiral in which negative results refuel the already imbedded NSDs over and over, they come to believe that *the world is the way they think it is.*

Some people distinguish themselves as the black sheep of the family. If I think of myself as the black sheep (negative *self-definition*), then I will act in objectionable and disturbing ways (negative *behavior*), resulting in fights, criticism, arrests, jail time, and so on (negative *results*) that make everybody, including me, conclude that I *am* the black sheep (the cycle repeats). Every time the cycle repeats, I see the world as a place that's "out to get me," as cold and hostile. But I'll cling to my distinction of being unconventional, a black sheep, unlike all those other conventional sheep I think of as boring (in other words, I'll start to take pride in being "bad").

We see the world not as it is, but as we are.

So if we were to listen in to people as they "talk" to themselves, what would we hear? Below is a partial list of the kinds of statements many people say to themselves subconsciously:

- I'll never be popular.
- My opinions don't matter.
- People like me only for what I do for them.
- It's safer to bury my feelings.
- I'm undeserving.
- I was born a rebel.
- I'll never be good enough.

The original events that generated statements like these, which eventually develop into NSDs, are long gone, and long forgotten. Our subconscious "parks" the NSDs in our "implicit memory," which prevents them from being conscious and therefore

accessible. Neuroscientists define *implicit memory* as "the powerful emotions and messages from an earlier time that flood our
present experience, usually without our recognizing the connection to past events."4 The trouble is, they were all just events —
nothing more. *We added our perception or opinion to them*, thus
generating the self-definition (negative or positive), and that
perception, notes Larsen, frequently is from the child's limited
point of view. The same event for different people is colored by
their perceptions, which are based on their self-definitions.

Can you see how entirely different perceptions result from
the same event? Why, for example, will three eyewitnesses to an
automobile accident tell three different stories? Why did my
twin brother Dave's reaction to our mother's outrageous behavior in her dream house differ from mine? His reaction, largely
tolerance, never led to feelings of homicidal urges and rage, as
mine did.

Here in Minnesota where I live and work, we get huge snowfalls in the winter. To a child huge snowfalls mean running outside to play, throwing snowballs, and sledding down steep hills.
To an adult, the same snowfalls mean getting mired in traffic,
shoveling the driveway, and having to take care of kids who stay
home unexpectedly from school. For the child, paradise. For the
adult, vexation.

The formula? Same event + different perspectives = different reactions and realities.

We see the world not as it is, but as we are.

And thankfully, this worldview can change. When I was in my
thirties I used to think, "I'm alone in this mess, and the world is out
to get me." I believed this even to the point of pondering suicide.
But many things happened that helped me change my thinking
to: "I'm in this together with others, and everybody wants to
help." With these changes came changes in my self-definition(s),

such as self-talk that went from "I'm undeserving and a failure" to "I'm loved and blessed by God."

As adults we can reshape our worldview, if we understand how our mind stores long-held emotions that shape our present behavior and how our revised self-talk can shape new self-definitions. Millions of once heavy drinkers (with NSDs) have learned how to live sober, saner lives (using PSDs) — they've revised the words they tell themselves. Moreover, based on the knowledge that we can revise our old self-definitions, and therefore respond to events in the present rather than reacting to decades-old implicit memories, we can also learn to trust the freshness of the moment instead of the stale ghosts of the past.

DALE: A REAL-LIFE EXAMPLE OF A NEW WORLDVIEW

I still remember the day Dale stepped into my office. He was a downcast, bedraggled man of forty-two with long hair hiding his face. Dale's shoulders were rounded, and his tattered jeans were faded. To his credit he was punctual for our one-on-one progress review. He mumbled, "Hi," but avoided eye contact with me. I knew his drug history well by now — cocaine and alcohol dependence in remission, active marijuana dependence for twenty-seven years. I'd observed him six or seven times interacting meekly in group with men his age, the kind of client who "warms a chair" and no more.

We discussed the purpose of the private meeting: to examine his old beliefs and replace them with new ones. His face showed the same blank stare as it had the first time I'd interviewed him for placement in treatment. Fortunately we had developed a friendly rapport, and soon we were into the "meat" of our session:

how his dead-end job at a lumber-products factory, while fairly well paying after many years of steady employment, fit his negative self-definitions to a fault. When I showed him a worksheet listing various self-definitions, he spent a few minutes picking out, without my prompting, three NSD-forming self-talk statements out of several listed. He agreed that they had rumbled around in his mind nonstop since he was young:

- I am only as good as my work.
- I'll never amount to anything.
- Feelings are dangerous.[5]

We discussed Dale's feelings about his job, exploring the connection between pot smoking and his old thoughts. He did certain "outdoor things" well for the company (these gave him opportunities to smoke pot on the job), but he was never promoted; he'd stopped talking with the owner because they had nothing much to say to one another anymore; and his co-workers enjoyed his wry sense of humor, but his supervisor never seemed to notice it. I then asked him about his home routine after work and how his wife and three kids responded to him.

"Basically, I light up my bong the first five minutes after I get home," Dale replied. "Then I go to the garage to hang out." He added that his wife disliked his pot habit intensely. Their kids, eleven to seventeen, basically ignored him.

"Can you see by what you've described," I asked, "how these three negative self-definitions play out? At work? At home? Every day?"

Dale paused, swiped back the long hair from his face and said, "Yeah. I think I do."

From there we discussed how his thinking habits limited the results he experienced at work and at home. He acknowledged how it seemed practically inevitable that his relationships in both places had gotten stuck in a rut. I explained how to turn the three often-repeated self-talk phrases around. I asked him to say aloud the opposite thing that came to his mind when he read the statement "I am only as good as my work."

After a long silence, he said, " 'Work is only part of who I am'?"

I immediately nodded and said, "Yes, that's good. You *are* more than your job." Then I asked him to write the new statement next to the old one, and we went on to the second NSD: "I'll never amount to anything."

In a similar manner, he stammered a moment and then said, "'I *can* amount to something'?"

"Perfect!"

He wrote that down too, and we went on to the third NSD: "Feelings are dangerous." We had more of a discussion about this one because Dale said he'd shut down his feelings for as long as he could remember. I helped him to name some feelings and to see that he could express them safely. "Every time you recognize that you're mad or sad or glad," I said, "others will learn more about the real you because your feelings will be in the open." We settled on, "Feelings are safe."

I then asked him to repeat all three new statements aloud. You would think nothing so easy and simple could transform a man, but I heard a hint of change in his voice and saw the sparkle of new thinking in his eyes — which now met mine directly.

I gave Dale a homework assignment: to look in the mirror when he was brushing his teeth in the morning and evenings and to say these three new statements aloud for thirty days. He looked flabbergasted. "That's right," I said. "Sixty times, got it?" I explained that his subconscious would hear them and would come to believe them in the next month. Over time these new statements would crowd out the old, stubborn beliefs that had been shaping him and his world. I call this therapy "repeating affirmations." "*You*, Dale, have control over what you tell yourself," I declared. As he left my office, he shook my hand with unfamiliar vigor.

Dale went all out to follow my instructions. He even typed up the new statements on his work computer and printed them out on sheets of colorful paper with a fancy border, and he posted them by the mirror in his bathroom and in his pickup truck: "So I can say them more often during the day."

By the time he appeared for his discharge from my agency's treatment program five weeks later (sporting a haircut!), Dale said that his co-workers and his family were gradually seeing his "new self" emerge. And with that, he bowed slightly and turned to say farewell to his mates in group therapy. I have since learned that Dale has made good use of the weekly aftercare meetings he attended, and that the other clients who observed the visible changes in Dale were encouraged in their struggles.

YOUR TURN

Now it's your turn. Follow Dale's example and say aloud the direct opposite wording of these NSD phrases:

OLD NSD		NEW PSD
Change "I'm a loser"	*to*	"I'm a winner."
Change "I'll never be some-body"	*to*	"I will be somebody."
Change "I'm incapable and undeserving"	*to*	"I am able and deserving."
Change "I don't matter much"	*to*	"I matter a lot."
Change "Life is out to get me"	*to*	"Life has blessings for me."

Repeat the new phrases, or ones you make up on your own, aloud for thirty days, once in the morning and once at bedtime. If you listed "My opinions don't matter," then say aloud, "My opinions do matter," and so on. Remember:

- Keep your *thoughts* positive because they become your words.
- Keep your *words* positive because they become your actions.
- Keep your *actions* positive because they become your habits.
- Keep your *habits* positive because they become your values.
- Keep your *values* positive because they become your destiny.

EXERCISE
Beliefs about Secret Keeping

Since our self-talk develops into our beliefs, let's look at this dynamic in terms of our beliefs about secret keeping. Below are twenty-one statements. Rate each one and decide how much you agree or disagree with it using the following scale.

1	2	3	4	5
Totally Disagree	Disagree Somewhat	Neutral	Agree Somewhat	Totally Agree

_____ 1. Life without secret keeping is boring.

_____ 2. Secret keeping is the best way to cope with the pain of my life.

_____ 3. I can't function without secret keeping.

_____ 4. I am not ready to stop secret keeping.

_____ 5. Cravings and urges make me continue secret keeping.

_____ 6. My life won't get any better if I stop secret keeping.

_____ 7. The only way to deal with my emotions is by secret keeping.

_____ 8. Life would be depressing without secret keeping.

_____ 9. I am not a strong enough person to stop secret keeping.

_____ 10. Secret keeping is not a problem for me.

_____ 11. My secret keeping is caused by someone else (spouse, partner, parent).

_____ 12. Secret keeping runs in my family.

_____ 13. I can't unwind without secret keeping.

_____ 14. Having a problem with secret keeping means I'm a bad person.

_____ 15. I can't have fun without secret keeping.

_____ 16. I can't control my anxiety without secret keeping.

_____ 17. I can't express my feelings without secret keeping.

_____ 18. I reward myself by secret keeping.

_____ 19. My secret keeping is part of who I am.

_____ 20. I like my secret-keeping personality more than my "regular" personality.

_____ 21. Secret keeping will happen whether I want it to or not.

What four or five beliefs about secret keeping struck you the most? Look for the statements you marked with a "1" or a "5". What do these tell you about yourself? In general, which statements do you think stem from your old NSDs?

TRACY: NO MORE "FAT COW"

We first met Tracy, the former high school gymnast whose secretive eating disorder came to rule her life, in chapter 3. By age twenty she weighed less than ninety pounds. She experienced severe dehydration and thought about suicide daily, but she also refused to be hospitalized. Then one day she collapsed from malnourishment, and an ambulance brought her to the emergency room. Tracy tore the IV tubes from her arms and fled the hospital.

"I could not face that I had a real problem," she admits. At times she had to get up right away after eating a meal because her system was so trained by then to vomit. Ironically, when she bent over to purge in a toilet or a grocery bag that she kept in her car, sometimes her gag reflex failed and food would not empty from her stomach. Once she stuck a hairbrush handle down her throat trying to vomit and cracked a tooth. Another time, she vomited so forcefully that a blood vessel burst in her eye.

"Basically, I was a mess. I started staying away from people altogether. And I refused to see a doctor." Her mom insisted that she go to the dentist and eye doctor, but she couldn't bring herself to because doing so "would have meant their telling me that my eating disorder was real." Keeping everything a secret became second nature. In fact, the secrecy of concealing her bulimia became as much of a problem as the eating disorder itself. But the evidence was visible to everybody.

Tracy no longer dated or behaved like other college-age women; fashion magazines with their ads for cosmetics and clothes no longer held any appeal. Tracy would have continued down this destructive path had her friend not committed suicide. "The same girl who went with me to gymnastics years ago killed herself — from the very same illness! She couldn't deal with her bulimia any longer, and here I was one step in the grave, right behind her."

Tracy accepted help, crossed the threshold of an inpatient treatment center, and surrendered to her powerlessness and the unmanageability of her life. Aided by insurance and a loan from relatives, she was able to help her body establish a new rhythm around food intake. Sitting in therapy groups, she heard from others like herself. "Listening to them, I saw it was not my outside appearance that determined my happiness, but what I believed — what I was telling myself — that mattered." Tracy was relieved at not having to cover up or lie anymore to hide her secret. "Admitting all my tricks and recognizing that I was like the others in treatment helped so much. It reduced the isolation I felt and my constant efforts at lying or making excuses."

Off to a strong start, Tracy followed her counselors' advice and took responsibility in other ways: she began attending Eating Disorders Anonymous meetings, which she attends today. "In EDA, we admit how we were once sold a bill of goods by advertisers, that our weight, figure, clothes, makeup, and exercise could make us into better people. That we weren't okay just the way we are."

The emergence of a new worldview had begun.

Tracy also "plays offense" today. Now up to 115 pounds, she visits a nutritionist and sees a private psychotherapist who helps her understand the early childhood "fat cow" messages that developed into her distorted beliefs. She understands how she got sucked in as a young girl to what she calls "fat cow-ism." By working at changing her early self-definition, she now repeats affirmations such as "I like the person I am" and "I am more than my body." She has identified her highest risk situation, being alone, and ways to defend herself against the temptation to relapse when nobody is looking.

"I now realize that a red flag for me is when I start edging away from people, when I slip back into isolating." Tracy also took the step of going to the dentist for repairs to her chipped tooth and damaged enamel, and she no longer fears ruining her remaining teeth with regurgitated stomach acids.

For Tracy, God has changed as well. "My relationship has gone from God being a strict and stern taskmaster, the image I was taught growing up, to God being more of a loving and forgiving helper for me in my struggles. I'm not limited anymore by old ways of relating to God."

Tracy admits her former behavior harmed others, especially her mom. "I was too caught up, too much in a fog, to know that she and others who cared for me were worried and trying to help me." At family sessions, a vital part of Tracy's treatment process, she says, "I heard all kinds of things from relatives, that they'd felt my pain and had seen through me." Tracy has begun making amends to people she has hurt, and she feels their acceptance returning.

Her worldview is altogether new and different. Life now holds exciting possibilities. Currently in her third year of recovery, Tracy wants a genuine life for herself, including getting married and having kids. "I remember watching African children who were starving on TV, and here I was vomiting up food. What a conflict! Only in a rich country like ours could there be problems like mine when thousands are dying elsewhere of starvation."

Nowadays Tracy is focused on living from the inside out and is no longer forced to walking a tightrope between two opposing worlds. A significant difference in Tracy's story of changed beliefs is her acceptance of "what is." No longer does she find her body unacceptable and in need of improvement: "I'm okay just the way I am!"

In the next chapter we'll look at ways to stay authentic. Making choices to *be* authentic takes plenty of will- and "won't-power," but *staying* authentic takes another sort of effort and set of resources. Let's keep the ball rolling!

Chapter 14

AUTHENTICITY
IN A MESSY WORLD

Nature doesn't move in a straight line,
and as part of nature, neither do we.

— GLORIA STEINEM

*T*HIS CHAPTER IS ABOUT KEEPING the new fires burning.
It's about staying on track and going on the adventure of
becoming your best self. How do you manage the potholes, pit-
falls, and pratfalls ahead? How do you approach the months it
will take to turn around that old secret-keeping mind-set — and
succeed? How long will it take for you to believe the new PSDs
deep in your gut?

I like to think of this chapter as "pedaling uphill and enjoying it." For supercyclist Lance Armstrong, who trained daily for
the annual Tour de France and in 2005 set the record of seven
consecutive wins, it meant just that: pedaling daily and enjoying
it. Think of your old secret-keeping days as coasting down a
gradual hill on your bike. But now you've turned around and are
headed in a new direction, so you're pedaling uphill. The slope
is gradual, however, and, while you may get tired from pedaling,
you can hop off your bike, rest a while, and then continue on.
Just keep pedaling and enjoy the ride.

Striving for authenticity is noble; *maintaining* authenticity takes mental effort. You are saying yes to H.O.T. attitudes and behavior daily in an uphill world *when nobody is looking*. It is your private bike ride. Finding the strength to stay true to your new pledge, especially when you are alone for lengthy periods, is the challenge. Remember how secret keeping beckoned when you were alone and nobody was looking? *That* was your highest-risk situation, and now it is no different except you're pedaling on the Wholeness/Recovery arrow. It is precisely at this time that you will be tested to rise to your best. Nothing else counts. Because authenticity is, at its simplest, *the contract you make with yourself, by yourself, and for yourself.* When you make such an inner contract, you are promising to be accountable to Self, which means practicing the last of the six Blueprint for Gaining Freedom stages: *Accounting* for your present and future behavior.

Notice that this stage is not about accounting for your past behavior, which may certainly have resulted in dire consequences. Rather, it's about your new recovery-minded behavior — although you may still have to serve time in jail, spend months on probation, deal with hurt feelings, repair reputations, and pay fines or restitution for past conduct. But before you can focus on the present and future, you will need to commit to the mental fortitude to stay authentic. Part of that commitment will be to make amends to those you have harmed, most likely for betraying or disappointing or grieving them in dozens of ways.

CARING FOR THOSE WE'VE HARMED

When we become aware of the ways we've harmed people, our hearts' desire is to make things right. I call this process "relationship repairs." We want to fix what's broken, to make amends. More than merely saying "I'm sorry" or "I apologize" or "Please forgive me," we want to show *by our actions* that we have changed. We want our interactions with the people in our lives to flow freely again without the tension or friction our previous behavior and attitudes once caused. We want to *mend*, to make good as new, the bonds we share with these people. Frequently an apology just isn't enough.

The guide below will help you jog your memory about the ways your secret keeping has harmed others and hurt their feelings. Place a check mark next to each item that applies:

EXERCISE
Harmful Consequences Guide

RELATIONSHIP

__Arguments or fights

__Breakups or separations

__Broken promises to self and others

__Divorce

__Estranged children

__Lack of communication

__Lost friendships

__Physical or verbal abuse

__Promiscuous behavior

__Violence

__Withdrawal from family and friends

JOB

__Absenteeism

__Lost jobs (being fired)

__Lowered production

__Many job changes

__Morning-after effects on job

__Neglecting basic needs of family (workaholic)

__Neglecting necessary jobs at home

__Warnings from employer

FINANCIAL

__Bankruptcy

__Extravagant purchases beyond income limits

__Going without necessities (food, clothing, medicine)

__Repossessions

__Unpaid bills or collection agencies

SPIRITUAL

__Changed values (what was important is no longer important)

__Loss of faith in self or others

__Loss of self-esteem, self-worth

__Lying, cheating, or stealing

__Suicidal thoughts or attempts

PHYSICAL

__Accidents

__Damage to health, yours or others'

__Times in emergency rooms or mental health units

LEGAL

__Arrests, such as DUIs

__Court appearances

__Fines and fees

__Jail time

SOCIAL

__Avoidance of holidays and parties

__Isolation or withdrawal

Now, having marked the descriptors that relate to your secret keeping, list the people in your life whom you associate with each descriptor. Let's say you marked "Broken promises to self and others" in the relationships category. Now name people such as your spouse, children (individually), friends, and parents. You can also name yourself, because the relationship you have with yourself is active from cradle to grave — it is the only relationship of its kind. Have you ever noticed that "wherever you go, there you are"?

As you reflect on these names, consider how the harm you've done allows for new *thinking* about these people. Making amends can take many forms: a phone call, a letter, a visit to someone's grave, a personal visit. The main attitude you need is that of *empathy*, of saying to the person something like: "When I did X and Y, I realize now that it hurt you and made you feel disappointed, sad, and angry. Because I'm no longer doing X and Y, but A and B instead, I hope you will give me another chance. I know that saying 'sorry' or 'I apologize' is not enough, so please consider my actions from today on and determine for yourself the difference. I want to deserve your trust again and for us to get along."

Having empathy for those in your life means that you are viewing past circumstances from *their* perspective, not from your own. You are in their shoes, understanding their feelings and responses, because it was your behavior that prompted the tension and friction they had to cope with. You are on their side now. Make that clear to them. In each fresh moment, when you choose to act on these new recovery principles, the person you were born to be emerges. And others will see that person!

Accounting for Present and Future Behavior

Addressing past harms will take time and effort. Don't stop there. Your next step in the healing process is to focus on today, the here and now, and on what's ahead. Agreeing to stay authentic goes beyond the agreements you make with your counselor, spouse, employer, probation officer, 12-step sponsor, or anyone else — it is the agreement and promise you make with Number One. *You* come first. *Your contract with yourself, by yourself, for yourself* is the foundation of all meaningful change.

In a sense, only you know the bare-bones truth of your behavior anyway, and only you know when you're telling the truth. If you're determined to stay clean, however, then character changes will manifest, and changes of that magnitude depend on being fearlessly honest and transparent — letting others in. That's the exact opposite of your old strategy of keeping everybody out. Each coin has a flip side, and the process you've committed to means flipping yourself from tails to heads, or heads to tails.

During the months while you are seeking authenticity, a turnaround is psychologically taking place, and the new you is emerging. With more practice, should a triggering event occur, you'll be on more solid footing and better able to resist a relapse. You'll also be better equipped to select your self-talk, thereby mastering your feelings rather than falling back into the old "stinking thinking." As changes occur in your personality, changes in your character will follow.

So how *do* you take control of those pesky secret-keeping urges?

Be realistic. Like a growling bulldog that bites your leg and won't let go, old habits resist change — fiercely! Now your goal is to *stay* free of secret keeping, not just to get free of it, and that means pedaling uphill and enjoying it. And it also means long-term improvement, not short-term white-knuckle change. It's a long, uphill trek, like much of the Tour de France, and it takes perseverance. But it's also truly enjoyable. To put it very plainly, if your recovery doesn't lead to your feeling better about yourself, it won't last.

Remember that contests are won with offense, not defense. It takes commitment to your recovery to win in the long run. For a role model, look once again to Lance Armstrong. Even he had to reinvent himself and think of a new strategy after his seventh and final first-place victory: "I have to enter a new phase in my life, where I realize I'm not going to have the outlet of winning a big race or training hard for something, and ultimately having success and having the thrill of victory. That's done for me. I need to find a new high."[1]

Like Armstrong, who admits to needing a "new high," a new present and an exciting future are your focus as a committed-to-recovery Secret Keeper. Until now your focus has been on the past, on the time and energy misspent or wasted on secret keeping, on accompanying addictions, on what's wrong. From now on your aim will be your health and wholeness, on restoring positive feelings and rephrasing old self-talk, on recovery as it benefits both you and others, on what's right. You are *accounting* for your present and future behavior.

LOOKING BACK, LOOKING AHEAD

To boost your motivation to keep looking ahead, to keep pedaling, on the next page I have provided a simple breakdown of where many former Secret Keepers find themselves after starting their journey toward wholeness:

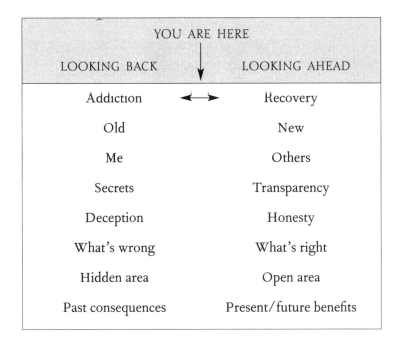

YOU ARE HERE	
LOOKING BACK	LOOKING AHEAD
Addiction ⟷	Recovery
Old	New
Me	Others
Secrets	Transparency
Deception	Honesty
What's wrong	What's right
Hidden area	Open area
Past consequences	Present/future benefits

What if Lance had looked back at his victories and not ahead to the next race? His path from cancer victim to cycling victor can serve as a model for your path as well. When you live out your values and commitments for all the world to see, your personality and character changes will show. Consider the changes that Dale, in chapter 13, faced and managed, although his, like yours, may never make headlines.

For you, as a Secret Keeper in recovery, the process of abstaining from secret keeping and the accompanying addictive behavior(s) has already started. You have already followed the Wholeness/Recovery arrow on the Four Squares of Life from square five, *feeling physically better*, to square six, *replacing distorted thoughts*. Next comes square seven, *restoring positive feelings*.

FIGHTING THE "VICTIM" MIND-SET

For many people, the hurts they experienced early in life have generated feelings of self-pity and vexation. Harsh self-talk and NSDs only add to the hurt. Environmental disparities and devel opmental deficits can lead to a steady stream of painful emotions, which generate wounded hearts and minds. It's tough to turn around twenty or more years of painful history in twenty or more weeks; it often takes about twenty months just to get off to a good start. Besides changing your old thinking, you will need to *heal the emotions attached to your old thinking*. Otherwise you will remain vulnerable to relapse, returning to your secret-keeping habits as a way to cope or escape, because these habits are familiar. Overcoming developmental deficits in your past (and major deficits mean that you were victimized) takes effort, time, and strategy.

Restoring positive emotions is possible. But how do you go about it?

One way to deal with old feelings of self-pity and en-trenched thoughts like "I've been cheated," for improving your moods and healing damaged feelings, is to practice *acceptance* and *forgiveness*. These are the next "biggies" for you to tackle. As full-grown adults with resources we didn't have when experiencing developmental deficits (including neglect or abuse), we have the ability today to make brand-new choices. *If* we choose. Regarding the *conditions* we endured or tolerated growing up, we can choose to practice acceptance. Regarding the *people* who did us harm or injury, we can choose to forgive them. Acceptance centers on uncontrollable environmental factors (poverty, racism, neglect). Forgiveness centers on specific individuals (the incestuous uncle, the verbally abusive mother). When we grow weary enough of the cycle of resentment, we can choose to accept the conditions under which we grew up and go one step further and choose to forgive the perpetrator(s).

Most people object strenuously to doing either!

Feeling justifiably, even correctly, that "it" should never have happened, they holler, "No way! Never can I forgive so-and-so!" But what happened *did* happen; you can't change that; only your attitude toward it today can change. Since you are living in the now, the choice facing you is to keep holding the grievance or to let it go. Otherwise your old damaged emotions continue fueling your distorted thoughts, which, as we know, lead to distorted views of ourselves and of the world.

Let's examine the underlying emotion that fuels our reluctance to accept or forgive — resentment. When you have been harmed unfairly, whether physically or emotionally, your very natural response is to feel hurt, and to grieve. Part of that response includes these impulses: 1) to strike back, 2) to air your grievance and be heard, and 3) to restore balance, often by expecting an apology from the perpetrator and immediate improvement in their behavior.

In a perfect world, the third option would settle most grievances. If only we lived in a perfect world. When none of these options is available, as is frequently the case, our pain from the injury gets internalized. Striking back, for example, is hardly ever feasible. A child gains nothing from kicking the shins of a grown-up, and may get even more of a licking for doing so. So he or she stuffs the pain of the injury. Since the pain has nowhere else to go, it slides quietly from short-term memory into implicit memory. What is left, then, is suffering.

Suffering arises when none of these three impulses gets a proper outlet. A victim, after all, is somebody lacking in power, control, influence, and status. This suffering is commonly borne silently and alone, and often it takes the form of resentment (nursing a grudge). Let's take a closer look at this word. The verb *resent* comes from Latin, and means to "feel again." The "sent" in re*sent* is Latin for "feeling," as in our English words *sent*imental, *sens*itive, *sens*ual, and *sens*ational. Applied to past injuries, resentment occurs when I feel *in the present* the pain of injuries from the *past*. And the nearly universal emotion linked with resentment is anger. Anger can be a justifiable emotion; it is triggered by unfair behavior or unjust conditions and can motivate efforts to reform, to prosecute crimes, to overturn slavery, and so on. Yet if held on to for too long, anger can also fester and feed our sense of victimhood.

If the pain you feel today concerns an event that happened twenty-seven years ago, then you are living in resentment. If you have felt it hundreds of times, then *you, not the perpetrator*, are injuring yourself. Any time we resurrect hurt from "back then" and feel it "now," we are reliving our original anger. The trap for many of us is that we don't realize consciously where the pain is coming from. Having only a vague sense of its origin, we still feel it very strongly. It's lodged in our implicit memory, just as our NSDs are lodged there. Whenever we feel resentful, we are living as powerless victims, lacking control, influence, and status. We hurt all over again.

Victims can hurt in thousands of quiet ways, suffering myriad health and emotional problems. Lila's story illustrates this mode of conduct well.

LILA: A SHOPLIFTER'S PATH TOWARD HEALING

When we last saw Lila in chapter 5, she "couldn't quit shoplifting completely," and her secret keeping was getting worse. In time her habit of stealing led to a loss of control and her "feeling like dirt." Seven arrests, jail time for two of them, low self-esteem, expensive court fines, plus the accompanying worries, delays, loss of serenity, and lowered quality of life finally got her attention. Her last arrest required her to meet specific legal obligations, one being mandatory attendance at a Shoplifters Anonymous program.

"At first it felt scary," Lila says. "Over time it really helped talking to others like me, but the reason I stole remained elusive. What I learned was that I needed to be *aware*. I had to quit, just quit." Lila needed to learn the times when it was unsafe for her to go into stores: when she was angry, down, happy, or excited. Lila came to understand that she was using the high she got from stealing to compensate for feeling underloved and underappreciated. It helped her get even. She also told herself that it provided the adventure and zest for life that seemed missing in her daily routine.

What she still did not recognize were her feelings of deep resentment from growing up as the oldest of four sisters on a farm. Always the one to take care of the younger ones, she bore the chief responsibility for doing the daily chores. She "plastered over" her feelings of being taken for granted and unappreciated by "wearing a mask carved with a permanent cheery smile," she says today.

Then came the day when Lila connected with a treatment specialist in Detroit, Michigan. Terrence Shulman, an attorney and consultant/therapist, was himself in recovery from addictive-compulsive shoplifting. He facilitated a weekly support group and had written the self-help book *Something for Nothing: Shoplifting Addiction and Recovery*.[2] In its pages Lila discovered clues to her own struggle.

Under a heading in the book, "My List of Unfair Things," Lila read: "Acknowledge that you feel like a victim and feel it as fully as you need to. Acknowledge that, in some way, what you have been attempting to do with shoplifting is to undo or make up for the past and to buffer future pain and disappointment. Think about all those things you hate about your life or feel are unfair."[3]

Lila began to realize she'd shoplifted as a way to cope with these feelings, to numb the nagging hurts, to transcend resentment in the same way that a drug addict uses drugs to numb her feelings. The accumulation of stolen objects made her feel she was getting something for nothing and tipping the scales of fairness back in balance. Says Lila, "The gamble itself — would I get away with it or not? — was the source of most of the adrenaline. Shoplifting was the high."

Lila contacted Shulman and told him about her struggles to recover. In the months ahead a network formed and grew steadily into an international conference on theft addictions and disorders featuring experts in psychiatry, psychology, and sociology.[4] Although Lila had helped spawn awareness in her local community and had written articles in recovery publications, she still felt her serenity invaded at times by decades of ingrained addictive thinking. "It has gotten easier as time goes by, but I have never felt that I am cured. Shoplifting as a way of keeping secrets was my first mistake. Nursing my resentments, although I never realized it at the time, was my second."

While interviewing her for this book, I asked her to list her resentments. Reviewing the list, I suggested Carl Jung's theory about the Shadow (see the seesaw diagram in chapter 5). Applying the theory to her upbringing, I offered the idea that she had grown up as a "squeaky-clean good girl" until eighteen, having denied her resentful feelings on the farm, at which time she moved away from home and parental restraints. For eighteen years she had perfected her persona (her shiny side) but had sublimated entirely her Shadow (her slimy side). Lila readily affirmed this view as accurate. Finding herself lonely, homesick, vulnerable, and insecure, she went shopping one day and, unconsciously, her Shadow side asserted those long-buried resentments by prompting her to steal.

When she saw things from this perspective, Lila understood more clearly why shoplifting had held her in such thrall. She came to accept her upbringing and her place in the birth order, then forgave her parents for their tight-lipped Scandinavian reticence. Today, Lila is carrying the message of recovery through service to fellow sufferers. She is pedaling uphill and enjoying it. She has found ways to live authentically, to free herself of resentments, and to replace old thoughts with new ones, all the while staying accountable to a national network. Staying clean for Lila has gotten easier, and the adventure of becoming her best self fuels her motivation.

The truth is that we can control our own resentment, just as Lila learned, and that we can *choose* to let go of it — for our own good. This process involves identifying and facing *consciously* the pain that is lodged in implicit memory, dragging it out of there, and then replacing the pain with peace, the anger with calm, the sorrow with serenity.

Let's return to the question, How, then, do you restore positive feelings?

To rid yourself of painful resentment and from ongoing anger and bitterness, you need not involve anybody else. You do not need to wait for somebody else to take action, as Lila discovered. The perpetrator doesn't have to come crawling or begging for mercy. The poverty of your childhood circumstances won't change because you want it to. The only one who can change your attitude about the past is you.

Only you can choose to free yourself. Do so today. Follow the steps outlined above, and "Just say yes."

Now I will tell you the story of how I did just that.

My Story of Forgiveness (Twice)

One April afternoon I was walking in a pensive state of mind on the hillside below the huge white H-O-L-L-Y-W-O-O-D sign in Los Angeles. There's a secluded footpath just below the concrete foundations of those thirty-foot-high letters, and I, in the intense heat and bright sunlight, suddenly felt a supernatural nudge: "Forgive your mother." I stopped, wondering if I was hearing things. The inner voice came again: "Forgive your mother." I couldn't fathom such a thing and walked a few more feet. Then it came again: "Forgive your mother."

I stopped, sat down in the dirt, and concluded that a divine voice must be beckoning. My thoughts rebelled. "Impossible! Forgive my mother?" It was 1978, and I was thirty-four years old. I'd been carrying resentful anger toward my mother for more than twenty years. In the next microsecond, I screamed aloud, *"No, no, no!"*

Silence. Very quietly, the nudge came again: "Forgive your mother."

For the next few weeks I held a running debate with God. I brought up every argument I could think of proving that Mom did not deserve forgiveness — she hadn't apologized or admitted to her faults, and she'd made Dad so miserable that he'd died young. Even if she begged, I reasoned, I wouldn't consider it. Memories of her tormenting House of Horrors and the endless work projects foisted on us as teenagers still upset me. On and on the list went.

But after days of realizing the many things I'd been forgiven for in my new walk with God, I returned to the spot near the huge white sign, knelt, and stammered aloud: "Mom, I...I... forgive...you." Instantly tears poured from my eyes. "I...I do forgive you, Mom. From my heart, truly." Huge waves of sorrow and grief dislodged and floated away from me. My entire body trembled. I sobbed like a prisoner released from a life

sentence. Oppressive, ugly, murderous grudges that I'd harbored for years lifted from me in waves. My soul groaned from
the release of these hurtful feelings. "Yes, I forgive you, Mom, I
forgive you, I forgive you."

Standing up, I felt freer than I'd ever felt as an adult. In the
weeks and months ahead, the same gentle nudge repeated itself,
triggering specific memories. Each time I presented my arguments against forgiving Mom to God, but each time his love
trumped my resistance and I obeyed "the nudge" with less resistance, letting go more easily. Each time another old hurt faded
and lost its power. And the long-buried urge to kill Mom less-
ened, then disappeared.

Yet more emotional lessons remained. Secret keeping had
made me feel like my whole life was a performance, that the
mask was always on. As I pondered past events in my life (more
developmental deficits), I also felt resentment about what was
missing in my growing-up years. Gradually I shifted from grieving about Mom to lamenting my hollow memories of Dad. With
one exception, the time I'd stopped the flurry of shots as a goalie
and Dad had cheered from the bleachers, I had no recall of his
ever having approved of me. Rather, I remembered the times
he'd been absent, the innumerable times when he'd said nothing
at all. Mom had meddled, Dad had looked the other way. As I
weighed each of their legacies, it hit me between the eyes that
Dad had as much to do with my wounds as Mom. He was a
bystander, she a perpetrator. Disturbed, I sat down and wrote
a soul-felt letter to him.

The letter was my attempt to purge myself of the hurt and
rage I'd felt for so many years and to release him from the hidden hold this anger had on us both. I wanted his soul and my soul
to be free of it once and for all. I concluded by saying, "I forgive
you now as totally as I am able, hoping this forgiveness reaches

you in your world. I love you, Dad. When we meet on your side of eternity, I eagerly want to throw my arms around you and begin anew. I hope and trust you're rejoicing like I am. Your loving son, Johnny."

My hands shook, and I felt shivers as I reread my letter. Instinctively, I was seeing old events with new eyes, perceiving history from a 180-degree perspective. Writing the letter helped free my grief and brought much-needed balance to an unbalanced, unhealthy era in my upbringing.

Like any letter, it needed to be delivered. Weeks earlier I'd worked on a camera crew at the windy shores of Palos Verdes, the rugged peninsula southwest of Los Angeles, a wildly barren outcropping of ocean-soaked rocks stretching for miles. After placing the letter in a sealed bottle, I climbed down the steep path to the shoreline, walked out on the blackened boulders as far as I dared, and waited for the right moment. Something very surprising happened next. Unexpectedly a new message came to me in that instant: "*I will be your Father.*"

These words came from God. I believed they were his answer to the heartfelt plea I'd sobbed at Dad's graveside ten years before when I'd asked, *Who will help me make the decisions a man needs to make? What model of manhood do I have to go by?* God was telling me that he would provide what was missing, that despite my past and the failures of my earthly father, he would be my new father.

Just then a large wave splashed at my feet. The moment to deliver the letter had arrived. I reached back, bent low, and hurled the bottle precisely as a roaring wave sucked itself back into the ocean. The bottle landed with a plop. I watched it float out beyond the jagged rocks. It floated farther out to sea, with each wave carrying it out until it became a speck on the wide expanse of seawater.

"Dad!" I shouted. "You have my blessing! Be at peace!"

In my heart came a warm feeling that circulated all through me. The precious bond between a father and a son, the assurance of belonging that every child needs, was no longer missing. I became very grateful.

"Thank you, Father!" I called to God.

Later, in the margin of my journal where I'd taped a copy of the letter, I scribbled:

> Forgiveness is setting a prisoner free
> and realizing the prisoner is you.

Chapter 15

TRANSFORMATION
FROM DEEP WITHIN

*A great part of our life is an invention to avoid
confrontation with our deepest self.*

— ANAÏS NIN, *DIARIES*, FIFTH VOLUME

NOW THAT WE'VE FOLLOWED the Blueprint for Gaining Freedom and covered some techniques to help you benefit from each stage, we are ready to transform. And that's a tall order. Transformation implies many things. Generally, it means a wholesale change from worse to better. And most of the time it means a wholesome improvement from within, a genuine reformation of heart or character. It's what classic movies or novels portray; think of how the hero transformed in stories like *A Christmas Carol* (Scrooge), *Jane Eyre* (Jane), or *Les Misérables* (Jean Valjean).

You too can be a hero who transforms. A hero to yourself and to those who love you.

By following the Wholeness/Recovery arrow to the Spiritual square (8) on the Four Squares of Life diagram (see page 134), *reconnecting with your spirituality*, you will reap the reward of a transformed life. We start to transform when we switch from living in ways that serve the ego to living in ways that serve the Spirit. So maybe you are asking, "How do I know I am living a spiritual life?" The answer is, "You know you are living a spiritual life when your life has *meaning*."

Authenticity and spirituality go together. Authenticity is the opposite of hypocrisy, and a meaningful life derives from living authentically. Meaning derives from acting consistently with your values. Meaning boosts self-esteem, empowers revised self-definitions, and results in lasting satisfaction. Meaning also derives from pursuing one's purpose. Finding your purpose may be a long and tricky process, but arriving at your personal answers to two questions can help you identify what's appropriate for you: What are my strongest *interests*? ("What do I love doing so much that I would do it even without being paid?") What are my greatest *gifts*? ("What special talents come easily to me and that others say I have?")

As you grow away from secret keeping, you will discover that *meaning follows from serving others with your special gifts and shared interests*. Serving others helps you to fulfill your purpose. Each time you set a goal that's in line with serving others and your life purpose, the meaning in your life expands. The challenges and joys of "stretching" to realize your dreams may lead to some mistakes, but ultimately they will lead to more successes. Celebrating your successes in healthy ways fuels your optimism, and goodwill from others will be reflected back to you.

So look again at the Continuum of Secrets in chapter 2 (page 23), and note the line dividing the more-harm-to-much-harm categories of Secret Keeping and Crime/Psychosis from the no-harm-to-less-harm categories of Simple Secrets and Silent Secrets — and then decide to go back over the line and return to the "simple" life! This process asks you to adopt a return-to-innocence attitude as you recover and mature in authenticity, much as a sea captain who has weathered many storms would enjoy the simpler pleasures of sailing a small sailboat more than he would maneuvering a battleship in enemy waters.

YOUR PERSONAL PATH TO WHOLENESS

Take a look at the bell-curve chart on the next page. It describes four ways to understand the changes that former Secret Keepers committed to recovery can make, showing how they can move from secrecy to transparency, from what is more selfish to what is more spiritual. Note the direction of the arrow, from left (secrecy) to right (transparency).

To find where you belong on the chart, read horizontally across the four rows. For example, read each of the four descriptions just under the shaded "bell" area. Reading across, you will see "Closed to others; 'loner,'" "Guarded with others," "More relaxed with others," and "Open with others." Now, decide which describes you best (and be honest!). Perhaps you can ask someone you know to tell you which of the four describes you, for verification. Once you've picked the column, read down it and decide whether each descriptor fits you. If it does, circle or highlight it. If it doesn't, read the descriptor to the left or right of it and decide if it fits. Circle or highlight it (but identify only one), and keep marking in the same manner until you reach the bottom.

What you have just determined is your baseline starting point — the personality and character traits you exhibit right now. Add all these descriptions together, and you should have a fairly concise summary of your current psychological traits. Look to the right (following the direction of the arrow), and you'll see some you may want to improve. Those you decide to improve become your next recovery goal. Ultimately, every descriptor in the far-right column under Recovering Secret Keeper could and should be your profile.

ESTIMATED PERCENTAGE OF ADULT POPULATION
WITH SECRET-KEEPING TRAITS

10%–15%	35%–40%	35%–40%	10%–15%
SECRECY →	→	→	→ **TRANSPARENCY**
ISOLATED SECRET KEEPER	SELFISH SECRET KEEPER	SENSITIVE SECRET KEEPER	RECOVERING SECRET KEEPER
Closed to others; "loner"	Guarded with others	More relaxed with others	Open with others
Everything to hide	Much to hide	Some to hide	Little to hide
Caves in to impulses; works at low-end jobs to make more indulgences possible	Protects her/his "own time"; holds down a job and has a family and home responsibilities	Ducks away and "steals hours" to indulge whenever nobody is aware; strives for fulfillment via career	Manages impulses by use of reason and divine power; career serves her/his life and meets the needs of others
Nonconformist/rebel; prone to crime	Conforms grudgingly; prone to outbursts	Conforms with apparent ease; prone to pouts/moods	Feels free to express her-/himself; conformity matters little
Denies/defies reason or logical feedback; stubborn self-will	May be sloppy about covering her/his tracks or making excuses/alibis	Clever and wise about covering her/his tracks or making excuses/alibis	No tracks to worry about or cover — hardly ever must make excuses/alibis
Self-sufficient even when bankrupt: "I live by my own rules"	Denies any wrongdoing or addiction — defensive and argumentative regarding feedback: "I can quit anytime"	Admits to wrongdoing or addiction; may seek counseling when in pain: "I can change my mind"	Admits to duality and self-defeating behaviors — actively follows path of recovery: "I am living a new life"
Scoffs at offers to help or at 12-step suggestions	Resists self-help resources or 12-step suggestions	Uses self-help books/resources or 12-step suggestions	Tends to join self-help groups and 12-step meetings
POOR FUNCTION	**LOW FUNCTION**	**RELIABLE FUNCTION**	**HIGH FUNCTION**

For instance, let's say "Much to hide" is your starting point. Look to the right and see the improvement: "Some to hide," then "Little to hide." In this case, these last two are your goals: first "Some," and then "Little" (even the healthiest people never have "None"). Study the items listed in the column on the far right and decide how willing you are to make those become realities in your life, then commit to those items. That's where you're headed.

Let's take a minute and ask a "big-picture" question:

Q: What is whole-mindedness?

A: It's everything you see in the right-hand "Transparency" column in the diagram on the facing page. Taking each descriptor in the column, let's add up what whole-mindedness means:

Being "open with others"	=	Considering them and their needs while meeting my own.
Having "little to hide"	=	Letting down my guard, relaxing more.
"Manages impulses"	=	Anticipating consequences and partnering with God.
"Freedom to express yourself"	=	What I have to hide no longer rules my life.
"No tracks to worry about or cover"	=	Fewer fear-based actions and feelings.
"Hardly ever making excuses"	=	Not having to apologize for deceiving.

"Living a new life"	=	Acting consistently with my values replaces the old ways of sneaking away to indulge secretly.
"Join self-help groups, go to meetings"	=	Collaborating with others like myself who understand and accept me.
Being "highly functional"	=	My efforts and choices weave together into satisfying and lasting results — for everyone who knows me and for myself.

Another answer to the question "What is whole-mindedness?" comes from practicing the opposite of the Triad of Secret-keeping Emotions, the Triad of Whole-minded Emotions:

1. the *excitement* of seeking God,

2. the *pleasure* of sharing divine presence and power,

3. the *delight* of belonging and being loved.

This amended triad came to me during silent, solitary moments while job hunting in Minneapolis in 1981. Whenever I took a break from interviews and walked alongside a tranquil creek in the woods — when previously being alone would have meant I'd certainly be secret keeping! — I prayed and recited verses from Scripture instead. How different that was from the sneaky excitement, pleasure, and delight I had earlier experienced from running in the woods naked or pot smoking and other secret-keeping behaviors. Now, by seeking authenticity and whole-mindedness, I was experiencing:

1. the excitement of seeking God rather than breaking rules,

2. the *pleasure* of sharing divine presence and power rather than indulging in what's forbidden,

3. the *delight* of belonging and being loved rather than not getting caught.

This new triad operated in my favor when I stood browsing at a magazine rack in LAX airport while waiting to board a job-hunting flight to Minnesota. My eyes went from *Time* to *Harper's* to *Fortune* past the sports magazines to the top row where *Playboy* and *Penthouse* beckoned. "No!" my inner voice shouted. "Don't be tempted! Don't even *think* of opening those magazines!" But the urge jabbed at me.

Months before I'd stuffed dozens of similar magazines from my fifteen-year collection into garbage bags and thrown them in the trash — having willingly chosen to remain faithful in my marriage. Now I felt shocked that the impulse seemed as strong as ever. I prayed silently for supernatural help, and the strength to turn away came to me right away. I was able to keep my "eyes-off" vow intact. No way was I going to plunge into that downward spiral again.

Another time I was attending a church retreat in the forests of California's San Bernardino Mountains. I'd snuck away to smoke a joint that I'd slyly tucked into my suitcase. I strolled among the majestic trees after twilight in search of an isolated place to toke up, fully aware of being a hypocrite. Stopping at a rugged precipice in dense shadows hidden from the lights of the resort, I started to light up. But abruptly I lost my footing and began falling, sliding down toward the sheer drop-off and the jagged rocks far below. Again I called out for divine help and, miraculously, my downward motion stopped — when I was only inches from the edge. Managing to pull myself back to safety, I praised God for saving me ... and turned this near-fatal warning into an arduous one-year recovery process of quitting pot. I haven't smoked marijuana since and am the happier for it.

At a neurological level, something wonderful was happening in my brain, and can happen in the brain of anyone who lives by the amended triad. As explained before, when nerve cells in our brains fire together, they wire together. The opposite happens too. To review for a moment, based on the sophisticated scientific principle of "use it or lose it," nerves cells that *don't fire together no longer wire together.* The cells lose their long-term relationship over time as new beliefs interrupt old thought processes. Of course, each individual Secret Keeper has to intervene on herself and do the interrupting by herself and for herself. With each interruption from a fresh thought (new self-talk) a stale thought (old self-talk) is replaced; the nerve cells that were once connected to each other start breaking up chemically, and the new cells start wiring together. By consciously interrupting the old triad of emotions and living out the new triad instead, you can gradually place new, even opposite, thoughts into your brain. These fresh positive thoughts then trigger fresh positive emotions.

Out with the old, and in with the new!

This process can lead you toward whole-mindedness. Along with replacing that old worn-out triad, you will also start to replace those old splintered mind-sets with the eight healthy mind-sets of whole-minded people:

Whole-minded people:

- live free of their secret attitudes and addictions
- are not threatened by the strengths of others
- see ahead to the result or conclusion of an action
- understand the difference between right and wrong
- do not obey their slimy motives
- behave spontaneously with nothing to hide
- are willing to show their true selves to others
- can love the essence of another person, regardless of the person's worldly status.

OBSTACLES ON THE QUEST
FOR WHOLE-MINDEDNESS

To go to the "next level," you will need to address the obstacles in the way of recovery and of reaching the goals of whole-mindedness and transparency. These could be anything from a lack of internal motivators to victim-based self-talk, from unaddressed developmental deficits to refusing to partner with a higher power. Let's say your starting point is "ducks away and 'steals hours' to indulge." To accomplish "manages impulses by use of reason and divine power," you will first need to ask, "What fears and beliefs are holding me back? What's making me duck re-sponsibility?" Then reread chapters 10 and 13 on those topics.

To help you discover what obstacles in your life you still need to overcome, I have provided the sample below. In a moment you will be asked to get out your notebook or journal and fill in the same blanks for yourself.

Exercise

Sample

(Your completed exercise could look like this.)

- List your fears and beliefs: *I will never amount to anything, I keep a low profile to avoid criticism, I'm not sure I can change, life won't be as exciting without secrets.*

- Next, list ways these fears could be reduced, refuted, or eliminated: *I'm part of a support group and not doing this alone, the Four Squares process is helping me, I've replaced distorted self-talk with realistic self-talk.*

- Then, apply one or more of the six stages from the Blueprint for Gaining Freedom: *I have surrendered my secret-keeping habits, I accept my duality, and I'm on my way to trusting in a new worldview.*

- Then, account for your present non-secret-keeping behavior, like *no more binging and purging in secret,* or *no more peeking at porn photos on the Internet.*

- Set some reasonable goals and time objectives, and write out a brief statement such as: *"I will practice or attempt disclosing my private thoughts to my spouse, my journal, or my support group sponsor once a week, then jot down my progress for each goal in a small notebook, then call a close friend, my sponsor, or accountability partner twice a week to report in. Each third Tuesday afternoon of the month we will sit together and assess my progress. I will be rigorously honest. If needed, I will repeat the above actions/objectives until authenticity (enjoyable abstinence) is accomplished. When I've succeeded I will know it because I'll feel less fearful and free of hypocrisy. My thoughts will have shifted from what I can get away with to what I can contribute to others. Along the way I will pay attention to any warning signs, such as H.A.L.T.* [Hungry, Angry, Lonely, Tired — more about this later in the chapter]. *With each small success I will celebrate by informing someone and by writing a new affirmation to repeat to myself like "I am becoming transparent."*

- List the internal motivators that will help you sustain longer-term consistency: *Honesty is helping to boost my self-esteem, I am getting more verbal approval from my family, and I feel less fearful.*

- Then list the character defects standing in your way that threaten to compromise the plan you've developed to reach these goals (always moving left to right): *self-pity, impatience, resentment, shame.*

- Use the same process for future goals.

EXERCISE
Your Turn

Now write your own information in your journal or notebook:

- List your fears and beliefs: _____

  _____

  _____

- Next, list ways these fears could be reduced, refuted, or eliminated: _____

  _____

  _____

- Then, apply one or more of the six stages from the Blueprint for Gaining Freedom: _____

  _____

  _____

- Then, account for your present non-secret-keeping behavior: _____
_____
_____

- Set some reasonable goals and time objectives, and write out a brief statement such as:

    "I will practice or attempt _____ once a week, then jot down my progress for each goal in a small notebook, then call a close friend or my sponsor or accountability partner twice a week to report in. Each _____ of the month we will sit together and assess my progress. I will be rigorously honest. If needed, I will repeat the above actions/objectives until _____ is accomplished. When I've succeeded I will know it because I'll feel _____ and _____ . My thoughts will have shifted from _____ to _____ . Along the way I will shrug off minor setbacks, such as _____
    _____
    _____.
    With each small success I will celebrate by _____
    _____.

- List the internal motivators that will help you sustain longer-term consistency: _____
_____
_____

- Then list the character defects standing in your way that threaten to compromise the plan you've developed to reach these goals (always moving left to right): _____
_____
_____

- Use the same process for future goals.

As you can decipher for yourself, the process of transformation takes some time and effort. Becoming whole again — becoming the same person wherever you go, or whoever you're with, including when you're alone and nobody is looking — means pedaling uphill. So enjoy it, right?

And, oh the rewards! You become fearless (no need to glance over your shoulder). You become honest (no need for alibis or fibs). You become transparent (people see the "real and only" you). You become whole (you are no longer divided mentally). You become your authentic self — honest, open, transparent — H.O.T.!

Your precious authenticity and new whole-mindedness may still be in danger, though. Just when you think your path to recovery may be secure, one possibility threatens it all, the risk of relapse.

AVOIDING RELAPSE: A FUTURE FREE OF SECRET-KEEPING

Much like former alcoholics with decades of successful sobriety who claim they are never cured, recovering Secret Keepers also claim that their secret keeping is never completely gone. There's that little voice that whispers, "Go ahead, nobody's looking." It remains stubbornly in our heads, perhaps at a very low volume, for a lifetime. After all, haven't you been obeying it for years? Though it remains, you can make it dormant — like something packed away in a chest and stored in the attic. It all depends on how you manage it.

Maybe you're asking, Is *anything* truly gone? Yes — the old way of making choices and dealing with them. For example, sober, recovering alcoholics can *think* about entering a bar or liquor store, but they *choose not to* because they risk returning to former destructive habits. So too can former recovering Secret Keepers *think* about old habits and old playpens (casinos, stores, X-rated websites), but they can *choose not to* go there for the same reasons. Having a thought does not mean you must act on it — it is only a thought. You might think of robbing a bank, but actually aiming a gun at a teller and demanding money is another thing entirely. Our thoughts do not have to lead to actions, not if we remain rooted in the values we profess and genuinely believe in abiding by them.

As a counselor, I use the following definition of *relapse*: A relapse is a break in one's recovery process due to former secret-keeping behavior that may last for one minute or for days and weeks…but it occurs only after a determined and genuine period of weeks or months of abstinence from secret keeping. If you have not first experienced a determined and genuine period of abstinence, it's simply a return to old behavior. In short, white-knuckling abstinence for a few days and giving up by going back to secret keeping doesn't count as recovery. Entire books have been dedicated to the "hows" of preventing relapse. For our purposes, let's start with this easy-to-remember acronym: H.A.L.T., which stands for Hungry, Angry, Lonely, Tired.

Essentially, H.A.L.T. acts as a reminder that any time we experience a combination of these four feeling states, we should watch out. A combination of any two states, say, Angry and Tired, should put us on notice. A combination of any three states, say Angry, Tired, and Lonely, should put us on high alert. And a combination of all four states should make us stop everything and call someone we trust, run to a support group meeting, or do anything that will prevent us from falling back into our old secret-keeping habits. Remember that your highest-risk situation is being alone, when those old familiar urges have a better chance of tempting you to indulge in familiar habits.

As a further aid to helping you understand when you are in danger of reversing course, below I have included a checklist of relapse warning signs. The warnings also act as reminders and will aid in raising your awareness. Again, be honest! If you have too many check marks on this "dirty dozen," you may be setting yourself up for a relapse.

CHECKLIST

Relapse Warning Signs: "The Dirty Dozen"

_____ 1. *Impatience*. Feeling that things aren't happening fast enough.

_____ 2. *Argumentativeness*. Arguing small or unimportant issues, always needing to be right.

_____ 3. *Depression*. Experiencing unreasonable or unexplained despair, hopelessness, feeling overwhelmed, dwelling on NSDs.

_____ 4. *Self-pity*. Feeling sorry for yourself, worrying about unfairness. Refusing to accept "what is."

_____ 5. *Cockiness* or *arrogance*. Believing you have got it all figured out, fixed, or solved. Flirting with former secret-keeping habits.

_____ 6. *Complacency*. Believing everything is going okay, forgetting about your recovery, not repeating your affirmations (PSDs).

_____ 7. *Exhaustion*. Allowing yourself to become overly tired or being in poor health.

_____ 8. *Dishonesty*. Telling unnecessary little lies to co-workers, family, and friends.

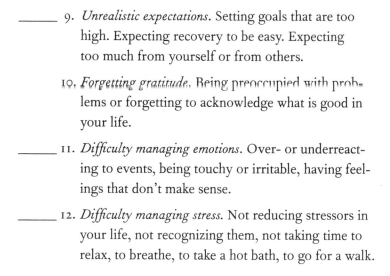

_____ 9. *Unrealistic expectations.* Setting goals that are too high. Expecting recovery to be easy. Expecting too much from yourself or from others.

_____ 10. *Forgetting gratitude.* Being preoccupied with problems or forgetting to acknowledge what is good in your life.

_____ 11. *Difficulty managing emotions.* Over- or underreacting to events, being touchy or irritable, having feelings that don't make sense.

_____ 12. *Difficulty managing stress.* Not reducing stressors in your life, not recognizing them, not taking time to relax, to breathe, to take a hot bath, to go for a walk.

Using H.A.L.T. and the list above will help spark your awareness before a relapse occurs, but it's up to you: Your contract is with yourself, by yourself, for yourself. Only you can intervene on you. In effect, these types of exercises are reminders not to cross the line on the Continuum of Secrets from simple or silent secrets to secret keeping again. They prompt you to continue replacing NSDs with PSDs, and to continue exploring the Wholeness/Recovery benefits of the Four Squares of Life: *feeling better physically*, *thinking more realistic thoughts*, *restoring positive feelings*, and *reconnecting with your spirituality*.

Dreaming Big

As we have seen, square eight of the Four Squares diagram, *reconnecting with your spirituality*, is where "transformation from deep within" fits. One thing veterans in recovery programs often express is that a vital spiritual awakening occurs as a result of "practicing these principles in all our affairs."[1] Living authentically, as mentioned earlier, means acting consistently with your values. Doing so boosts the meaning in our lives, which in turn boosts our self-esteem and lasting satisfaction. Meaning also derives from pursuing our purpose in life. Individuals who pursued great purposes in their time on earth (like Abraham Lincoln, Mahatma Gandhi, Nelson Mandela, Mother Teresa, and Martin Luther King Jr.) showed us how to practice these principles in their daily lives. They made huge contributions while partnering with God in serving others, despite overwhelming obstacles.

For you, the idea is to live out a dream so big (like theirs) that only your special gifts, along with the amazing partnership of your higher power, can make such "miracles" happen. Dream big! Then you and fellow human beings can reap the rewards of living happier, more fulfilling lives.

How do you know you are living a spiritual life? When you are doing exactly that.

Please note that arriving at the Spiritual square doesn't have to mean getting bogged down in debates about "religion" or the names for "God" or where one worships — church, cathedral, temple, mosque, tent, nature, and so on. Organized religion, doctrine, and dogma may enhance one's spirituality, or these may exhaust it. Examples of both dynamics are plentiful.

Alas, not all Secret Keepers attempt to recover or to invest their lives with meaning. They persist in their secret keeping, and the others in their lives suffer for it. Take Ted, for instance....

TED'S STORY: THE FLIP SIDE

When we last saw Ted, in chapter 8, he was parking his repair van at a motel advertising adult movies on cable TV. Meanwhile, his wife, Shelly, was planning the festivities for their fourth wedding anniversary. Using their home computer, she made an innocent click with the mouse, and the screen revealed Ted having sexual intercourse with a woman on their couch!

Shelly's world collapsed.

For months her gut had told her that something was wrong in their marriage, and now she knew what. More clicks revealed different women having sex with him, and a cursory search revealed similar photos of her nude husband in wild poses.

Shelly sought counseling and explored her feelings of betrayal. She learned from the therapist that the evidence she had uncovered showed classic patterns of sexual addiction. Armed with this information, Shelly confronted Ted. He blew up in anger and spewed blame and criticism. Shelly asked him to join her in marriage counseling. He refused. As if following a written script, Ted justified his behavior by using every excuse imaginable:

- You lost interest in sex with me.

- No one saw anything.

- You are making a big deal out of nothing.

- I was only testing the camera.

- I can stop anytime.

Fearful for her safety, Shelly moved out of the house and into a trailer. Discouraged, she studied books on the topic and learned that sex addicts act overly self-absorbed, objectify their partners, and have trouble with intimacy. Searching for answers, she read popular self-help books aimed at readers in abusive relationships and came face-to-face with her own codependence. Although never choosing to do so consciously, she had picked a man with abusive and addictive tendencies. Unless she stood up for herself and somehow reversed his violations of her boundaries, and of their marriage vows, she would ultimately be condoning his misbehavior. This pitfall of codependency she could no longer tolerate. "Ted never addressed the core problem, his sexual obsessions, but then I realized how my codependency had only exacerbated the underlying sickness in our marriage. It was time for a change."

Divorce ensued. Shelly started attending COSA Anonymous meetings (Codependents of Sexual Addicts) and accepted the fact that she hadn't recognized the glaring red flags while they were dating. "When we want something a certain way," she says, "we make our reality fit that." She also discovered another uncomfortable reality: Often when you tell someone else's secret, you become the bad guy. "The negative feedback I got for 'tattling' on Ted floored me. I took the brunt for *his* defects of character. Almost everybody I knew treated me like I was the one with the problem." Regardless, she stuck to her mission of growing her authenticity and continued to believe that revealing the truth was healthier than concealing it.

Empowered by her readings and encouraged by support groups, Shelly wrote her own articles and books and attended conferences, with the purpose of reaching out to others like her. Her message was "stand up for yourself." After writing out a fearless personal inventory of her life history and values, after looking deeply within herself for who she wanted to be, she started her own website, YouAreATarget.com, to offer help and insight to anyone who, like her, has been victimized by someone else's secrets.

"When the divorce was final," Shelly states, "it no longer bothered me that Ted had never admitted that his addiction had sabotaged our marriage. I'm so much stronger now, and he is still out there somewhere in never-never land."

She smiles and says, "I spent years always doing what I

thought was best for him. Now I'm doing what's best for me and for others, serving people like me and refusing to protect anyone's secrets or image. How refreshingly uncodependent!"

—⚹—

Like Shelly, perhaps you are living with a Secret Keeper. Perhaps you are only a mouse click (or an overheard phone call) away from the Discovery That Changes Everything. If you suspect that you are living with a Secret Keeper, you would do well to emulate Shelly's assertive ways when dealing with your loved one's secrets. In the next chapter you will meet another spouse who faced some uncomfortable choices.

Chapter 16

YOUR RECOVERY
FROM TODAY ON

Be the change that you want to see in the world.

—— MAHATMA GANDHI

Y OU'VE COME THIS FAR. You've looked into the motives
and mind-sets of several Secret Keepers, and you've
observed where secret keeping fits on the Continuum of Secrets.
You've explored each of the Eight Splintered Mind-sets, and you
have learned ways to reverse those mind-sets, including the distorted thinking and emotions that can trap you. You've examined the stages of the Blueprint for Gaining Freedom and some
useful 12-step principles. Finally, you've traveled both directions
on the Four Squares of Life diagram and seen how youthful
development can be twisted physically, mentally, emotionally,
and spiritually — but, more important, also how one's enthusiastic recovery can heal, restore, rejuvenate, and reconnect us to
wholeness.

Take a deep breath. You have just a little way to go before
you reach the beginning. Yes, you read that right — I said, "the
beginning." That's because your new life is starting as you read

this. One way to think of your recovery journey from today on is that you are traveling:

1. from the insanity of secret keeping to the sanity of personality change,

2. from the sanity of personality change to the stability of character change, and

3. from the stability of character change to the serenity of spiritual change.

To see how these shifts can work for you, take a look at the chart below. It shows a series of "milestones" in your future, the potential stages of the new you that is now emerging. Note especially the differences in self-talk at each milestone:

MILESTONE	TIME FRAME	SELF-TALK
Transitional	Indefinite	Do I have a problem? Should I stop secret keeping?
Stabilized (no secret keeping)	1–2 years	I'm tired of faking it. I want my authenticity back.
Early Recovery	2–7 years	I am building a new life of integrity and wholeness.
Middle Recovery	7–15 years	I'm living the H.O.T. life, free and whole, and loving it.
Late Recovery	15 years +	I am a new person helping others deal with their secrets.

Once a stressed-out, weary (Transitional) Secret Keeper, at some point you no doubt said to yourself, "I have a problem. How can I quit?" Having admitted as much, you've now begun taking the actions that are helping you reach the Stabilized milestone, like surrendering, seeking help, preparing to disclose, and disclosing. You've already been saying, "I'm tired of faking it. I want my authenticity back." As you reap the rewards of Stabilized authenticity, you will know when you have reached the end of this stage because you'll no longer wake up thinking, planning, plotting, scheming how to sneak off and drink, gamble, shoplift, look at porn, and so on. Instead, you will have been practicing the Blueprint for Gaining Freedom, replacing NSDs with PSDs, and accepting and forgiving, long enough to reach the Early Recovery milestone.

Now let's review the tasks related to each milestone:

MILESTONE	TASKS
Transitional	Surrendering; seeking help; acknowledging pain and guilt over secret keeping; accepting and understanding your duality.
Stabilized	Preparing to disclose and then disclosing the true facts to self, God, others; replacing old distorted thoughts; restoring positive feelings; relying on internal motivators.
Early Recovery	Trusting in a new worldview; accounting for present and future behavior; telling your "Four Squares" story; joining and staying active in your support group.

MILESTONE	TASKS
Middle Recovery	Spelling out the benefits of a H.O.T. life to others; leading your support group; coaching others on how to make personality and character changes.
Late Recovery	Celebrating your transformation; leading an active and visible spiritual life; starting new groups; teaching the Blueprint for Gaining Freedom and the Four Squares of Life; attending conferences.

As you continue on in your new life, you will one day find yourself saying: "I am building a new life of integrity and wholeness." Your internal motivators will be solid, and those once-powerful secret-keeping urges will have gone dormant. As you live authentically and complete the tasks in each phase, the years pass, and the day will come when you find yourself shifting into the Middle Recovery milestone period: "I'm living an honest, open, and transparent (H.O.T.) life, free and whole, and loving it." Then one day you will greet the morning and humbly say, "I am a new person helping others deal with their secrets," leading an active and visible spiritual life, happy that you've stayed on the path to freedom.

Think about it for a minute. Secret keeping and its accompanying addictions, compulsions, and delusions can be behind you, and recovery and a brand-new life are before you. That means you can focus on the present and future instead of on the past, on recovery rather than addiction, on what's right rather than on what's wrong. Recall how our brains make new circuits — "neurons that fire together wire together"— while old circuits that go unused fade away, "neurons that don't fire together no longer wire together." Even biology is in your favor!

Review how the Wholeness/Recovery arrow goes in the opposite direction of the Dysfunction/Addiction arrow on the Four Squares of Life diagram (page 134). By choosing to intentionally go in the direction of Wholeness/Recovery, you are moving naturally from insanity to sanity (personality change), to stability (character change), to serenity (spiritual change). It's a learning process. As a recovering Secret Keeper you are saying yes to being a lifelong learner — with a twist. As I once jotted down in my journal: "In school, the lesson comes first, then the test. In life, the test comes first, then the lesson."[1]

What lessons are you drawing from the tests you've faced so far? Regardless of the answer, the attitude we take toward learning (always a venture into the unfamiliar) is vital to our growth and overall satisfaction.

Sometimes we can overthink things and stay in our heads too long. Our next topic, about "mindfulness," is actually based on the way we breathe. Stop reading, close your eyes, and take a deep breath. Really. Put this book aside and think only of inhaling and exhaling. Take your time. Slow down. Breathe in, breathe out. Allow in as much air through your nose as possible, hold it a second or two, then slowly let the air out through your mouth. Repeat slowly. Repeat again. Notice how your chest expands and contracts. Feel your mind drifting, floating. Put your full attention on the air going in and going out...in and out....

THE IMPORTANCE OF MINDFULNESS

You have just practiced mindfulness. Ironically, when we focus solely on our breathing, the clutter and constant churning in our minds loosen their grip and release fresh, new sensations. When we direct our awareness, when we aim our attention, the cacophony of thoughts we cope with gradually settles into a quiet reverie. Our self-talk is silenced, and new possibilities emerge. We become self-affirming human *beings* again, not just task-oriented human *doings*. We experience recovery — the enthusiastic energy of transforming — not just the planning and implementing of cognitive restructuring (much of what we've been exploring up till now).

Actually, the concept of mindfulness has been an underlying theme in all our discussions. Mindfulness, or higher consciousness, is about increased awareness. It's about switching off our "autopilot" and switching on "fresh eyes." It's about seeking increased consciousness *and* conscience.

Mindfulness is about looking beyond your current state of mind to the conditioning in your past that shaped your current outlook. It's the silent signal in us that says, "Use power, not force." Remember who won India's independence from British rule; a skinny little bespectacled "nobody" who used power, not a mighty army that used force.

To cultivate this state of mind, start by trying to see today's events without instantly judging them. If you are liberal, try reading conservative op-ed pieces — and vice versa. Take a second look at your first impression. Choose your response rather than living to regret your reaction. A response implies making a reasoned choice, whereas a reaction implies a choiceless habit. We are creatures of choice, not cretins of habit.

Many of us have an automatic tendency to judge, to evaluate others quickly and ourselves slowly. Cultivating a higher consciousness automatically means thinking about and caring for others. It means we see outside ourselves. Also, we often tend to appraise our overall experience as being not quite right. With this tendency comes the uneasy emotions that trigger blame. We may ponder what's missing in our careers or marriages or families, judging these things as being not quite good enough, then think-ing about how things could or should be different — *how my way is best*. This is the opposite of accepting *what is*. Blaming sets us up for another negative feeling state. And negative feeling states, as we know all too well by now, trigger numbing or escaping. Before we know it, especially when we're drifting on autopilot, we go looking for relief, and secret keeping, our old friend, comes knocking at the door.

Unless we interrupt this ingrained reaction by staying alert to our recovery goals, we'll get hooked once more and face a relapse, with all the ugly consequences that follow. The best way to stop reacting is to be mindful, to simply be attuned to what is. Cheri Huber, author of *The Key*, a book of mindful wisdom, reminds us: "When you can let it be the way it is and not how you've decided it should be, you can begin to see that the only thing making you unhappy is your idea of how it should be."[2]

Mindfulness releases us from the grip of blaming, of insist-ing that things should go our way. Immaturity shouts, "It's my way or the highway!" Maturity whispers, "My way may be the wrong way." Immature people pound their fists, while mature people acknowledge "things happen the way they do for a rea-son." By practicing mindfulness, we become more aware of those warning signs that may be telling us we are getting hooked (or stuck) again. At just such a time we can focus on *what is*, on *everything we have*, and be grateful. It's as simple as shifting our attention and choosing to be thankful.

This is freedom, from the inside. Our new Self empowers us to generate positive emotions based on new habits, instead of demanding to get its way and refusing to change our self-talk or to forgive those who once hurt us.

Whenever we "take a second look at our first reaction," says Terry Fralich, leader of mindfulness seminars, "we have a real opportunity to make a more intentional choice. Many times we discover that our first reaction is not constructive or healthy. In a very real sense, the practice of mindfulness allows the old brain circuits conditioned by fear to die out as we replace them with new neural circuits created by our best intentions.... The ability to self-regulate our states of mind, emotion, and body is one of the keys to living a balanced and satisfying life."3 Indeed, it's a skill we can all develop that will pay diverse dividends.

SEEKING PROFESSIONAL HELP

Another way to attain this all-important mindfulness is to receive professional help. Go see an acupuncturist, yoga instructor, massage therapist, or another of the many practitioners who are ready, willing, and able to assist you in practicing mindfulness.

Think of a three-legged stool. Let's name one leg *awareness*, another *understanding*, and the third *readiness*. Former Secret Keepers yearning for wholeness benefit from the awareness of the harm caused by their secret keeping; and they want to build on their understanding of duality; and they seek to nurture their readiness for character change. When combining all three, they can stand securely on such a "stool" to reach a higher state of consciousness and enjoyable authenticity. (Any dairy farmer who has milked cows will tell you that a three-legged stool seldom tips over.)

Professional help also comes in myriad forms. Psychotherapists run the gamut, and talking to a compassionate trained counselor about your troubles is a wise option. If you can pay, or have insurance, or are mandated by a court of law, then such help is advisable. If not, it's still a wise choice to make, despite the obstacles. For the people we have met in these pages, myself included, it proved to be.

Professionals offer:

- consistent openness and support of client — no recriminations
- a pledge to act in your best interests
- a model of open, nonjudgmental communication
- a forum for the discussion of options
- clarity regarding standards of normal/abnormal, healthy/unhealthy
- trustworthiness, in the form of returning calls, being on time, acting professionally
- confidentiality, making disclosure safer.

Is a therapist right for you? After so many years of perfecting my secret-keeping "skills," there came a time when I sought out a professional therapist — and I'm glad I did. My head was so jumbled with alibis and fatigued from twisting the truth that I needed to sit down with an objective listener and voluntarily sort it all out. After several sessions, some things became clear: that I was ruining my mental health and had sullied my character; that emotional issues were the basis of my "secrets" problem; that other people were being harmed, even if they didn't realize the cause; that God was not pleased by my hypocrisy; and that the time had come when change was absolutely necessary. All this helped, and my therapist offered homework assignments and exercises to get me started on making those changes (pedaling uphill and enjoying it).

Then, during one session, he asked me what positive lessons I'd learned from secret keeping. Could I name any transferable skills? I sat there in his office tongue-tied. Slowly, gradually, the creativity and finesse I'd developed while juggling two opposing worlds dawned on me, as well as the dexterity and shrewdness

I'd mastered in walking the "tightrope." He helped me see that while secret keeping demanded a lot from me, it also offered positive lessons and certain skills that could apply to numerous areas of life. At once I felt jolts of internal motivation! With fresh enthusiasm, I developed my own program of recovery, stuck to it, and harvested multiple benefits in my life. Later, I applied this learning to my professional counseling with troubled clients who had their own secret-keeping messes.

Seeking professional help is a wise choice to make for other reasons. Because the Secret Keeper has done harm to other people, you may think that the therapist will side naturally with the partner or family. Not so. It is his or her job to resist being pulled into the middle of the conflict, and to facilitate the communication between the parties, rather like an interpreter fluent in the language spoken by both parties who can speak clearly and accurately for both sides.

The therapist helps interpret what is happening and discusses the differences between how each person views the reality of their situation, while striving to validate each one's feelings.[4] As a coach, the therapist suggests strategies to prevent an attack-defend mode of interacting and helps both parties to work productively at handling disagreements. He or she offers insights into past behavior and consequences, clarifies treatment goals, uses methods to reach those goals and to set measurements of improvement, provides time lines and accountability for present and future conduct, and refers clients to other sources of aid.

Psychologist Anita Kelly cites findings by counseling researchers Fong and Cox about the critical importance of addressing secrets in therapy. "Until clients can expose their innermost secrets and make themselves vulnerable to the counselor, the real work of counseling cannot begin."[5] Barry Farber, another research psychologist, states, "Revealing hidden thoughts, feelings, and experiences is an essential aspect of the therapeutic process and a critical component of healing. Approximately 50 percent of clients keep secrets from their therapists."[6] Assuredly, keeping secrets inhibits the work of therapy, whereas disclosure facilitates it. Research clearly shows that the person who discloses often experiences a sense of relief from physical and emotional tension.

In my own counseling practice, I've observed the benefits of "just talking" to be profound. Talk therapy, after all, is the bedrock of mental health therapy, according to many psychotherapists, including pioneer Sigmund Freud. Combining respectful listening and up-to-date, accurate information, professional counselors help clients focus on the harmful issues they need to examine.

In the early days of my training as a counselor, I had to sit back and learn to listen. Really listen. I had to learn to hear what the client *wasn't* saying, to pay attention to tone of voice and pace of speech, to hear the emotions behind the words and beneath the pauses. It became evident to me that listening, without jumping in with snappy replies or quick bits of advice, was one of the most respectful things one human being can do for another. Not to interrupt. To shut off the voice in one's own head. To seek to enter the head — and heart and soul — of the hurting person in the opposite chair.

Seeing the changes in people's lives became its own special reward for me. My overall aim in counseling clients and families has remained the same, to help them move in the three directions stated earlier:

1. to the sanity of personality change,

2. to the stability of character change,

3. to the serenity of spiritual change.

A simplified way of thinking about these three aims is that recovery helps you:

- Manage better
- Feel better
- Get along better.

Manage better refers to how you balance your career, finances, civic duties, and relationship issues (think King Arthur and his knights). You no longer drive drunk, for example, because doing so endangers every other driver on the road. Moreover, you know you can get into a legal labyrinth and/or injure or kill yourself.

Feel better refers to your "inner landscape," your emotional health and restored positive feelings. You no longer suffer acute bouts of depression or attacks of anxiety, because you are less captive to negative feeling cycles or unexamined self-talk.

Get along better refers to how you contribute at home, to the lives of your spouse and kids, as well as to those of co-workers and neighbors — thanks to those newly replaced thoughts and restored positive feelings. You no longer think like a victim, because the positive self-talk you are practicing more closely matches the reality you want, and that's healthy. As the benefits of recovery pile up, you become the "change that you want to see in the world."

For a visual picture of how these dynamics interact, see the diagram on the next page.

BRAD: RELATIONSHIP REPAIRS AND THE ROUGH ROAD AHEAD

Sadly, not everyone walks the path of mindfulness or seeks the transformative rewards of recovery. One such individual is Brad, whom we met way back in chapter 1, then a schoolboy betting

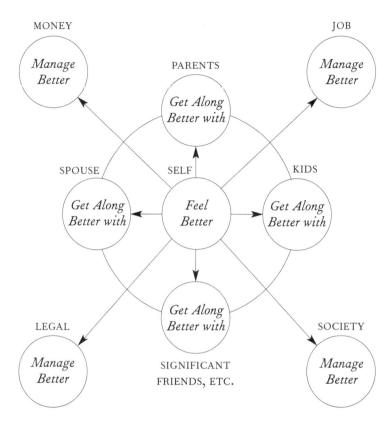

on marbles. We're returning to his story because Brad is thirty years older now and has followed none of the advice in this book. His condition has worsened over the three decades of his secret keeping. Perhaps you, or someone you love, are stuck in the same kind of predicament and need to really soul-search about what your own next steps will be. If you identify with Brad and his wife, I hope that you are yearning to avoid their misery and are prompted to take healthy action instead.

Here we meet up with Brad again at forty-six, employed, educated, married, a father of twins, and condemned to walking a tightrope between two opposing worlds. A typical day in Brad's life goes like this:

8:47 A.M.

Brad arrives at the offices of CompuMax lacking sleep. He carefully avoids his boss's office in the hopes of concealing his red, puffy eyes. This morning, like most, Brad's inner world is chaotic. Two pressing thoughts disturb him: (1) the wrenching sense of regret about staying out till 3:30 A.M. at the casino and then sneaking back into bed with his wife, Nancy, and (2) a gnawing urge to win back the $1,700 he squandered at the craps table last night. He fears the bank may cancel his account today because of too many overdue payments.

Brad's desk is messy. His phone light is blinking. A proposal for CompuMax's computer hardware customers is just where he left it yesterday, when he ducked out early to run to the casino, after asking his fishing buddy, Randy, for some cash. *I should've quit before I lost it all. Now Randy will be mad again.*

Brad boots up his PC and resumes writing the proposal. Reaching for the phone, he dials a familiar number. *I wonder if Mom has cashed her check from dad's annuity yet?*

His mother answers. After chitchatting, she expresses surprise when he asks about the annuity check. "With your salary, Brad, why are you asking for money?" Just then his boss pokes her head in the doorway. "Morning, Brad. How's that deadline coming?" She detects his sluggish, sleepy-eyed appearance. "Out late again, Brad? What adventure was it this time?"

He turns jovial, smiles. "Private business, just a little fun." He promises to have the proposal to her two hours ahead of schedule. Skeptically, she leaves. *Whew, that was close!* Brad grimaces, feeling severe abdominal pain.

At lunchtime, Brad stays at his desk hammering away at the proposal. Worry deepens the wrinkles on his brow. He remembers the special birthday plans for his twin girls tomorrow. He has promised to take them to Six Flags amusement park. *But I don't have a cent! And my credit cards are maxed out. Nobody else to borrow from.* Frowning, he frantically tries to come up with a solution. Another abdominal attack makes him wince.

1:09 P.M.

At Brad's home in an upscale suburb, Nancy sees a collection notice from the bank among the envelopes in the mail. The phone rings. It's Brad. "I'll be leaving work a little late, Nancy. Another bust-my-butt proposal. Can you hold dinner an hour or so?"

Nancy's face falls. "You've been late for dinner twice already this week."

"Honey, I'm sorry."

Nancy bites her lip.

"Look," Brad hems and haws, "I'll be home for dinner no later than 6:45, okay?"

She rolls her eyes. "Brad, I really think —"

"Deal?" says Brad, hurriedly. "I love you, bye."

5:22 P.M.

At a scenic overlook in a sunlit nature reserve, Brad sits in his parked car, glassy-eyed. His downcast mood contrasts starkly with the natural beauty around him. He stares out the windshield, barely focused on the trees or wildlife. On the passenger seat beside him lie scattered numerous instant lottery scratch-off cards, each ripped and shredded. He hangs his head. His shoulders start to shake. He grabs the steering wheel.

What has gotten into me? It can't go on like this. I'm sick of making excuses, of covering up. I'm sick of dodging creditors and sneaking out of the house at night. My whole life is a lie. It can't keep on like this. I can't put up with it. Neither can Nancy or the kids. Nancy must think I'm having an affair, always wondering why I'm gone somewhere.

Opening the car door, Brad walks to a nearby footbridge spanning a steep embankment to railroad tracks below. With shoulders hunched, he stares straight down at the tracks. His eyes get watery, and his lips tremble. Brad stifles sobs.

7:04 P.M.

Brad's family is eating dinner without him. One of the ten-year-old twins stares at her food, barely eating it. Her sister gazes down at her plate.

"I don't really care if we go tomorrow or not!" blurts the first girl.

Nancy tries to calm her. "But of course you're going. Dad promised."

"Yeah, right," chimes her sister. "And we all know what *that* means."

"Jennifer!" protests Nancy. "That's your father you're talking about."

The twins share knowing looks. The family hears a car driving into the driveway...fast. It screeches to a stop. A door opens and slams shut.

Brad rushes in, sits at the table, smiles, acts chipper and upbeat (no sign of the downcast mood at the bridge). The glum faces of his children greet him. "Hi, everybody! Sorry I'm late....Is there a funeral or something?"

"Late? What's new?" mutters Jackie, the first girl.

"Hey, if I didn't stay late at work once in a while," he protests, "we wouldn't be eating like this every night, now would we?" *If only they knew!*

Nancy puts her finger to her lips. "Honey, the less said the better."

Sarcastic looks circulate around the table. Nancy clears her throat. "It's about Six Flags, Brad. Nobody's sure if they're really going or not."

"Of course we're going. Who said otherwise?"

Silence blankets the room. One by one, everybody stands and scatters, leaving Brad to eat alone.

11:23 P.M.

Nancy brushes her teeth in the bathroom of their master bedroom. As Brad gets into his pajamas, she mentions the collection notice from the bank that came in the mail. "It's the third or fourth one this month, Brad. Are we in some kind of financial trouble I don't know about?"

"Uh, our investments have been taking a horrible beating lately."

"But it's the bank. It's not about our stocks or mutual funds."

"I'll look into it tomorrow," he says, waving it off. *What stocks or mutual funds? You must be dreaming!* Another stomach pang grips Brad. *Is she on to me this time?*

"You've been acting strange again, Brad. Coming in at four in the morning last night. Were you where I think you were?"

Brad collects himself, walks over to her, gently puts his arms around her, and whispers, "Everything is fine and dandy. The kids are going to have a fabulous 'day with Dad' tomorrow. You'll have all the time you need to set up their birthday party. I admit I've been edgy and hard to get along with lately. Please forgive me. Can we go to bed now and let it rest?" *When we switch cars tomorrow and I take the kids in her van, I'll have to make sure she doesn't find any of those lottery tickets in my car.*

Nancy rests her head on his shoulders. "It gets to me at times. The way we live. Does it have to be this way? Am I doing something wrong?"

Nothing, Nancy. Nothing at all, believe me. "No, honey, you're not doing anything wrong."

They head for bed and turn out the light. Under the covers, they lie beside one another, back to back. In the dark, Brad looks up at the ceiling. *Whew! I made it through another tough day! How many more like this can there be? But I still haven't a clue where the money for tomorrow will come from.*

Brad's inner life is no less chaotic now than when he started the day. Pressing thoughts still disturb him as he tries to fall asleep. Like it will for millions of others trapped in stealing hours to indulge in secret habits, tomorrow will bring more stress and more disappointments for Brad and his loved ones...until he summons the courage to confront the toll his double life is taking on him, until he voices the truth about his insanity and unmanageability, until his secrets become known.

FOR EVERY SECRET KEEPER OUT THERE

I saved Brad and Nancy's story for last because it represents the millions who are in predicaments like theirs — Secret Keepers who are still stuck and the family members who remain stuck with them. This book is for them, both the person trapped in secret keeping and the loved ones who suffer alongside them.

As an "everyman" Secret Keeper, Brad is hiding deep in the Hidden area of the Johari Window, unaware of the healthy actions that make up the Blueprint for Gaining Freedom, having surrendered nothing, trusting in a self-absorbed worldview, accountable to nobody but himself, and headed for disaster.

He is dancing on the thin line between secret keeping and crime/psychosis, is plagued by medical issues due to high stress, is pestered by NSDs buried in his implicit memory, and is ill from distorted thoughts and beliefs. He appears to have no internal motivation to change, no relationship with a higher power, no readiness for personality or character change, and no way to stop victimizing himself and his family.

As an "everywoman" Secret Keeper's spouse, Nancy is caught between loyalty to her husband and love for her children. She is lacking encouragement and effective ways to cope and feels weary from constantly guessing what her out-of-control adult partner will do next. Unlike Shelly, she has yet to confront Brad's secret keeping and the compulsive behavior that goes along with it, has yet to get the counseling she needs to determine healthy boundaries and new options, and still hasn't fathomed the full extent of devastation awaiting her when she finally learns the truth.

Unfortunately, Brad and Nancy don't know the Secret Keepers featured in previous chapters who found ways to break free from the stressful captivity of secret keeping. Surely they would benefit from hearing about their struggles and triumphs. To that end, I have included some brief hypothetical comments from those who have triumphed to encourage Brad to come clean and Nancy to stand her ground — so they both might begin the journey toward wholeness.

Caroline's advice to Brad: "I finally faced how really rotten I felt. My cry for help led to getting professional help. Despite my initial resistance, I found one-on-one and family therapy to be effective answers."

Bonnie's advice to Brad: "Opening up in a support group motivated me. It was the exact thing I needed. By associating with others, like you could in Gamblers Anonymous, I no longer withdrew as much or isolated like I always had. I gradually let others in on my secrets and felt waves of healing."

Mitch's advice to Brad: "I allowed the reality of God's grace and redemptive power to happen for me. My connection with a higher power helped me deal with a tough divorce, a court trial, and massive debt issues. I know the agony you're in. Just do it, Brad."

Earl's advice to Brad: "I spent hours of solitary time looking out a window and writing down my weaknesses and strengths, my character defects and distorted beliefs, and I gained so much.

I wrote down my life history in a journal that I still keep to this day. It's a safe outlet for my wounds and pain."

Tracy's advice to Brad: "So much changed when I repeated affirmations to myself, 'I like the person I am' and 'I am more than my body' made a real difference. I identified my highest risk situation, being alone. Now I have ways to defend myself against temptations and to keep from relapsing when nobody is looking. Get honest. Stop wasting time."

Lila's advice to Brad: "My secret keeping was my attempt to fill the missing feelings in my life. What I didn't recognize were the deep resentments from growing up that I'd numbed by stealing. Getting high secretly is a vain attempt to tip the scales of fairness back in balance. Surrender. Get help."

And, finally, Shelly's advice to Nancy, one spouse to another: "I spent years doing what I always thought was best for my husband, for us. But there was no 'us.' I'm so much stronger now because I'm doing what's best for me, refusing to protect anyone's secrets or image. I am finally my own person. Stop being codependent. It works!"

For the Brads and Nancys of this world, this book is for you. May it help you start on the path to recovery today.

ACKNOWLEDGMENTS

*M*ANY PEOPLE CONTRIBUTED to this book. High up on the list is Georgia Hughes, editor extraordinaire and all-around genius, cheerleader, and collaborator. Copyeditor Mimi Kusch also added her brilliant touches, as did Managing Editor Kristen Cashman. And Louise Woehrle saw the potential of this project early on and championed it with New World Library. My deepest thanks to each of you.

Then there is David Prin, my brother and encourager, who believed in the secret-keeping concepts as they developed and supported me during the infancy of this book and at numerous challenging times.

I wish to also express thanks to everyone who encouraged me or made a difference in some other way. Please regard the following as a gesture of my heartfelt appreciation. I truly feel grateful for everything you've done and wish you all many rich blessings.

People who have supported my writing over the years or this project in particular:

Carrie Almaer, Roy Arnold, Kathryn Bode, J. Marie Fieger, Katy Ingle, Cheris Garrison, Dan Humiston, Connie Hurtt, Dave Koehser, Cindy Lamont, Ian Leask, Don Leeper, Richard Leider, Doris Little, Jane MacCarter, Rick Mattson, Dorothy Molstad, Ed Newman, Gary Rosch, Julie Saffrin, Pat Samples, Paul Walker, Stan West, Betsy Williams, and Bob Wuornos. Special thanks to Tanya Dean for her help and encouragement in the early stages of writing about this topic.

There are other groups of folks I wish to thank: Mindy Caron and Frank Miller of SASSI Institute; Marty Hesselroth and her book club pals; Jane Smalkoski, Steve Pipkin, and the legendary serving staff at the Original Pancake House; and Rick Sanders and the design staff at Allegra Print & Imaging.

People who have supported my alcohol/drug recovery or professional development as a counselor and researcher over the years:

Dakota Baker, Dan Barmettler, Mark Brandow, Tom Berscheid, Don Caplinger, Patrick DeChello, Stephan Dilchert, John Driscoll, Russ Engle, Carlton Erickson, Fred French, Janie Hartnett, Priscilla Herbison, Tom Huberty, Earnie Larsen, John Magnuson, Shelly Marshall, William Cope Moyers, Mike Olson, Deniz Ones, Ron Potter-Efron, Mary Regnier, Jack Rowe, David Schreiber, Bev Sockwell, Terry Shulman, Dar Trnka, and "Vish" Viswervaran.

Thanks also to my AA home group: Jeff, Dave, Tom, Terry, Henry, Gary, Gene, Ward, and the remainder of the rowdy Boiler Room Gang.

People who have supported my spiritual development over the years:

Jack Blackburn, Al Bloch, Mary Ellen Conners, Greg and

Barb Cornell, John DeJong, Rev. Bob Dickson, Jack and Anna Kerr, Fred Kopplin, Rev. David Lenz, Larry Lorence, Rosie Maykowski, Dennis and Ann Monikowski, Eric and Jeanne Ness, Ed Newman, Mike and Susie Northrop, Rev. Lloyd Ogilvie, Rev. Ralph Osborne, Ted and Hildur Perkins, Carol and Bob Steere, Joe Steward, Roger and Debbie Stoesz, Rev. Allan Talley, and Rob and Joan von Edeskuty.

Thanks too to the many friends from the vibrant communities of Hope Presbyterian Church and River Valley Church in Minnesota, and Hollywood Presbyterian Church in California. I also thank the God "of my understanding," Jesus Christ and the Holy Spirit, which connect me with the Father's love, and the community of people of all faiths and doctrines who lovingly serve the common good.

Last, thanks to the people who contributed their stories to this book who remain anonymous.

NOTES

CHAPTER 1. WHO ARE THE SECRET KEEPERS?

1. This calculation is based on U.S. Census data for 2000 times the current agreed-on SAMHSA (Substance Abuse and Mental Health Services Administration) percentage of Americans with addictive disorders.
2. I based this estimated calculation on U.S. Census data and SAMSHA statistics.
3. Daniel Golcman, *Emotional Intelligence* (New York: Bantam, 1997), 8
4. Goleman, *Emotional Intelligence*, 9–10; emphasis added.
5. Goleman, *Emotional Intelligence*, 113.
6. Robert Louis Stevenson, *The Strange Case of Dr. Jekyll and Mr. Hyde*, 1886, chap. 10, available at www.online-literature.com/stevenson/jekyllhyde.

CHAPTER 2. WHAT ARE UNHEALTHY SECRETS?

1. Sissela Bok, *Secrets: On the Ethics of Concealment and Revelation* (New York: Vintage Books, 1989), 7.
2. *Alcoholics Anonymous: The Big Book*, 4th ed. (New York: Alcoholics Anonymous World Services, 2001), 76.
3. Bok, *Secrets*, 11.

4. Anita Kelly, *The Psychology of Secrets* (New York: Kluwer Academic/Plenum Publishers, 2002), 5.

5. Daniel Wegner and Julie Lane, "The Allure of Secret Relationships," *Journal of Personality and Social Psychology* 66, no. 2 (1994): 288 (paraphrased).

6. Julie Lane and Daniel Wegner, "The Cognitive Consequences of Secrecy," *Journal of Personality and Social Psychology* 69, no. 2 (1995): 237.

7. Anita Kelly, "Revealing Personal Secrets," *Current Directions in Psychological Science* 8 (1999): 106.

8. Aldert Vrij et al., "Characteristics of Secrets and the Frequency, Reasons and Effects of Secrets Keeping and Disclosure," *Journal of Community & Applied Social Psychology* 12 (2002), 56–70.

Chapter 3. How Secret Lives Seduce Us

1. Home page of postsecret.blogspot.com.

2. Joe Klein, "Citizen Clinton," *TIME* magazine, June 28, 2004, 32.

3. "Jesse Jackson Fathers Child Out of Wedlock, Asks Forgiveness," January 18, 2001, Web posted on CNN.com.

4. "Kuralt's Mistress Awarded Montana Property," *Minneapolis StarTribune*, March 23, 2000.

5. Mark Landler, "A Secret Life for Lindbergh?" *Minneapolis StarTribune*, August 2, 2003.

6. Erving Goffman, *The Presentation of Self in Everyday Life* (New York: Doubleday, 1959), 71.

7. William Shakespeare, *As You Like It*, Act 2.

8. Goffman, *Presentation of Self*, 62,71.

9. M. Scott Peck, *People of the Lie* (New York: Simon and Schuster, 1983), 75.

10. Peck, *People of the Lie*, 76.

11. Peck, *People of the Lie*, 124.

12. Pew Internet and Family Life Project, Teens and Technology, available at pewinternet.org/PDF/r/a62/report_display.asp.

Chapter 4. Where Our Secrets Stay Hidden

1. Joseph Luft and Harry Ingham, "The Johari Window," in *Of Human Interaction* (Palo Alto, CA: National Press, 1969), 13.

2. See *Stolen Hours: Breaking Free from Secret Addictions* (St. Paul, MN: Syren Book Co., 2004), my memoir, for a full discussion of this mind-set.

3. Edwin Arlington Robinson, "Richard Corey," available at Bartleby.com.

CHAPTER 5. WHO ARE YOU WHEN NOBODY IS LOOKING?

1. Daniel Goleman, *Emotional Intelligence* (New York: Bantam, 1997), 113.
2. Credit for the seesaw analogy goes to Robert Johnson, *Owning Your Own Shadow* (San Francisco: HarperSanFrancisco, 1991), 10–11.
3. Anthony Stevens, *On Jung* (Princeton University Press, 1999), 42.
4. Stevens, *On Jung*, 47–48.
5. Stevens, *On Jung*, 51, 45, 206.
6. Stevens, *On Jung*, 204.
7. *American College Dictionary* (New York: Random House, 1969).
8. Terrence Shulman, *Something for Nothing: Shoplifting Addiction and Recovery* (Haverford, PA: Infinity, 2004), 77.
9. "Living a Secret Life," transcript, *Oprah Winfrey Show*, September 21, 2004, 6.

CHAPTER 6. MAXIMIZING PLEASURE, MINIMIZING PAIN

1. Robert Ornstein, *The Roots of the Self: Unraveling the Mystery of Who We Are* (San Francisco: HarperSanFrancisco, 1993), 54, 63.
2. Ornstein, *Roots of the Self*, 74.
3. Developmental Chart adapted from Erik H. Erikson's website, Psychology.About.com/Library/weekly/aa091500a.htm.
4. Viktor Frankl, *Man's Search for Ultimate Meaning* (New York: Fine Communications, 2002), 32.
5. Terry Fralich, *Through the Path of Mindfulness* (Eau Claire, WI: PESI Health Care, 2005), 17.
6. Craig Nakken, *The Addictive Personality* (Center City, MN: Hazelden Foundation, 1988), 15.

CHAPTER 7. THE QUEST FOR AUTHENTICITY

1. Mark Wexler, "Conjectures on the Dynamics of Secrecy and the Secrets Business," *Journal of Business Ethics* 6, no. 6 (1987): 470, 474.
2. Robert Ornstein, *The Roots of the Self: Unraveling the Mystery of Who We Are* (San Francisco: HarperSanFrancisco, 1993), 81.
3. Wexler, "Conjectures," 475, 471.
4. James W. Pennebaker, *Opening Up: The Healing Power of Expressing Emotions* (New York: Guilford, 1997), 62.
5. Pennebaker, *Opening Up*, 61, 66, 69.
6. *Alcoholics Anonymous: The Big Book*, 4th ed. (New York: Alcoholics Anonymous World Services, 2001), 60, 62.

7. Joseph Dispenza, interviewed in *What the Bleep Do We Know!?* (film), Twentieth Century Fox, 2004.

CHAPTER 8. WHEN SECRET KEEPING GOES TOO FAR

1. Ralph Blumenthal, "Boy Scouts Executive Surrenders in Fort Worth on a Child Pornography Charge," *New York Times*, March 30, 2005.
2. Jayne O'Donnell, "Former 'Duo of Deceit' Now Lecture Students About Ethics," *USA Today*, April 19, 2005.
3. Nick Coleman, "Guerin Packs Up Mistakes, Seeks Healing," *St. Paul Pioneer Press*, September 17, 2000.
4. "Slain 6th-Grader Led Two Lives," *Minneapolis StarTribune*, May 22, 2002.

CHAPTER 9. SEEKING THE HELP YOU NEED

1. The original model is credited to Hazelden Spiritual Director John MacDougall; however, the title "Four Squares of Life" and the text explaining the diagram are my own.
2. *Alcoholics Anonymous: The Big Book*, 4th ed. (New York: Alcoholics Anonymous World Services, 2001), 59.
3. William James, "The Sentiment of Rationality," in *The Writings of William James*, ed. John J. McDermott (University of Chicago Press, 1977), 337.

CHAPTER 10. FINDING YOUR MOTIVATION

1. David R. Hawkins, MD, *Power vs. Force: The Hidden Determinants of Human Behavior* (Carlsbad, CA: Hay House, 1995 and 2002), 37.
2. Ernest Kurtz and Katherine Ketcham, *The Spirituality of Imperfection: Modern Wisdom from Classic Stories* (New York: Bantam, 1992), 20–21.
3. Kurtz and Ketcham, *Spirituality of Imperfection*, 28–31, 53.
4. John MacDougall, "Spirituality and the Family," lecture (Center City, MN, November 12, 1999).
5. John Driscoll, "So That's How It Works: A Practical Understanding to Working the 12 Steps" (Center City, MN: self-published, 1998), 31–34.
6. Driscoll, "So That's How It Works," 31.
7. "Bill's Story," in *Alcoholics Anonymous: The Big Book*, 4th ed. (New York: Alcoholics Anonymous World Services, 2001), 10.
8. "Bill's Story," 11.
9. "Bill's Story," 12–13.

10. Portia Nelson, "Autobiography in Five Short Chapters," in *There's a Hole in My Sidewalk* (Hillsboro, OR: Beyond Words Publishing, 1994).

CHAPTER 11. PREPARING TO LIVE AUTHENTICALLY

1. Ironically, my book *Stolen Hours: Breaking Free from Secret Addictions* (St. Paul, MN: Syren Book Co., 2004) emerged from my fourth-step inventory.
2. Earnie Larsen, *Life Management Program: Stage II Recovery Training Manual* (Brooklyn Park, MN: E. Larsen Enterprises, 1990), 2, 22.
3. John Driscoll, "So That's How It Works: A Practical Understanding to Working the 12 Steps" (Center City, MN: self-published, 1998), 6–10.
4. *Alcoholics Anonymous: The Big Book*, 4th ed. (New York: Alcoholics Anonymous World Services, 2001), 64.
5. Driscoll, "So That's How It Works," 6–10.
6. *Alcoholics Anonymous: The Big Book*, 4th ed., 84.

CHAPTER 12. COMMITTING TO COMING CLEAN

1. James W. Pennebaker, *Opening Up: The Healing Power of Expressing Emotions* (New York: Guilford, 1997), 28.
2. Pennebaker, *Opening Up*, 2.
3. Pennebaker, *Opening Up*, 34.
4. Anita Kelly, "Revealing Personal Secrets," *Current Directions in Psychological Science* 8 (1999): 106.
5. Deborah Corley and Jennifer Schneider, *Disclosing Secrets: When, to Whom and How Much to Reveal* (Wickenburg, AZ: Gentle Path Press, 2002), 53.
6. Corley and Schneider, *Disclosing Secrets*, 53.
7. Barry A. Farber, "Clients' Perceptions of the Process and Consequences of Self-Disclosure in Psychotherapy," *Journal of Counseling Psychology* 51 (2004): 340.
8. Corley and Schneider, *Disclosing Secrets*, 58.
9. Corley and Schneider, *Disclosing Secrets*, 61.
10. Corley and Schneider, *Disclosing Secrets*, 60.

CHAPTER 13. SEEING THE WORLD THROUGH NEW EYES

1. Earnie Larsen, *Life Management Program: Stage II Recovery Training Manual* (Brooklyn Park, MN: E. Larsen Enterprises, 1990), 15, 16.
2. Larsen, *Life Management Program*, 15.
3. Adapted from Larsen, *Life Management Program*, 17.

4. Terry Fralich, *Through the Path of Mindfulness* (Eau Claire, WI: PESI Health Care, 2005), 15.

5. Larsen, *Life Management Program*, 17, 18.

CHAPTER 14. AUTHENTICITY IN A MESSY WORLD

1. Interview with Lance Armstrong, *Larry King Live*, August 25, 2005.

2. Terrence Shulman, *Something for Nothing: Shoplifting Addiction and Recovery* (Haverford, PA: Infinity, 2004), 126–27.

3. Shulman, *Something for Nothing*, 74–75.

4. For details, call (248) 358-8508 or visit www.shopliftersanonymous.com.

CHAPTER 15. TRANSFORMATION FROM DEEP WITHIN

1. *Alcoholics Anonymous: The Big Book*, 4th ed. (New York: Alcoholics Anonymous World Services, 2001), 60.

CHAPTER 16. YOUR RECOVERY FROM TODAY ON

1. Author's proverb.

2. Cheri Huber, *The Key: And the Name of the Key Is Willingness* (Mountain View, CA: Zen Center, 1984), 73.

3. Terry Fralich, *Through the Path of Mindfulness* (Eau Claire, WI: PESI Health Care, 2005), 7, 13, 39.

4. Deborah Corley and Jennifer Schneider, *Disclosing Secrets: When, to Whom and How Much to Reveal* (Wickenburg, AZ: Gentle Path Press, 2002), 60.

5. Anita Kelly, "Clients' Secret Keeping in Outpatient Therapy," *Journal of Counseling Psychology* 45 (1998): 50.

6. Barry A. Farber, "Clients' Perceptions of the Process and Consequences of Self-Disclosure in Psychotherapy," *Journal of Counseling Psychology* 51 (2004): 340.

Cudney, Milton, and Robert Hardy. *Self-Defeating Behaviors: Free Yourself from the Habits, Compulsions, Feelings, and Attitudes That Hold You Back.* San Francisco: HarperSanFrancisco, 1991.

Full of useful ideas and practical exercises, this book gives insightful examples of ways we can master the conflicting urges and behaviors that often defeat our goals and spoil our intentions.

Driscoll, John Patrick. "So That's How It Works: A Practical Understanding to Working the 12 Steps." Center City, MN: self-published, 1998.

A rich commentary with imaginative instructions for assisting anyone practicing the steps to successful recovery. Full of easy-to-learn and memorable methods.

Fralich, Terry. *Through the Path of Mindfulness.* Eau Claire, WI: PESI Health Care, 2005.

A workbook that accompanies Mr. Fralich's seminars, this offers straightforward ideas on meditation, breathing, the role of emotions, and effects on brain pathways.

Frankl, Viktor. *Man's Search for Ultimate Meaning.* New York: Fine Communications, 2000.

The author, a Holocaust survivor, found meaning in the senseless cruelty that he experienced in Auschwitz for several years. The fact that he found meaning in severe suffering helped him to survive his ordeal.

Goffman, Erving. *The Presentation of Self in Everyday Life.* New York: Doubleday, 1959.

Although this book is written in dense academic prose, its message that humans are really just clever actors wearing masks shouldn't be missed. Incisive, irreverent, and at times witty.

Goleman, Daniel. *Emotional Intelligence.* New York: Bantam, 1997.

We have two minds, says the author, one that thinks and one that feels. Moods are molded by cultural influences, and this shows how the individual can tap into the power of positive thinking by choosing actions that generate harmonious feelings.

Hafner, A. Jack. *It's Not As Bad As You Think*. Center City, MN: Hazelden Foundation, 1981.

A great booklet that examines why people become upset. The reasons are as simple as what we tell ourselves. The tips contained in this easy-to-read primer explain the ABCs of adjusting our self-talk.

Hawkins, David R. *Power vs. Force: The Hidden Determinants of Human Behavior*. 1995. Reprint, Carlsbad, CA: Hay House, 2002.

Hawkins presents a compelling premise: that societies often resort to force, which is extremely costly, instead of employing power, which is very economical. With power, all fear and pain disappears, and joy becomes unending and ever-present.

Huber, Cheri. *The Key: And the Name of the Key Is Willingness*. Mountain View, CA: Zen Center, 1984.

How we see things matters more than what we see. A Zen approach to helping us find ways to comprehend how our mind works (the internals) rather than the ways we can manipulate people, money, jobs, opinions, and so on (the externals).

Kaufman, Gershen. *Shame: The Power of Caring*. Cambridge, MA: Schenkman Books, 1980.

A definitive work that describes the inner torment of shame and how it acts as a source of splitting and self-hatred, "dividing us both from ourselves and from one another." Very helpful for increasing one's awareness of why we sometimes act as we do.

Kurtz, Ernest, and Katherine Ketcham. *The Spirituality of Imperfection: Modern Wisdom from Classic Stories*. New York: Bantam, 1992.

Forget being perfect, it'll never happen — for you or anyone else. Using a variety of examples, the authors suggest that embracing our imperfection is necessary for spiritual growth.

Larsen, Earnie. *Destination Joy: Moving Beyond Fear, Loss, and Trauma in Recovery.* Center City, MN: Hazelden Foundation, 2003.

In easy-to-read language, Larsen points the way to the goal of recovery: abundance and joy. Exploring the Three Stages of Recovery, he outlines the decisions based on "our new reality, our new truth, and our new chosen path."

Nakken, Craig. *The Addictive Personality.* Center City, MN: Hazelden Foundation, 1988.

The explanations in this informative volume will help shed understanding on the mysteries of the Self and the Addict in a human's split psyche.

Ornstein, Robert. *The Roots of the Self: Unraveling the Mystery of Who We Are.* San Francisco: HarperSanFrancisco, 1993.

Delivered in a refreshing style, this potpourri of observations on genetics, biology, and psychology presents intriguing insights and provocative illustrations.

Peck, M. Scott. *People of the Lie: The Hope for Healing Human Evil.* New York: Simon and Schuster, 1983.

These case studies describe the kind of mind-boggling behaviors that many Secret Keepers engage in growing up. It offers hope by diagnosing the bizarre mixture of motivations that can prompt such mental dysfunctions.

Pennebaker, James W. *Opening Up: The Healing Power of Expressing Emotions.* New York: Guilford, 1997.

The experiments in this user-friendly volume demonstrate the powerful benefits of writing about one's feelings and how doing so improves a person's inner temperament and positive outlook on life.

Seligman, Martin. *Authentic Happiness: Using the New Positive Psychology to Realize Your Potential for Lasting Fulfillment.* New York: Free Press, 2002.

The focus of psychology since its earliest beginnings has been on pathology. This book turns that focus upside down and claims that the recent field of "positive psychology" offers numerous benefits. It asserts that happiness is a practice that can be cultivated when people focus on their strengths.

Shulman, Terrence Daryl. *Something for Nothing: Shoplifting Addiction and Recovery.* Haverford, PA: Infinity Publishing, 2004.
Presents evidence and research pointing to shoplifting as an addiction and emotional disorder stemming from destructive, unresolved beliefs. The author started a self-help group for shoplifters in 1992, called CASA, and leads national seminars and conferences on the topic.

Stevenson, Robert Louis. *The Strange Case of Dr. Jekyll and Mr. Hyde.* 1886. Reprint, New York: Bantam, 1994.
A fictional portrayal of the duality of opposing selves in a human being. Loaded with literary insights into the split psyche that science later named and explained.

Zweig, Connie, and Jeremiah Abrams, eds. *Meeting the Shadow: The Hidden Power of the Dark Side of Human Nature.* Los Angeles: Tarcher, 1991.
A rich assortment of writings about the dark side, or Shadow, in human beings. Examines the many possibilities of how our dark sides can both harm and heal us.

INDEX

A

abstinence, authenticity vs., 151–52
acceptance
  of duality, 130, 150
  practicing, 227–28
accountability for present/future behavior, 130
  case study, 229–36
  looking back/ahead, 225–29
  maintaining authenticity and, 220, 224–25
  relationship repairs, 220–23
acting one way while feeling another (first splintered mind-set), 10, 13, 16, 38, 39, 68, 151, 174
addictions
  fundamentals of, 84
  Lie of Addiction, 82–86
  powerlessness and, 137
  sexual, 124–25, 253–56
  shoplifting as, 81–82
  See also alcoholism; drug abuse; eating disorders; gambling, compulsive; *specific addiction*
Adelphia, 37
alarm circuit, 12, 94–95
Alcoholics Anonymous (AA), 138, 156, 204
alcoholism
  abstinence vs. authenticity, 151–52
  case studies, 82–84, 99–100
  dysfunction/addiction cycle and, 134
  powerlessness over, 137
  recovery case studies, 161–63, 210–13
  as secret-keeping behavior, 4
alibis, 180–81
alienation, 73–74, 109–11
altered mental states
  case studies, 97–101
  developmental deficits and, 90–94
  inadequacy of, 94–96
  secret keeping as shortcut to, 103
  voluntary altered perspective, 151–52, 162–63

ABOUT THE AUTHOR

*J*OHN HOWARD PRIN is a licensed alcohol and drug counselor, speaker, and teacher. Formerly an in-patient counselor at Hazelden, he currently serves out-patient treatment centers in the Twin Cities area. He speaks throughout the country to a variety of audiences on addiction and recovery topics aimed to help people discover healthy ways to think, behave, and live. He also offers seminars in conflict management, self-esteem, and individual and team development for Fortune 500 companies.

Before becoming a counselor, Prin worked for ten years in Hollywood as an art director and set decorator. Prin's scripts and productions have won nineteen national and international awards. He lives in Minneapolis, Minnesota. His website is johnprin.com.

SEEKING STORIES
If you know of a secret-keeping story
and would like to contact the author,
please notify him at
www.johnprin.com.
THANKS!

NEW WORLD LIBRARY is dedicated to publishing books and other media that inspire and challenge us to improve the quality of our lives and the world.

We are a socially and environmentally aware company, and we make every attempt to embody the ideals presented in our publications. We recognize that we have an ethical responsibility to our customers, our employees, and our planet.

We serve our customers by creating the finest publications possible on personal growth, creativity, spirituality, wellness, and other areas of emerging importance. We serve our employees with generous benefits, significant profit sharing, and constant encouragement to pursue our most expansive dreams. As members of the Green Press Initiative, we print an increasing number of books with soy-based ink on 100 percent postconsumer waste recycled paper. Also, we power our offices with solar energy and contribute to nonprofit organizations working to make the world a better place for us all.

Our products are available
in bookstores everywhere.
For our catalog, please contact:

New World Library
14 Pamaron Way
Novato, California 94949

Phone: 415-884-2100 or 800-972-6657
Catalog requests: Ext. 50
Orders: Ext. 52
Fax: 415-884-2199

Email: escort@newworldlibrary.com
Website: www.newworldlibrary.com